IDIOMS

This comprehensive, up-to-date, and accessible text on idiom use, learning, and teaching approaches the topic with a balance of sound theory and extensive research in cognitive linguistics, psycholinguistics, corpus linguistics, and sociolinguistics, and informed teaching practices. *Idioms* is organized in three parts.

- Part I includes discussion of idiom definition, classification, usage patterns, and functions.
- Part II investigates the process involved in the comprehension of idioms and the factors that influence individuals' understanding and use of idioms in both L1 and L2.
- Part III explores idiom acquisition and the teaching and learning of idioms, focusing especially on the strategies and techniques used to help students learn idioms.

To assist the reader in grasping the key issues, study questions are provided at the end of each chapter. The book also includes a glossary of special terms and an annotated list of selective idiom reference books and student textbooks.

Idioms is designed to serve either as a textbook for ESL/applied linguistics teacher education courses or as a reference book. No matter how the book is used, it will equip ESL/applied linguistics students and professionals with a solid understanding of various issues related to idioms and the learning of them.

Dilin Liu, Ph.D., teaches at The University of Alabama, USA.

ESL & Applied Linguistics Professional Series
Eli Hinkel, Series Editor

Liu • *Idioms: Description, Comprehension, Acquisition, and Pedagogy*

Chappelle/Enright/Jamieson, Eds. • *Building a Validity Argument for the Text of English as a Foreign Language*™

Kondo-Brown/Brown, Eds. • *Teaching Chinese, Japanese, and Korean Heritage Students: Curriculum Needs, Materials, and Assessments*

Youmans • *Chicano-Anglo Conversations: Truth, Honesty, and Politeness*

Birch • *English L2 Reading: Getting to the Bottom, Second Edition*

Luk/Lin • *Classroom Interactions as Cross-cultural Encounters: Native Speakers in EFL Lessons*

Levy/Stockwell • *CALL Dimensions: Issues and Options in Computer Assisted Language Learning*

Nero, Ed. • *Dialects, Englishes, Creoles, and Education*

Basturkmen • *Ideas and Options in English for Specific Purposes*

Kumaravadivelu • *Understanding Language Teaching: From Method to Postmethod*

McKay • *Researching Second Language Classrooms*

Egbert/Petrie, Eds. • *CALL Research Perspectives*

Canagarajah, Ed. • *Reclaiming the Local in Language Policy and Practice*

Adamson • *Language Minority Students in American Schools: An Education in English*

Fotos/Browne, Eds. • *New Perspectives on CALL for Second Language Classrooms*

Hinkel • *Teaching Academic ESL Writing: Practical Techniques in Vocabulary and Grammar*

Hinkel/Fotos, Eds. • *New Perspectives on Grammar Teaching in Second Language Classrooms*

Hinkel • *Second Language Writers' Text: Linguistic and Rhetorical Features*

Visit www.Routledge.com for additional information on titles in the ESL & Applied Linguistics Professional Series

IDIOMS
DESCRIPTION, COMPREHENSION, ACQUISITION, AND PEDAGOGY

Dilin Liu

NEW YORK AND LONDON

First published 2008
by Routledge
711 Third Ave, New York, NY 10017

Simultaneously published in the UK
by Routledge
2 Park Square, Milton Park, Abingdon, Oxon OX14 4RN

Routledge is an imprint of the Taylor & Francis Group, an informa business

© 2008 Taylor & Francis

Typeset in New Baskerville by
Keystroke, 28 High Street, Tettenhall, Wolverhampton

All rights reserved. No part of this book may be reprinted or reproduced or utilized in any form or by any electronic, mechanical, or other means, now known or hereafter invented, including photocopying and recording, or in any information storage or retrieval system, without permission in writing from the publishers.

Trademark Notice: Product or corporate names may be trademarks or registered trademarks, and are used only for identification and explanation without intent to infringe.

Library of Congress Cataloging in Publication Data
Liu, Dilin.
Idioms : description, comprehension, acquisition, and pedagogy / Dilin Liu.
p. cm.— ESL & applied linguistics professional series)
Includes bibliographical references and index.
[etc.]
1. English language—Idioms. 2. English language—Study and teaching—Foreign speakers. 3. English language—Terms and phrases. 4. Americanisms. I. Title.
PE1460.L493 2007
428—dc22
              2007023914

ISBN 10: 0–805–86345–1 (hbk)
ISBN 10: 0–805–86346–X (pbk)
ISBN 10: 1–410–61807–2 (ebk)

ISBN 13: 978–0–805–86345–1 (hbk)
ISBN 13: 978–0–805–86346–8 (pbk)
ISBN 13: 978–1–410–61807–8 (ebk)

TO YUN, MY DEAR WIFE,
WITH LOVE AND DEEP AFFECTION

Contents

List of tables — xi
Preface — xiii

Part I: Idioms and Their Use — 1

1 Idiom Definition and Classification — 3

Introduction 3
Defining idioms: Diverse views 4
A perspective from language learners 13
Classification of idioms 16
Phrasal verbs: A unique group of idioms 21
Summary 23

2 Idiom Use: Function, Variation, Frequency, and Register — 25

Introduction 25
The idiom principle 25
Function 27
Variation 36
Frequency 39
Register 40
Culture and idiom use 41
Summary 42

Part II: Idiom Comprehension — 45

3 L1 Idiom Processing and Comprehension — 47

Introduction 47
Five major processing models 48
The "syntactic and semantic processing disassociation" hypothesis 56
The "idiom key" hypothesis 59
Summary 63

4 L2 Idiom Processing and Comprehension — 65

Introduction 65
Major strategies used in L2 idiom comprehension 66
Heuristic approach: A distinctive L2 idiom processing model? 73
Summary 74

5 Factors that Affect Idiom Comprehension — 77

Introduction 77
Factors relating to idioms and their use 77
Factors relating to language users 84
Factors affecting L2 idiom comprehension only 87
Summary 88

Part III: Idiom Acquisition and Pedagogy — 91

6 Idiom Acquisition and Its Importance in Language Development — 93

Introduction 93
Knowledge and skills required for idiom acquisition 94
The role of rote learning in idiom acquisition 98
The effect of different types of idioms and sequence of idiom acquisition 101
The importance of idiom acquisition in language development 103
A caveat 105
Summary 105

7 Selection and Organization of Idioms for Learning and Instruction — 107

Introduction 107
Selection criteria and useful selection practices 107
Types of idiom information that need to be provided 113
Organizing idioms for instruction and retention 115
Passive versus active idioms 118
Summary 118

CONTENTS

8 Idiom Pedagogy: Macro-strategies and General Approaches — 121

Introduction 121
Raising students' awareness of and interest in idioms 121
Incorporating idiom learning into the entire curriculum 124
Advancing a heuristic approach with discovery learning activities and adequate contextual information 126
Promoting "conceptual motivation analysis" and developing L2 cultural knowledge 128
Employing a variety of activities to deal with different types of idioms and to accommodate diverse learners 131
Using direct study as a supplement to contextualized learning 132
Enhancing idiom retention with effective mnemonic strategies 134
Training and boosting learning strategy use 134
Conducting unplanned teaching of idioms 135
Overcoming avoidance error and encouraging creative idiom use 135
Pros and cons of proactive and retroactive approaches 136
Summary 137

9 Idiom Pedagogy: Micro-strategies and Techniques — 139

Introduction 139
Noticing and identifying idioms 139
Understanding idioms and developing interpretation strategies 143
Analyzing idioms for register, connotation, and other in-depth understanding 149
Retrieving and using idioms for comprehension 152
Retrieving, generating, and using idioms for production 156
Using effective mnemonic techniques for retention 159
Explaining idioms to help students notice and understand them 162
Using idiom dictionaries 164
Summary 166

10 Error Treatment and Assessment in Idiom Instruction — 169

Introduction 169
Errors and their treatment 169
Assessment 173
Summary 174

Glossary — 177
Annotated list of Selected Idiom Reference Books and Textbooks — 181
Notes — 185
References — 191
Index — 201

Tables

1.1	Summary of Major Scholars' Views on Criteria for Idioms	14
2.1	Major Functions of Idioms	29
3.1	Empirical Predictions Made by the Three Models	58
5.1	Percentage of Idiomatic Answers by Age Groups and Context	85
5.2	Percentage of Completion Answer Types by Two Age Groups	86
8.1	Summary Chart of Intelligences and Suggested Activities for Teaching and Learning Idioms	133

Preface

Because of the ubiquity of idioms in human language, a decent command of a language entails a grasp of some of its basic idioms. In fact, the level of command of idioms is an important indicator of second language (L2) proficiency (Howarth, 1998; Weinert, 1995; Yorio, 1989). Yet the acquisition of idioms in L2 is no easy task. According to many scholars (Boers & Lindstromberg, 2005; Cooper, 1998, 1999; Cornell, 1999; Irujo, 1986a, 1986b, 1993; Grant & Bauer, 2004; Kővecses and Szabó, 1996, to cite a few), idioms are one of the most difficult aspects in L2 acquisition due to the fact that they are conventionalized expressions peculiar to a language community and they are usually frozen in form and often unpredictable in meaning—that is, their meaning cannot always be derived from the literal meanings of the components involved. Many L2 learners probably have a few anecdotes to tell about the difficulty they have experienced with idioms.

For example, Makkai (1993), a Russian immigrant turned professor of linguistics, recalls the following incident to illustrate the problem that idioms might present to L2 speakers:

> I was a recently arrived refugee immigrant in the United States when, shortly before the end of my 6th month in Boston, someone said, "You can't be serious, you're pulling my leg." I was startled and in broken phrases apologized, "pardon me, Sir, I did not mean to touch your foot." (p. 303)

As an immigrant and an English as a second language (ESL) learner-turned L2 educator myself, I also have quite a few anecdotes to share. An international student of mine once told me of an embarrassing experience he had. One day, the professor of one of his classes told the class that their plan to visit a museum had fallen through. Hearing that, the student voiced a cheer of joy because he thought it meant the visit was going to happen, for in his mind the particle "through" in the phrase meant "no glitches" and hence "fall through" implied the same thing as "go through." Obviously, he was wrong. Of course, Makkai and the student of mine are not the only ones to have made this type of mistake. Many L2 educators also have anecdotes about their students' misunderstanding of idioms. Larsen-Freeman (2007) in her plenary speech at the Forty-first Teachers of English to Speakers of Other Languages (TESOL) Convention told the following story. One day she was late for her class and she explained to the students that she had *run across* an old friend. Her students were all startled, thinking she had literally run a person over, and asked if the person was all right. Misunderstanding or feeling lost is very common for L2 learners when they encounter a new idiom.

It is, thus, no wonder that L2 teachers are constantly bombarded by students' complaints about the difficulty of idioms and by their questions about these expressions. Yet despite the challenges that idioms present, the issue of L2 idiom acquisition and instruction has so far failed to receive adequate attention. Although one can find some idiom textbooks for L2 students and some articles about idiom use, acquisition, and teaching, to my knowledge there has not been a professional book devoted to the topic. A lack of comprehensive coverage on the issue is really unfortunate, because for L2 teachers, especially those who are new to the field or still in training, a basic understanding of idiom use and learning is extremely important to their success in dealing with this difficult aspect of language.

For more than a decade, I have been reading and doing research on idioms in preparation of a book that I hope will provide teachers with this basic knowledge. I have approached the task from two angles: that of an ESL learner and that of an ESL educator and researcher. From the perspective of the former, I have been reading and learning about various English idioms and their usages; from that of the latter, I have been studying what idioms really are and how they are learned and taught in general. In the process, I have learned to appreciate the complexity of many of the issues involved with idioms, the lack of consensus among scholars regarding, among other things, idiom definition, and the inadequacy of our understanding of how idioms are processed and acquired and what strategies learners use in understanding idioms. As a result, in this book I have decided to take the approach of presenting and assessing all the different views scholars hold on many of these issues, rather than embracing just one view, so as to give the reader a more complete understanding. For example, my discussion concerning what constitutes an idiom covers the entire echelon of positions ranging from those who advocate an unusually broad definition, to a few who espouse an extremely narrow one.

PREFACE

OVERVIEW

Comprising ten chapters in three parts and drawing from the existing theories and research that date back to the 1950s, this book aims to offer a comprehensive, up-to-date coverage of idioms, the comprehension and acquisition of idioms, and the learning and teaching of idioms. This book is designed to serve either as a textbook for ESL/applied linguistics teacher education courses or as a reference book. In the former capacity, the book may either serve as a textbook for courses on teaching specific language skills such as vocabulary and idioms or function as a recommended reading or reference book for other TESOL courses such as L2 language acquisition and teaching methodology. No matter how the book is used, a reading of it should equip an ESL/applied linguistics professional with a solid understanding of various issues related to idioms and the learning of them.

Specifically, Part I of the book discusses, among other things, idiom definition, classification, usage patterns, and functions. Part II investigates the process involved in the comprehension and the factors that influence individuals' understanding and use of idioms in both L1 and L2. Part III explores idiom acquisition and the teaching and learning of idioms, focusing especially on the strategies and techniques used to help students learn idioms. To assist the reader in grasping the key issues, study questions are provided at the end of each chapter. The book also contains a glossary of special terms and an annotated list of selective idiom reference books and student textbooks.

ACKNOWLEDGMENTS

First, I would like to thank Eli Hinkel, the editor of the ESL and Applied Linguistics Professional Series (to which this book belongs), for giving me invaluable advice and suggestions over the course of the development of the book. I owe the same gratitude to Paul Nation, who in his review of the book proposal and most of its chapters provided me with extremely helpful comments and suggestions for developing and revising the book. Similarly, I need to express my appreciation to Naomi Silverman, the LEA ESL/Applied Linguistics editor, for her encouragement and clear directions in the preparation of the manuscript. I would also like to convey my appreciation to an anonymous reviewer of the manuscript for the useful comments and suggestions. Finally, my graduate students Jennifer Colvard, Adam Copeland, Kelly McPherson, Pat Norton, and Rui Zuo either proofread the manuscript or helped with the index and I would like to thank them for helping improve the accuracy of the book. Of course, I alone am responsible for whatever errors and shortcomings remain.

PART I

IDIOMS AND THEIR USE

Chapter **1**

Idiom Definition and Classification

INTRODUCTION

What constitutes an idiom is a very important yet difficult initial question for all those interested in the study of idioms, including those in the business of learning or teaching idioms (Cornell, 1999; Fernando, 1978, 1996; Grant & Bauer, 2004; Liu, 2003; Moon, 1998; Tabossi & Zardon, 1993; M. M. Wood, 1981). A fairly extensive reading of publications on idioms will reveal that the definition of idiom often varies considerably from scholar to scholar. For some scholars, and in a broad sense, the term is rather inclusive, covering, among other things, all fixed phrases, clichés, formulaic speeches, proverbs, slang expressions, and, at the extreme, even single polysemic words. For example, Cooper (1998), Hockett (1958), and Katz and Postal (1963) have included as idioms individual words, especially those used metaphorically such as the word "weigh" in the phrase "weigh a decision." Yet for other scholars, and in a more restrictive use, "idiom" is a much narrower term, referring only to those "fixed and semantically opaque or metaphorical" expressions such as *kick the bucket* or *spill the beans* (Moon, 1998, p. 4); for a very few, the concept of "idiom" even excludes metaphorical idiomatic expressions (Grant & Bauer, 2004). Confronted with these diverse definitions of idiom, one will have to agree with Moon (1998) that "[i]diom is an ambiguous term, used in conflicting ways" (p. 3). What makes the term ambiguous is, of course, the fact that idioms are "multifaceted objects" that are "not only complex, but also in many ways elusive" (Tabossi & Zardon, 1993, p. 145). For such a complex and elusive concept, perhaps no single definition can be adequate or even possible, certainly not for scholars whose research interests vary significantly.

This chapter will first review the major theories and practices concerning the definition of idiom so as to provide the reader with a basic understanding of what scholars in general believe constitutes an idiom.[1] It will then briefly explore the perspective of second language learners on idiom definition. Addressing the issue from the learners' perspective is necessary because learners' criteria for identifying idioms may sometimes differ from those of researchers due to the learners' unique interest in idioms: to learn to understand and use them. The chapter will end with a discussion of the major approaches and systems that scholars have employed in classifying idioms.

DEFINING IDIOMS: DIVERSE VIEWS

Of the scholars who have dealt with the issue of defining what constitutes an idiom, Hockett (1958) appears to espouse the broadest definition. To him, any language element whose meaning cannot be deduced from its structure is an idiom, including units as small as morphemes (e.g. *work, ed, tele, phone, class*, and *room*) and as large as clauses (e.g. *What's up?*). Because Hockett is perhaps the only person who has considered individual morphemes as idioms, it is important that we understand his reasons for doing so. In his theory, *work, ed, class*, and *room* are each idioms because one cannot deduce the meaning of each of the morphemes from its structure. On the other hand, the words *worked, biology*, and *classroom* are not idioms because one can easily determine the meaning of each of these words by looking at its two composing morphemes or idioms. *Work-ed* means the past tense of *work*, *biology* refers to "life study" or the study of life, and *class-room* signifies the room for classes. In fact, in Hockett's theory every morpheme is an idiom except "when it is occurring as a constituent of a large idiom, since a morpheme has no structure from which its meaning could be deduced." (1958, p. 172). Hockett illustrates his point as follows:

> Thus *new* is an idiom in *She wants a new hat*, but not in *I'm going to New York*, because it is part of the larger idiom *New York*. *New York*, in turn, is an idiom in the preceding sentence but not in *The New York Times* or *The New Yorker*, since in the latter expressions *New York* occurs as part of larger idioms. (p. 172)

However, if we use Hockett's definition we will soon discover that there are simply too many language items that will be labeled idioms. Hence, his definition of idiom is too broad to be of much practical value in idiom research, learning, and teaching.

While Hockett appears to be the only scholar who has considered individual morphemes as idioms, there are a few who believe that individual words consisting of polymorphemes such as *greenhouse* and *telephone* should be classified as idioms. Katz and Postal (1963) and Makkai (1972) are representatives of this group. To Katz and Postal (1963), "[t]he essential feature of an idiom is that its full meaning, and more generally, the meaning of any sentence containing an idiomatic structure, is not a compositional function of the meanings of the idiom's elementary grammatical parts" (p. 275). In other words, any linguistic structure (including polymorphemic words) whose meaning is not the compositional meaning of its constituent parts is an idiom. On such a definition, *greenhouse* is an idiom because its meaning as a place for nursing plants is not the composite meaning of the morphemes *green* and *house*. Similarly, *telephone* is an idiom because its meaning as a device for long-distance talk does not really come from the composite meaning of the morphemes *tele* (far) and *phone* (sound)—that is, a "far sound" does not equate to a "long-distance talk device" (although one may infer the meaning from the context in which the two-morpheme word is used). In contrast, words like *unsafe* and *overestimate* are not idioms because the meaning of each is indeed the compositional meaning of its constituents. For example, the meaning of "not safe" comes directly from the combined meanings of its two constituent morphemes, *un* and *safe*.

Of course, according to Katz and Postal's definition of idiom, not only can polymorphemic words be idioms, but so too can phrases whose meaning is not the composite meaning of their elementary structures, such as *kick the bucket*. Katz and Postal differentiate these two types of idioms, though. They call the idioms made up of polymorphemic words "**lexical idioms**" and those consisting of multiple words "**phrase idioms**" (Katz & Postal, 1963, pp. 275–276). In their theory, one that Katz further elaborated in an article in 1973, the two types of idioms differ in two important aspects. First, they differ in structure, with lexical idioms belonging to "the lowest syntactic categories (noun, verb, adjective, and so on)," and the second type falling into "higher syntactic categories (phrases, clauses, and sentences)" (Katz, 1973, p. 360). Second, the types of idioms also differ in the way they are stored in a speaker's language system. Lexical idioms, like all other individual words, are stored in a person's lexicon, but phrasal idioms are registered differently in an idiom list because these idioms may have two possible meanings, with one being the composite or literal meaning of its syntactic elements (*kick the bucket* = "strike the bucket with one's foot") and the other being the idiomatic meaning, one that is not derived from its syntactic elements (*kick the bucket* = "die"). Using a generative-transformational approach, Katz and Postal's identification of "phrase idioms" relies largely on the test of whether a phrase is productive and transformation-permissible. Phrase idioms are not productive or transformation-permissible. For example, "put one's foot in the mouth" and "eat one's words" cannot be turned into passive without losing their idiomatic meaning. This use of generative-transformational approach is the trademark of Katz and Postal's study and it makes their analysis rather formal.

Makkai (1972) also considers some polymorphemic words as idioms, but, unlike Katz and Postal (1963), Makkai believes that only polymorphemic words consisting of at least two free morphemes, such as *blackmail*, may qualify as idioms. In other words, polymorphemic words made up of only one free morpheme plus one or more bound morphemes, such as *telephone* (*tele* as a bound morpheme or an affix and *phone* a free morpheme), cannot be classified as idioms because there are adequate morphological rules for decoding first the bound morphemes and then the words containing the morphemes. For example, knowing the meaning of the affix *tele*, one may fairly easily predict the meaning of a word containing it, such as *telescope*. In other words, the meaning of such a polymorphemic word is deducible from its constituent parts. In contrast, the meaning of an idiom is not deducible from its elementary parts because, Makkai (1972, p. 120) argues, these elementary parts so put together can "potentially mislead" or "disinform" a listener or reader. For instance, the meaning of *blackmail* as "extortion by threats" is not derived from the meanings of the two free morphemes, *black* and *mail*. So it seems that Makkai's and Katz and Postal's definitions are really the same in the sense that both insist that the meaning of an idiom cannot be derived from its individual components. Yet they disagree on whether the meaning of a word consisting of one bound and one free morpheme can be derived from its components, with Katz and Postal saying yes and Makkai claiming no. Thus, in terms of polymorphemic idioms, Makkai's definition appears narrower than Katz and Postal's. Yet Makkai's overall notion of idioms is much broader than Katz and Postal's, as will be shown below.

Applying Lamb's (1962) stratificational grammar, Makkai renders a very formal study of idioms. He identifies two major types of idioms: **idioms of encoding** (also called **phraseological idioms**) and **idioms of decoding** (also known as **semantic idioms**). The former refers to stable collocations peculiar to a language. An example cited in his discussion is *drive* **at** *70 m.p.h.* rather than **with** *70 p.m.h.*, as is used in French. These expressions are called idioms solely for their phraseological peculiarities (Makkai, 1972, pp. 56–57). The latter type, **idioms of decoding**, on the other hand, comprise expressions that possess a non-literal meaning such as *red herring* and *come up*. These idioms are all potentially misleading or have "disinformation potential," as can be seen in the two examples just mentioned. Each of them has both a literal and a figurative meaning: *red herring* = (1) a type of fish that is red, and (2) a phony issue; and *come up* = (1) move to a position as in "come up to the front," and (2) occur or be mentioned as in "the issue came up at the meeting." All idioms of decoding are, of course, idioms of encoding because they are also rather fixed and unique in composition. Because of their meaning opacity and structural uniqueness, idioms of decoding are the focus of Makkai's study.

Like Katz and Postal (1963), Weinreich (1969), another important scholar on the topic, also employed the principles of generative-transformational

IDIOM DEFINITION AND CLASSIFICATION

grammar in defining and identifying idioms, but his definition of idiom is much narrower than those given by any of the aforementioned scholars. Because his generative-transformational analysis is highly technical and is not directly relevant or important to the purpose of this book, our discussion will focus on his theory and criteria for defining and identifying idioms. First, he does not believe that single polymorphemic words like *telephone* and *greenhouse* can be idioms. To him, only multiword expressions like *blind date* and *pull someone's leg* may qualify as idioms. Second, while agreeing with Katz and Postal (1963) that only expressions whose meaning is not the composite meaning of their syntactical elements may be labeled idioms, Weinreich further limits the scope of idioms by reserving the term only for those expressions that have both a literal interpretation and an idiomatic one and, more importantly, are potentially ambiguous, as in the case of *pull someone's leg* (a literal meaning and an idiomatic/figurative one = "to tease someone") and *be in hot water* (a literal meaning and an idiomatic/figurative one = "be in trouble"). Such a criterion will disqualify as idioms expressions like *by and large, blow to kingdom come, assets and liability*, and *Two wrongs don't make a right* because these expressions either have no literal meaning (e.g. *by and large* and *as of*) or no idiomatic/figurative meaning and no real phraseologicality (e.g. *assets and liability* and *Two wrongs don't make a right*) (Weinreich, 1969, pp. 68 and 71). In fact, Weinreich makes a strict distinction between idioms and **stable collocations** such as *assets and liability* and *Two wrongs don't make a right*. Expressions of the latter type are not idioms because they "have nothing idiomatic or even phraseological about them. They are merely stable and familiar" (ibid., p. 71). Weinreich's definition of idiom is thus very narrow.

Fraser (1970) also employed the generative-transformational approach in his examination of idioms. Yet his focus differs from those of Katz and Postal (1963) and Weinreich (1969) in that he is interested in the transformational potential of idioms rather than the lack or limit of idioms' ability in transformation and productivity. In other words, he disagrees with Katz and Postal's and Weinreich's view that idioms are not productive or transformation-permissible. From a close analysis of the variability of idioms, Fraser came up with a six-level scale to account for the degrees of variation that idioms may be able to undergo. The following lists and summarizes Fraser's description of the scale (pp. 39–41):

L6 – **unrestricted** (no true idioms, according to Fraser, may permit this level of variation);

L5 – **reconstruction** (only one type: nominalization of a verbal idiom: from "He *lay down the law*" to "*his laying down the law* . . .");

L4 – **extraction** (e.g. "passive transformation," as can be seen in *The buck has been passed too often here*, and "particle and noun inversion in a phrasal verb idiom," as can be seen in *look the information up*);

L3 – **permutation** (e.g. "inverting the indirect and direct object," as in *can't teach an old dog new tricks*, and "particle and noun inversion in a phrasal verb where the noun is part of the idiom," as in *put some weight on*);

L2 – **insertion** (the placement of some non-idiomatic constituent in the idiom such as adding an indirect object to an idiom that usually does not contain one, as in "He *read the riot act to the class*";

L1 – **adjunction** (gerundive nominalization transformation, as in "Tom's *dropping the ball*" from "Tom dropped the ball." *It is important to point out that idioms which allow such gerundive nominalization transformation do not allow other higher levels of transformation, a fact that differentiates them from those that allow nominalization at the reconstruction level (level 5).*

L0 – **completely frozen.**

Note: *If an item is able to undergo variation at a higher level (say level 5), then it should allow lower levels of variation. For example,* lay down the law, *mentioned in level 5, will also permit variation types 1–4.*

Despite holding a different view on whether idioms are transformation-permissible, Fraser concurs with Katz and Postal (1963) and Weinreich (1969) in believing that only expressions whose meaning cannot be derived from their individual components can be classified as idioms. For Fraser, an idiom is "a constituent or a series of constituents for which the semantic interpretation is not a compositional function of the formatives of which it is composed" (1970, p. 22). Of course, like Katz and Postal, Fraser does not share Weinreich's view that an idiom has to possess both a literal and a figurative meaning. Nor does he make a swift, clear-cut distinction between idioms and stable expressions. Of the definitions of idioms using the generative-transformational approach, Fraser's is perhaps the broadest.

Though not from the generative-transformational camp, M. M. Wood (1981) offers a rather narrow idiom definition, one that is close to Weinreich's. In her book *A definition of idiom*, Wood, after a rather exhaustive review of literature and a close analysis of previous research, arrives at the conclusion that "[a]n idiom is a complex expression which is wholly non-compositional in meaning and wholly non-productive in form" (p. 95). The definition lists two strict criteria that an expression has to meet in order to be called an idiom: it must be (1) "wholly non-compositional in meaning," and (2) "wholly non-productive in form." The former insists that the meaning of an idiom does not come from its individual components. The latter stipulates that the structure of an idiom is frozen, allowing no productive transformation. For example, unlike non-idiom expressions like "catch a bus," where "bus" may be changed to "train" while still keeping the meaning

IDIOM DEFINITION AND CLASSIFICATION

of "catch" in the expression, *kick the bucket* does not allow similar changes, because any change of the components will totally alter the original idiomatic meaning. Although Wood contends that an expression has to meet both criteria to earn idiom status, she disagrees with Weinreich in insisting that idioms do not have to be ambiguous, i.e. do not have to have both a literal and an idiomatic (figurative) meaning. So, for Wood, *by and large* and *as of* are both idioms.

One point that needs to be made here about Wood's definition of idiom is that she believes that her definition is "more precise" and "accurate," for she uses the word "wholly" in her definitions: "wholly non-compositional in meaning" and "wholly non-productive in form." Yet her definition, as she explains, is built on the "gradience" nature of language: "Our definition has been put forward in the context of an account which accepts and uses the concept of gradience as an important feature of natural language" (1970: p. 97). The concept of "gradience" suggests that linguistic categories are not clear-cut. The boundaries between these categories, such as lexicon and syntax, are not always straightforwardly defined. Instead, they often gradually extend into another. In terms of the relationship between idioms and the non-idiom expressions, Wood supports Bolinger's idea (1975) that, depending on the degree of their compositionality in meaning and their productivity in form, expressions may be placed on the continuum ranging from idioms to collocations, clichés, formulae, and finally free forms. Because of this gradience nature, it is not always easy to decide whether an expression is an idiom or collocation, since it is not always clear whether it is "wholly" or "partially" non-compositional in meaning and "wholly" or "partially" non-productive in form. In that sense, despite Wood's claim that her definition is precise and accurate, applying her definition in identifying idioms is not always unproblematic. Furthermore, there is a clear tension between her clear-cut definition and the "gradience" principle that she claimed to have followed in developing her definition.

Unlike most other scholars, who view as idioms only those fixed expressions whose meanings are opaque and/or ambiguous, Fernando (1978, 1996) includes as idioms all fixed expressions that allow no or little variance in structure regardless of their degree of transparency in meaning. It thus appears, at least on the surface, that Fernando's idioms are quite similar to Makkai's "idioms of encoding"—that is, expressions with structure peculiar to a language (of course, Makkai's definition of idiom also contains idioms of decoding, i.e. expressions with idiomatic or opaque meanings). Yet examined closely, Fernando's concept of idiom and Makkai's notion of "idioms of decoding" are not entirely the same, because Fernando excludes from idioms what she calls idiomatic expressions that show "habitual collocations" such as "take a bus" and "drive at 65 miles per hour." She does not consider these habitual expressions idioms because they allow fairly free word substitution, or what she calls "adjective and normative variants" (Fernando, 1996, p. 30). For example, the word "bus" in "take a bus" can be replaced by "a train" or "a taxi," and the "65 miles" in "at 65 miles per hour" can be changed to any number of miles. Here is how Fernando defines the difference between idioms and habitual collocations:

> Idioms are indivisible units whose components cannot be varied or varied only within definable limits. No other words can be substituted for those comprising, for example, *smell a rat* or *seize/grasp the nettle*, which take either these two verbs but not others: thus *grab* is unacceptable. Nor are the words of an idiom usually recombinable.
> ... However ... habitual collocations such as *rosy cheeks, sallow complexion, black coffee* or *catch a bus*, etc. are not idioms for they are relatively unrestricted in their adjective and normative variants: *rosy/plump cheeks, rosy down* and *sallow skin* are all possible. Similarly, we can have *strong coffee* and *catch a tram*. (p. 30)

Thus, for Fernando, the key difference between idioms and habitual collocations is the degree of variability of the word combination of an expression. As long as the structural composition of an expression is "invariant" or has only "restricted variance," the expression is an idiom. Otherwise, it is merely a habitual collocation. Fernando emphasizes the point by stating specifically that "only those expressions which become conventionally fixed in a specific order and lexical form, or have only a restricted set of variants, acquire the status of idioms. Combinations, showing a relatively high degree of variability ... are not regarded as idioms" (p. 31).

Despite its exclusion of "habitual collocations," Fernando's definition of idiom remains rather broad, compared especially with definitions that confine idioms only to expressions that are ambiguous or opaque in meaning (cf. Weinreich; Moon; M. M. Wood). Fernando's definition is broad because there are numerous expressions with an invariant or restricted variant composition in English, or in any language for that matter. Given such a broad definition, a very large number of expressions of various types may be labeled idioms. Hence, identifying and classifying idioms so defined will be a very challenging task. Fernando thus employs a combined semantic and structural approach and system in dealing with the issue. She classifies idioms first on the basis of their degree of transparency in meaning, and then on their degree of variance in constituent elements. Idioms thus fall into three categories semantically: "**pure** (non-literal)," "**semi-literal**," and "**literal idioms**," and they are divided structurally into two types: "**invariant idioms**" and "**idioms of restricted variance**" (Fernando, 1996, p. 32). For example, both *smell a rat* and *get cold feet* are pure idioms because of their opaque idiomatic meaning, but while *smell a rat* is an invariant idiom wherein not a single word may be changed, *get cold feet* is an idiom of restricted variance in which the verb "get" is sometimes replaced by "have." Similarly, *fat chance*

IDIOM DEFINITION AND CLASSIFICATION

and *blue film* are both semi-literal idioms, but while *fat chance* is invariant, *blue film* has restricted variance, for a few nouns such as "joke" and "story" can replace "film" with the meaning "blue" remaining the same—that is, "obscene."

Of course, as Fernando herself admits, making a strict, clean-cut distinction between idioms using the above semantic or structural criteria is not an easy task at all. While it may be fairly straightforward to differentiate between a pure and a literal idiom, it is sometimes very difficult to decide whether an idiom is pure or semi-literal, or whether an idiom is semi-literal or literal. Similarly, with regard to the issue of variance in structure, it is also not always an easy undertaking to judge whether an expression has only restricted variance or a high degree of variability. As a result, it is sometimes difficult to determine whether an expression is an idiom or a habitual collocation. The task may become very arbitrary in some cases. That is why Fernando concedes that literal and semi-literal idioms sometimes overlap with habitual collocations—that is, some literal and semi-literal idioms that have restricted variance may be simultaneously called habitual collections.

Moon (1998), a corpus lexicographer, differs from Fernando, for she appears to share, to a fairly large extent, Weinreich's view on what constitutes an idiom. First, Moon distinguishes idioms from **fixed expressions**, a term similar to Weinreich's **stable collocations**, although Moon's term is a little more inclusive than Weinreich's as it covers "frozen collocations, grammatically ill-formed collocations, proverbs, routine formulae, sayings and similes" (1998, p. 2). Second, Moon defines idioms as "semi-transparent and opaque metaphorical expressions such as *spill the beans* and *burn one's candle at both ends*" (p. 5). These expressions have both a literal and a figurative meaning, a point that Weinreich also insists on as a criterion for defining what an idiom is. Of course, such a definition of idiom, as is pointed out above, is very narrow. Furthermore, identifying idioms by relying exclusively on whether an expression's meaning is transparent is a rather subjective undertaking. It appears that Moon understands the difficulty or sees the futility in clearly separating **fixed expressions** and **idioms** in actual practice. After discussing the difficulty of finding precise terms for these different expressions, Moon writes, "I will retain it [fixed expressions] for simplicity's sake. I will hereafter refer to fixed expressions (including idioms) as **FEI**s" (p. 2). In other words, by labeling all these expressions **FEI**s, she basically avoids the problem of separating idioms from the other fixed expressions. Of course, this does not mean that Moon does not distinguish the two categories in theory. She does, and somewhat vehemently, although she does not quite maintain the distinction in practice.

Like Moon, Grant and Bauer (2004) also espouse a very narrow definition of idioms, one that is in fact much narrower even than Moon's. For them, idioms, or what they call **core idioms**, are not only non-compositional (i.e.

not literal) but also non-figurative—that is, their meanings cannot be interpreted figuratively from their constituents. On their definition, *kill two birds with one stone* and *a dog in the manger* are figurative expressions, not idioms, because one can recognize the untruth or non-literalness of the expression and arrive at their intended figurative meanings by "pragmatically reinterpreting" them (p. 52). True idioms or core idioms, on the other hand, cannot be interpreted meaningfully either literally or figuratively via compositional analysis. *By and large* and *so long* are examples of core idioms. Grant and Bauer's rigid definition, which leaves few expressions as idioms, is, to a great extent, pedagogically motivated. They argue that traditional idiom definitions are too broad and often too vague, resulting in a mammoth number of expressions being classified as idioms, which in turn makes the learning and teaching of idioms an almost impossible task. They also contend that core idioms are processed and learned differently from the other multiword units (**MWUs**), a point that will be discussed in Chapters 6, 8, and 9 regarding idiom acquisition and teaching. Grant and Bauer's endeavor in making idiom definition more precise and the number of idioms more manageable for learners is both theoretically and pedagogically sound and deserves applause from language teachers and students alike. Yet their non-figurative criterion for idiom identification appears fairly subjective and, hence, not always easy to apply. Grant and Bauer themselves seem to be aware of the problem, because they acknowledge that "[s]ome MWUs may be judged borderline" (p. 54)—that is, they may be considered either figurative or non-figurative. What complicates the matter further is the fact that whether an MWU can be pragmatically reinterpreted to make sense often depends on who is doing the reinterpretation. For example, according to Bauer and her associates *a dog in the manger* is a figurative expression (Grant & Bauer, 2004) but *have a bone to pick with someone* is a core idiom (Grant & Nation, 2006) because, in their analysis, while it is possible to pragmatically reinterpret the meaning of the former expression in a correct way (hence, it is figurative), it is impossible to do the same with the latter (hence, it is a core idiom). Yet one may find this distinction questionable, because it appears that, without any knowledge of its origin and relying completely on cognitive analysis and common sense, a person might find it equally difficult to discern the former expression's figurative meaning. In fact, in an informal survey of advanced ESL learners about what they believed the two MWUs meant out of context, more figured out the meaning of *have a bone to pick* than that of *a dog in the manger* because many of the learners had little knowledge about "manger" and its functions but they were familiar with the concept or image of "bone picking"—one often associated with quarreling or fighting.

 The above review of the major existing idiom definitions indicates clearly the challenge of the task and also the diversity of views on the issue. Yet despite the differences, our review also reveals some important agreements among the scholars. To help us understand better the differences and similarities among the various views, I have created a table (Table 1.1) that summarizes the representative scholars' main syntactical and semantic criteria for defining and identifying idioms. From this table we can see that the most noticeable agreements among the various scholars are that (1) idioms are often but not always non-literal or semi-literal in meaning—that is, their meaning is not completely derivable from the interpretation of their components; (2) they are generally rigid in structure, with some being completely invariant and some allowing some restricted variance, as demonstrated by Fraser (1970) and Fernando (1996); and (3) idioms are multiword expressions consisting minimally of two words, including compound words. Using these three criteria that most scholars appear to agree on to define and identify idioms will place a person somewhere in the middle of the continuum on the issue of what constitutes an idiom. The number of idioms identified using such criteria will also be close to the median, greater than the number that the proponents of a narrower definition of idiom (e.g. Grant & Bauer; Weinreich) would allow but smaller than the number that the advocates of a broader notion of idioms (e.g. Hockett or Makkai) would come up with.

A PERSPECTIVE FROM LANGUAGE LEARNERS

What constitutes an idiom from a language learner's perspective? It is a question well worth exploring. As Makkai (1993) and especially Ruhl (e.g. 1989) have argued rather convincingly, the question of whether an expression is an idiom cannot be really answered without dealing with the question "For whom?". Ruhl (1989) has even gone so far as to claim that idioms exist only for foreigners, because mature native speakers do not have any problem understanding these idiomatic expressions. Of course, he forgets that idioms are also often regional and it is not uncommon for speakers of one dialect of the same language to have difficulty understanding idioms used in other dialects. Controversial as Ruhl's claim is, it at least highlights the fact that idioms are problematic, especially for L2 speakers. Fortunately and interestingly, the properties of idioms that most scholars have agreed on as key criteria for defining idioms, such as opaqueness in meaning and frozenness in structure, also appear to be the most appropriate criteria for defining and identifying idioms from the perspective of L2 learners.

When learners approach a new language item, the level of difficulty in understanding its meaning and the effort required to grasp its structure are two extremely important issues they have to consider in deciding whether the item deserves their special attention. From this learners' perspective, the degree of an expression's opaqueness in meaning and the extent of its

TABLE 1.1
Summary of Major Scholars' Views on Criteria for Idioms

Syntactical and Semantic Criteria

Scholars	Mono-morpheme (free or bound)	Polymorphemic Word (Semantically Unpredictable) 1 free + bound morphemes	Minimally 2 free morphemes	Literal	Multi-word (Phrase) (structural variance restricted) Non/semi-literal	Totally opaque (excluding figurative/non-literal)	Clause/Sentence (proverbs, sayings, etc.)
Hockett	Yes						
Katz & Postal		Yes		Yes	Yes		Yes
Makkai			Yes	Yes	Yes		Yes
Weinreich				(idioms of encoding)	(idioms of decoding)		
Fraser			Yes		(including phrasal verbs) Yes		
Wood, M. M.			Yes		(including phrasal verbs) Yes		
Fernando				Yes	Yes		Yes
Moon*					(including phrasal verbs) Yes		
Grant & Bauer†						Yes	Yes

* As stated in the discussion, Moon distinguishes, in theory, idioms and fixed expressions but, in practice, she groups them together as FEIs (fixed expressions and idioms). Her FEIs include formulae, proverbs, and sayings.

† Grant & Bauer's definition of idioms (or what they call "core idioms") is the narrowest because it excludes even figurative idiomatic expressions such as *kill two birds with one stone* and *a dog in the manger*. They seem to be aware of their extreme narrow view so they use the term "core idioms" instead of "idioms."

invariance in structure should perhaps constitute the two most important criteria in determining whether an expression is an idiom. If an expression is fairly loose in structure—that is, it has very high "compositionality" and its meaning is quite literal or self-evident—then it should not be considered an idiom, because such an expression does not present any special difficulty for L2 learners to process. In contrast, an expression with a fixed composition and an idiomatic meaning is extremely difficult for L2 learners to process and understand. In fact, for L2 learners even fixedness in form alone (that is, there is no opacity in meaning involved) should perhaps make an expression an idiom because the compositional invariability itself presents learners with the difficulty of having to grasp the expression as a whole (including all of its lexical items and the sequence they are in, with no room for error) if they want to use it correctly and meaningfully. For example, they need to learn to say "*call* it a day," not "*tell* it a day," and "make up *for* something," not "make up *to* something" (compare, though, "make up *to* someone").

The view that idiomatic meaning and institutionalized structure constitute the two most important criteria for defining idioms for L2 learners has also been supported by the fact that idiom dictionaries and textbooks often use them as the main criteria in selecting idioms for inclusion. For example, Biber et al. (1999, p. 1024), in their comprehensive English grammar book, define idioms as "expressions with a meaning not entirely derivable from the meaning of their parts." Similarly, the *Cambridge dictionary of American idioms* (2003), for example, defines idioms as follows: "An idiom is a phrase whose meaning is different from the meanings of each word considered separately. These phrases have a fixed form—they usually cannot be changed" (p. ix). ESL idiom publications often place a special emphasis on the invariance of structure as the most important feature of idioms. For instance, McMordie (1972), in the book *English Idioms*, states emphatically, "As a general rule an idiomatic phrase cannot be altered; no other synonymous word can be substituted for any word in the phrase, and the arrangement of the words can rarely be modified" (p. 6). This invariance feature presupposes that idioms are multiword expressions. Cowie and Mackin (1975) make the point very clear in their *Oxford dictionary of current idiomatic English*, for they begin their idiom definition by saying, "an idiom is a combination of two or more words which function as a unit of meaning" (p. ix). The reason for excluding single words as idioms for L2 learners is rather simple and obvious: no matter how difficult it is, a single word is just an individual vocabulary item, and to learn it is basically the same as to grasp any other regular individual word. Learning idioms, on the other hand, is a different matter as it involves the challenge of not only figuring out their unique meanings but also dealing with their invariance or restricted variance in form.

In short, for L2 learners, idioms are perhaps best defined as multiword expressions that are invariant or variance-restricted in structure and **often** (not always) non- or semi-literal in meaning. In other words, all idioms are invariant or variance-restricted, but **not** all of them are non- or semi-literal, for there are quite a few fairly literal idioms that are fixed in form such as *according to*, *by word of mouth*, and *on foot*. Literal idioms, as stated earlier, are usually not difficult for L2 learners to understand but are difficult to use because L2 learners have to memorize these idiomatic expressions as a whole unit in order to use them correctly and effectively in communication.

CLASSIFICATION OF IDIOMS

Our discussion so far has shown that idioms vary in terms of their degree of semantic transparency and structural variability. They also differ significantly in syntactic composition. For example, some idioms are phrasal verbs such as *put up with* and *give in*; others are verb + noun phrases or what Makkai (1972) calls **tournures** such as *kick the bucket* and *pull someone's leg*; some are simply noun phrases such as *red herring* and *hot potato*; still others are prepositional phrases like *in the long run* and *by far*. Given that idioms are not a uniform group, it is important for the purpose of both research and teaching to classify them appropriately and systematically. As has been shown in the above discussion, idioms may be classified in many different ways, including, among others, Katz and Postal's (1963) division of **lexical idioms** (idioms made up of one individual word each) and **phrase idioms** (idioms consisting of more than two lexical items), Makkai's (1972) stratification-based dual system of **idioms of encoding** versus **idioms of decoding**, and **lexemic idioms** versus **sememic idioms**, Fernando's (1996) **pure** (non-literal), **semi-literal**, and **literal idioms**, and Grant and Bauer's (2004) **core idioms**. Some of these classifications are primarily semantically based; others are, in essence, structurally motivated; some use both criteria; still others are functionally driven.

Given that perhaps no individual words should be treated as idioms for L2 learners, Katz and Postal's lexical and phrase distinction is of little relevance from the perspective of language learners. Makkai's encoding versus decoding distinction is not of much practical value, either, because all decoding idioms are also encoding idioms, or because many of what Makkai includes as encoding idioms such as *at x miles per hour* are just habitual collocations, according to other scholars such as Fernando (1996). Makkai's other classification, the lexemic versus sememic distinction, appears, however, to be of significant practical value because the classification is based on both structural and functional differences. On the basis of Makkai's definition, a **lexemic** idiom consists of more than one word but its meaning is not the cumulative sum of the meanings of its parts. Furthermore, this type of multiword structure functions as one lexeme, a "polylexonic lexeme" (e.g.

give in = succumb and *kick the bucket = die*). In contrast, a **sememic** idiom is a multiple-word structure whose meaning is "derived from its constituent lexemes" and it additionally has "an unpredictable sememic network" or, to paraphrase, an unpredictable pragmatic function. Examples of sememic idioms include sayings and proverbs (e.g. *don't put all the eggs in one basket* and *no pain, no gain*) and familiar quotations (e.g. *Brevity is the soul of wit*). Thus, generally speaking, sememic idioms are longer expressions than lexemic idioms, and they are often complete utterances rather than noun or verb phrases (lexical items), as lexemic idioms are. Being complete statements, sememic idioms may perform as a variety of speech acts such as advice, warnings, and requests. For that reason, Makkai (1972) also calls sememic idioms "cultural-pragmatic idioms" (p. 169).

Makkai's distinction between lexemic and sememic idioms is useful for language teachers and learners also because it includes a detailed systematic analysis of the various subcategories of each of the two types of idioms. With regard to lexemic idioms, there are six subcategories (Makkai, 1972):

1. **phrasal verbs**—structures each consisting of a verb plus one or two particles (e.g. *come across* and *put up with*);
2. **tournures**—structures each made up of a verb plus at least two lexons (e.g. *take the bull by the horns* and *bite the bullet*);
3. **irreversible binominals**—structures each composed of two nouns in a fixed order (e.g. *friend or foe* and *safe and sound*);
4. **phrasal compounds**—compound nouns and adjectives (e.g. *stalemate* and *high-handed*);
5. **incorporating verbs**—compound verbs (e.g. *eavesdrop* and *brainwash*);
6. **pseudo-idioms**—compound words or phrases in which one of the constituents is a "cranberry morph" or in which one or more lexons are "banned" (e.g. *chit-chat* and *hanky-panky*, where "chit" and "hanky" are two cranberry morphs, ones that have no meaning by themselves). (pp. 135–165)

Except for the cranberry morph or the banned lexons, the last category overlaps, to a large degree, with "irreversible binominals" or "phrasal compounds."

Sememic idioms, according to Makkai, include eight major subcategories:

1. **"first base" idioms**—expressions based on "nationwide" cultural institutions such as American baseball, football, etc. (e.g. *step up to the plate* and *hit a home run*);
2. **idioms of institutionalized politeness**—conventional polite expressions (e.g. *Could you please . . . ?* and *Would you mind X-ing . . .*);

3. **idioms of institutionalized detachment or indirectness**—conventional expressions indicating detachment or indirectness (e.g. *It seems that/to X...*);
4. **idioms of proposals encoded as questions**—conventional expressions of making proposals (e.g. *How about...?, Would you like to...?*);
5. **idioms of institutionalized greeting**—conventional expressions of greeting (e.g. *How do you do?, So long*, etc.);
6. **proverbial idioms with a "moral"**—well-recognized proverbs in a language (e.g. *Don't count your chickens before they are hatched* and *Birds of a feather flock together*);
7. **familiar quotations as idioms**—quotations from well-known figures or sources (e.g. *Brevity is the soul of wit* [from Shakespeare's *Hamlet*] and *Ask not what your country can do for you; ask what you can do for your country* [from John F. Kennedy's presidential inaugural address);
8. **idiomaticity in institutionalized understatement**—conventional expressions of understatement to lesson the impact of a blunt statement (e.g. *I wasn't too crazy about it* and *It wasn't the smartest move*).

Examined closely, some of Makkai's subcategories of sememic idioms are problematic. The first subcategory, "first base" or cultural institution-based idioms, should be classified as tournures in the lexemic idiom type, for two reasons. First, like all the other lexemic idioms, most of the cultural institution-based idioms are "lexemes," such as *to have two strikes against one* and *to hit a home run*. In other words, they are not like the other sememic idioms, which are all complete statements. Second, if Makkai classified these "first base" idioms as sememic simply because of the fact that they are based on cultural institutions, then many of the tournure idioms may also be so classified, because they too can be considered to have derived from cultural institutions, broadly defined. For example, the idiom *kick the bucket* is tied to the meat industry because the expression is said to have originated from an old pig-slaughtering practice.[2] Similarly, the idiom *play second fiddle* is derived from the musical profession.

Compared with Makkai's complex classification, Fernando's (1996) **pure/non-literal**, **semi-literal**, and **literal idiom** categorization appears much simpler. Yet in practice Fernando's system is not easy to implement, a problem that can be seen in the examples she offers in her classification (1996). For instance, she labels the idiom *chin-wag* non-literal but *foot the bill* literal (1996, p. 32). Yet for most people, *chin-wag* is perhaps more literal than *foot the bill*. Similarly, she considers *good morning/day* semi-literal but *on foot* literal (1996, p. 32), a classification that many would probably challenge on the grounds that the phrase "good morning/day" is as literal as "on foot." These examples indicate that determining the degree of an idiom's opaqueness is largely a judgment call, and a very difficult one. Also, in Fernando's classification table, in addition to the non-literal, semi-literal, and literal categorization she further divides idioms into "invariant" and "restricted variance" types according to their degree of fixedness in form. Such a classification is useful for L2 learners because it helps to highlight the structural features of the idioms that L2 learners need to know so they can use the idioms more accurately in structure.

Using an eclectic approach, including lexicogrammar, pragmatics, and semantics, Moon (1998) classifies idioms (or what she calls **FEI**s, meaning fixed expressions and idioms) into three major categories: **anomalous collocations**, **formulae**, and **metaphors**. **Anomalous collocations** refers to all the uniquely or unusually formed collocations, which include four subcategories: "ill-formed collocations," "cranberry collocations," "defective collocations," and "phraseological collocations." "Ill-formed collocations" are those that violate grammatical rules such as *all in all, day in and day out, by and large,* and *stay put.* "Cranberry collocations" refers to those that contain items in them that are peculiar to the collocation—that is, the items do not exist in other collocations. Examples include *kith and kin, on behalf of someone/ something, safe and sound,* and *to and fro.* "Defective collocations" are a complicated subgroup. According to Moon,

> These are collocations that cannot be decoded purely compositionally either because a component item has a meaning not found in other collocations or contexts, although it has other compositional meanings, or because one or more of the component items is semantically depleted.
> (1998, p. 21)

Beg the question is such an example because the verb "beg" in the phrase means "to assume as established or proved," which constitutes a unique meaning not found in its collocations with other nouns. Other examples include *foot the bill* and *in time.* "Phraseological collocations," the last subcategory, differs from the previous three subtypes in that such idioms are not entirely invariant in structure. Instead, they possess what Fernando calls "restricted variance," although they are not completely productive. Examples of this subgroup include sets of idiomatic expressions such as *with regard to* and *in regard to; to a degree, to a certain degree,* and *to an extent;* and *on show* and *on display.*

Formulae are those expressions that are generally grammatical in structure and compositional in meaning but have specialized pragmatic functions; they include the following subcategories: "simple formulae" (e.g. *safe and sound*), "sayings" (e.g. *an eye for an eye*), "proverbs" (e.g. *every cloud has a silver lining*), and "similes" (e.g. *as good as gold*).[3] Metaphors are divided into three types based on their degree of transparency in meaning: "transparent" (e.g. *stepping stone*), "semi-transparent" (e.g. *throw in the towel*), and "opaque" (e.g. *pull someone's leg*). Of course, as Moon acknowledges, some FEIs or idioms may be classified as belonging to more than one category. According to her analysis, 25 percent of the FEIs in her database have dual-type status and 1 percent enjoy all three classifications.

Grant and Bauer's (2004) **core idioms**, as explained earlier, are largely semantically defined and refer to an extremely small group of idioms, because the concept excludes not only literal but also figurative idioms, the latter being arguably the largest group of what most scholars consider idioms. In Grant and Bauer's classification, in addition to core idioms there are three other groups of MWUs: literal (e.g. *in summary* and *Merry Christmas*), figurative (e.g. *keep a low profile* and *put the cart before the horse*), and **ONCE** (i.e. only one word in the MWU is non-compositional or literal—for example, *the dog days* and *have designs on something*, because *dog* and *designs* are each the only one non-literal word in their respective MWUs). According to Grant and Bauer, a ONCE can also be figurative.

Besides the above approaches, scholars have also used a functional approach, one that classifies idioms according to functional categories (Fernando, 1996; Lattey, 1986). Because the issue of functional categorization will be addressed again in more depth in the discussion of idiom functions in the next chapter, only a brief introduction of the functional categories is given here. In her functional classification, Fernando applied Halliday's semantic functional analysis model in sorting out idioms and identified three major types of semantic functions that idioms fulfill: (1) ideational, or "the state and the way of the world", (2) interpersonal, and (3) relational. Most of the idioms, especially phrasal idioms, are ideational idioms. They are primarily informational, either expressing *message content* or characterizing the *nature of the content*. These idioms fall into various subtypes. Message content types can be divided into:

1. **actions**: *twist somebody's arm, spill the beans, rock the boat*, etc.;
2. **events**: *the bottom drops out, the straw that breaks the camel's back, the shoe drops*, etc.;
3. **situations**: *in hot water, on the fence, hang in the balance*, etc.;
4. **people and things**: *a back-seat driver, a pain in the neck, a red herring*, etc.;
5. **attributes and evaluations**: *cut and dried, turn back the clock, emperor's new clothes*, etc.;
6. **emotions**: *green with envy, a lump in one's throat, on cloud nine*, etc.

Message characterization types can be divided into:

1. **specific information**: *to be exact, in fact, the truth of the matter is*, etc.
2. **non-specific information**: *kind of/sort of, off the top of my head, so to speak*, etc. (adapted from Fernando, 1996, pp. 72–74)

IDIOM DEFINITION AND CLASSIFICATION

As for interpersonal idioms, they are those that either perform an interaction function or characterize the nature of the message. Idioms in this category are mostly formulaic sayings such as *What's up?* (greeting), *You're right on the money* (agreement), *As a matter of fact* (expressing sincerity) and *cut the cackle* (calling for brevity). Relational idioms, on the other hand, serve to provide cohesion in discourse. Examples of these idioms include *on the contrary* (adversative), *on the other hand* (comparison), and *in the meantime* (concessive).

In addition to semantic, structural, and functional classifications of idioms, some other approaches have also been proposed. For example, Kővecses (2002) and Kővecses and Szabó (1996) have categorized idioms according to the sources that motivate their use or the cognitive mechanisms on which idioms are based, such as metaphor-based idioms (e.g. "Something is *a piece of cake*," where the easiness of doing something is compared to that of eating a piece of cake) and metonymy-based idioms (e.g. "Someone *met his/her Waterloo*," where Waterloo stands for defeat[4]). They also emphasize the distinction between conceptual metaphor-motivated idioms and the other idioms because they argue that the use and understanding of the former idioms hinge on the possession of knowledge of the conceptual basis behind the idioms, a point that will be explored in the discussion of idiom processing and comprehension in Chapters 4 and 5, and again in Chapters 6 and 9 when we address how to assist students in better understanding these idioms. Finally, some idiom teaching material writers (Genzel, 1991; Lindstromberg & Boers, 2005; Wright, 1999) categorize idioms by their original sources such as business (*the bottom line* and *get more than one bargains for*), sports (*hit a home run* and *whole nine yards*), and eating/food idioms (*bite more than one can chew* and *compare apples and oranges*). They contend that such classifications or organizations help L2 learners to better grasp idioms.

PHRASAL VERBS: A UNIQUE GROUP OF IDIOMS

Phrasal verbs deserve some special attention because of their enormous number and because of a lack of consensus among scholars regarding whether they should be considered idioms. For the latter issue, while some scholars (e.g. Fernando, 1996; Makkai, 1972) readily include phrasal verbs as idioms, others (e.g. Moon, 1998; Grant & Bauer, 2004) do not. There are also those who appear to take an ambiguous position on the issue. For example, Cambridge University Press (1997, 1998) and Oxford University Press (2001) each published a dictionary of idioms and a dictionary of phrasal verbs, but neither stated why they opted for two separate publications. The practice may be interpreted in two different ways: (1) the two publishers did indeed consider idioms and phrasal verbs to be two entirely different linguistic categories; or (2) they treated the two basically the same, as evidenced by their production of a dictionary of phrasal verbs to accompany their idiom dictionary, and they may have placed phrasal verbs in a separate publication simply because of their overwhelmingly large number. Lack of consensus on the issue aside, if we apply the two most important criteria for identifying idioms—non- or semi-literalness in meaning and invariance in structure—then most phrasal verbs should be considered idioms. As far as meaning is concerned, many phrasal verbs are figurative (some of them may have literal meaning) such as *close in on, fall apart, go after, round up, run into, wrap up*; some are entirely opaque (i.e. non-compositional and non-figurative in Grant and Bauer's (2004) terms) such as *boil down to, come by* (acquire), *put up with* (tolerate), and *turn up* (appear). What makes phrasal verbs even more challenging for ESL students is the fact that some of them have multiple meanings. For example, *turn on* in "*turn on* the light" means to switch on, but *turn on* in "*turn on* the audience" means to excite.

In terms of structure, phrasal verbs allow little variation. Of course, it must be pointed out that not all verb + particle (either an adverb or a preposition) phrases are phrasal verbs according to the criteria that many linguists have established for identifying them. These criteria include:

1. Whether an adverb may be inserted between the verb and the particle. Phrasal verbs do not allow such insertion. For example, we cannot say, "He *came slowly across* a large sum of money" or "She *turned quickly down* the proposal."
2. Whether the particle can be forefronted in a sentence. Phrasal verbs do not allow such forefronting. For example, we cannot say, "*Across* a large sum of money he *came*" or "*Down* the proposal he *turned*."
3. Whether the meaning is completely literal. Phrasal verbs are often not completely literal in meaning, as is shown in *come across, put up with* and *turn down* (adapted from Celce-Murcia and Larsen-Freeman, 1999, pp. 428–433).

Verb + particle phrases that do not meet all or some of these criteria are not phrasal verbs. *Listen to, look at, come in,* and *talk about* are a few examples. First, one can insert an adverb between the verb and the preposition in these verb phrases, e.g. *listen closely to* and *look carefully at*. Second, one can forefront the particle in the verb phrase, e.g. "*In* he *came*" and "*About* what did he *talk?*" Finally, all these verb phrases are completely literal in meaning.

Phrasal verbs are not uniform in structure and usage, however. First, there are transitive and intransitive phrasal verbs (e.g. *make up something* versus *give in*). Furthermore, according to Quirk et al. (1985), phrasal verbs can be classified into three subcategories. The first type refers to those separable idioms made up of a verb plus an adverb such as *turn down* (*turn down an offer*

IDIOM DEFINITION AND CLASSIFICATION 23

or *turn an offer down*). The adverb in such a phrasal verb may be placed either after or before the noun complement. In fact, if the complement is a pronoun, the adverb particle has to be placed after it, as in *turn it down*. Phrasal verbs of the second type are those consisting of a verb and a preposition, such as *come across* and *run into*, where the preposition particle cannot be moved (e.g. *come across something* but not *come something across*). The third type includes phrasal verbs that are composed of a verb plus two particles (one adverb and one preposition), such as *put up with* and *look down upon*. Another important characteristic of phrasal verbs is that many of them have multiple meanings. For example, *round up* can mean either to gather and arrest (e.g. *The police rounded up all the suspects*) or to finish (e.g. *They plan to round up their research next spring*). This interesting feature of some of the phrasal verbs adds to the difficulty in learning this unique group of idioms.

SUMMARY

There have been very diverse definitions of idiom. Scholars often approach the issue from their unique perspectives based on different research purposes. However, it appears that there are three criteria that most scholars agree on in defining and identifying idioms: (1) Idioms are often non-literal or semi-literal in meaning—that is, an idiom's meaning is often not completely derivable from the interpretation of its components. (2) They are generally rigid in structure—that is, some of them are completely invariant but others allow some restricted variance in composition. (3) Idioms are multiword expressions consisting minimally of two words, including compound words.

Besides the diverse views on what constitutes an idiom, there have also been many different approaches used to classify idioms, such as semantically based, structurally motivated, and functionally governed (an issue that will receive thorough coverage in the next chapter). Classified by meaning, idioms may fall into three subcategories: **pure**, **semi-literal**, and **literal** idioms. Sorted by structure or form, idioms may be categorized using two different systems: (1) They can be dichotomized as idioms of **invariance** and those of **restricted variance**. (2) They can also be divided into **lexemic (phrasal)** idioms, which include phrasal verbs, and **sememic (sentential)** idioms, which include sayings and proverbs.

Questions for Study or Discussion

1. On the basis of your reading and understanding, define "idiom" in your own words.

2. As was mentioned in the chapter, Ruhl (1989) contends that idioms exist only for second language speakers because mature native speakers do not have any problem understanding the idiomatic expressions in their language. Argue for and against this view. Then discuss whether you believe the definition of idiom for L2 speakers should be different from that for L1 speakers and why.

3. First decide whether the following expressions are idioms or not and explain why.

Come in.   *Drop by*
Fair and square   *Face the music*
Let one's hair down   *Look at*
Give in   *Day in and day out*
How do you do?   *Not all that glitters is gold.*
Put one's best foot forward

4. Of the various classifications of idioms discussed in the chapter, which one do you think is most systematic and comprehensive? Can you think of any other ways to classify idioms?

5. Fernando classifies idioms according to their degree of transparency in meaning (pure/non-literal, semi-literal, or literal) and their degree of variance in form (no variance or restricted variance). Categorize the following idioms using her classification system:

(Be) in the driver's seat   *Get more than one bargained for*
Blow off steam   *(Go) down the drain*
Break up with someone   *Go up in smoke*
Come across something   *Hit a home run*
Eat one's words   *Put up with someone/something*

6. Makkai divides idioms into lexemic (phrasal) and sememic (mostly sentential) categories. Use his system in classifying the following idioms.

Beat a dead horse   *On and off*
Come up with something   *Put one's foot in one's mouth*
God helps those who help themselves   *Throw out the baby with the bathwater*
Jump the gun   *What's up?*
Meet one's Waterloo   *You can't have your cake and eat it, too.*

Chapter **2**

Idiom Use: Function, Variation, Frequency, and Register

INTRODUCTION

After we learn what idioms are, we need to know why and how they are used. In other words, we need to understand idiom use in terms of purpose, context, form, and frequency. Such information about idiom use is crucial in order to make appropriate decisions in rendering idiom learning and teaching effective. Historically, because of limitations in the research tools and resources available, idiom usage questions have not been adequately examined. In recent years, with the advances made in corpus linguistics, these issues have begun to receive due attention. A few extensive corpus-based studies (Biber et al., 1999; Fernando, 1996; Liu, 2003; Moon, 1998) have examined a variety of idiom use issues in English, including their discourse functions, usage patterns, frequency, and register distribution. This chapter discusses these important idiom use issues, and the discussion is based primarily on findings from corpus research and other linguistic studies.

THE IDIOM PRINCIPLE

In studying idiom use, the first question to ask is why we use idioms. The answer may lie in the way language operates. According to Sinclair (1987), language operates on two principles: the **open choice principle** and the **idiom choice principle**.[1] The two principles are complementary, and **both** are needed to account for language use. The open choice principle posits that in constructing phrases and sentences, language users possess relative freedom in word choice, a freedom restricted only by grammaticality.

The idiom principle, on the other hand, postulates that word choices or combinations are not random and language users also have available to them "a large number of semi-preconstructed phrases that constitute single choices, even though they might appear to be analyzable into segments" (p. 320). *Of course* and *take something/nothing for granted* are two examples of preconstructed or semi-preconstructed phrases. *Of course* is a **prefabricated phrase** because it is completely invariant in structure, allowing no word movement or substitution, and its meaning is idiomatic, not derived from its two components: *of* and *course*. *Take something for granted* is a **semi-prefabricated phrase** as it allows some variations in its structure. For example, it may appear in any one of the following forms: *take* or *not take something/ nothing/anything/everything for granted* or *take for granted what someone says*... When we speak or write, the topic, context, register, etc. of our conversation or text may severely condition or limit the choice of words at hand, making us resort to preconstructed and semi-preconstructed phrases.

Research shows that the open choice principle and the idiom principle are simultaneously at work in our language production (Erman & Warren, 2000; Wray, 2002). While few sentences in any written or spoken text are exactly identical, preconstructed phrases (many of which are idioms) abound in these very sentences. Take, for example, a short paragraph from the beginning of Sinclair's seminal (1987) article on the topic:

> It is contended here that in order to explain *the way in which* meaning *arises from* language text, we *have to* advance two different principles of interpretation. One is not enough. No single principle has been advanced which *accounts for* the evidence *in a satisfactory way*. (p. 319; italics added)

All the italicized phrases are either prefabricated or semi-prefabricated to a certain degree. *It is contended that* is a semi-prefabricated phrase based on the sentence pattern *It is argued/ believed/reported that*... *In a satisfactory way* is also a semi-prefabricated phrase based on the pattern, *in a/some/no way*. *In order to, arise from,* and *account for* are prefabricated phrases allowing little variation.

Thus, the idiom principle is also evidenced by a variety of longer idiomatic linguistic units such as formulaic sentences and proverbs: *What's up?, You bet,* and *Don't throw out the baby with the bathwater*. Like phrase idioms, these longer formulae often constitute single choices in language production (Wray, 2002). As Moon (1998) points out, these idiomatic expressions are often "prompted discoursally as stereotyped responses," and they usually serve as "predictable comments on common experiences"—for example, "(*every cloud has) a silver lining* or *no news is good news*" (p. 29). The use of these idiomatic expressions or idioms is often dictated by the language use maxim articulated so well by Searle (1979): "Speak idiomatically unless there is some special reason not to" (p. 50), a maxim that speakers, consciously and unconsciously, generally follow. Of course, Searle is not enjoining us to use idioms here; he is urging us to make our language idiomatic. Yet idiomaticity involves the appropriate use of idioms.

Psycholinguistic research findings about language processing (Bolinger, 1975; Erman, 2007; Nagy, 1978; Steinberg, 1993; Underwood et al., 2004) also indirectly support the idiom choice principle. Quite a few studies on lexical storage and retrieval suggest that lexical items are stored not only as individual words but also as elements of preconstructed phrases, and they are often retrieved from memory as such chunks in language processing. For example, Erman's (2007) research about pauses in spontaneous speech indicates that the retrieval time required for filling variable slots in prefabricated phrases is significantly less than that needed for filling slots in computed or constructed phrases. Similarly, in an experimental study examining the time subjects needed to recognize the terminal words in formulaic sequences versus the time required for recognizing the same words in non-formulaic text, Underwood et al. (2004) found that "the terminal words in formulaic sequences are processed more quickly than the same words when in nonformulaic contexts," providing further evidence that "formulaic sequences are stored and processed" as whole units (p. 167). More importantly, the use of such prefabricated idiomatic expressions has been found to be extensive (Nagy, 1978). According to Nagy, in many instances "sentences are constructed out of prefabricated chunks rather than being built from scratch on the spot," and these instances "may also be typical of a far wider range of phenomena, making semi-productivity in natural language more prevalent than one might have otherwise thought" (p. 289).

As additional evidence of the idiom choice principle, research on language description and learning (Bahns et al., 1986; Howarth, 1998; Nattinger & DeCarrico, 1992; Schmitt, 2004; Stubbs, 2001; Wray, 1999, 2002; Yorio, 1980, 1989) has demonstrated that idiomatic linguistic chunks figure prominently in actual language use data (more so than previously recognized) and that they also play a very important role in language acquisition. The level of command of such idiomatic expressions that an L2 learner possesses has been shown to be a very good indicator of his or her proficiency in the language. Of course, we also use idioms for different functional purposes for effective communication, which will be discussed below. In short, to learn to use a language effectively, one has to grasp its idioms.

FUNCTION

Research has shown that, like non-idiomatic linguistic items (lexical, phrasal, or clausal), idioms are used for a variety of functions (Aijmer, 1996; Fernando, 1996; Fraser, 1996; Lattey, 1986; Moon, 1998; Schmitt, 2004; Strässler, 1982;

Stubbs, 2001; Wray, 1999, 2002). Because of the diverse approaches used in the research, such as Halliday's (1973, 1994) Systemic Functional Grammar and the Speech Act theory (Austin, 1962; Searle, 1969), various terms have been employed in describing idiom functions: **ideational, interpersonal, relational, evaluation and interactional, cohesive/textual**, and **pragmatic**. Of course, some of the labels differ mostly in terminology. They either mean the same or they overlap in what they refer to. For example, "evaluation" is a type of ideational function; "cohesive" and "relational" both deal with textual functions (i.e. textual organizations); "interactional" is basically interpersonal; and pragmatics is often at the center of many of the other functions, such as interpersonal and interactional. For the sake of simplicity and clarity, we will group the functions under three major categories: **ideational, interpersonal**, and **textual**, terms that Halliday (1978, p. 116; 1994, p. 179) used in defining the functional components of meaning in language. There are two reasons for using Halliday's terms: (1) Halliday's theory and classification of language functions are comprehensive and systematic, and (2) many existing studies on idiom functions (Fernando, 1996; Moon, 1998) have relied heavily on this theory. In fact, Fernando (1996) used basically the same classification system with the same labels for her three categories of idioms except that she used the word "relational" for the "textual" category. There are two plausible reasons for her selection of the word "relational" over "textual." First, the word "textual" might be mistakenly taken to refer to organizational components in written texts only, although in discourse analysis "textual" refers to organizational issues in both spoken and written discourses, since from a discourse analysis perspective any given speech is a text. Second, and more importantly, in Halliday's discussion, logical and organizational relationships are treated as ideational as well as textual functions, with logical and organizational relationships below the clause level being considered ideational, and those contributing to the cohesion of an entire text being regarded as textual.[2] Perhaps in order to avoid confusion, Fernando has placed all elements dealing with logical and organizational relationships under the "relational" category. Regardless of Fernando's reasons for using the term, "relational" is identical to "textual" in our discussion.

To better understand the three major functions, some additional explanation of the terms is in order. Ideational refers primarily to the use of language (or idioms in our specific case) to convey a person's experience, ideas, and views of the world, e.g. *passed out, kick the bucket*, and *dropped the ball*. Idiom uses in this function are mostly informational (i.e. to communicate ideas) and evaluative (i.e. to express views). Interpersonal uses are interactional in nature and serve primarily to facilitate communication between the interlocutors, e.g. *What's up/cooking? I don't mind giving you my two cents* (*worth*), *by and large*, and *by any stretch of the imagination*. The first two examples are formulaic sayings that speakers frequently use in interactions. The latter two are idiomatic adjuncts or adverbials that speakers often use to convey what Moon (1998) calls "modality" in interaction. In other words, these idiomatic adjuncts are usually epistemic or deontic in nature, and they help speakers to qualify or modify their message for more effective communication. In general, interpersonal idioms serve to create and maintain conviviality (e.g. *You made my day* and *You bet!*), while occasionally they are used to mark conflicts or disagreement (e.g. *Knock it off, please!* and *Give me a break/rest!*). Textual uses, on the other hand, are those that help to organize information, highlight a theme, and provide textual cohesion (e.g. *in sum* and *to make a long story short*). In our discussion, we will place all organizational uses under "textual." In other words, organizational uses will not be treated as part of the ideational function, a practice that Fernando followed. Table 2.1 is a summary of the three major functions that Fernando (1996) renders.

Some more examples of idiom uses from Barlow's (2000) Corpus of Spoken Professional American English (CSPAE) and Liu's (2001) Corpus of Spoken American Median English (CSAME) are offered below to help illustrate the various functions of idioms.[3]

TABLE 2.1
Major Functions of Idioms

Ideational	*Interpersonal*	*Relational or textual*[*]
Contribute to the subject matter of a discourse by functioning as impressionistic packages of information	Organize the flow of verbal exchanges and facilitate interactions between language users, especially in promoting conviviality	At the micro level they relate phrases or clauses within sentences (intra-sentential) or relate sentences within a discourse (inter-sentential); indicate a point in time, or temporal duration.
		At the macro level they relate portions of a discourse, for example paragraphs introducing new topics (meta-discoursal). Macro-relational expressions also indicate a global temporal frame.

Source: From Fernando's (1996, p. 188) table 5.2 with the word "expressions" under each column heading removed.
* "Textual" is my addition because it is now a more commonly used term for this function. Used by permission of Fernando's estate.

1. *Ideational*
   a) informational:
      - The President's [Clinton] inclination is not to *give up*. He doesn't *give up easily*. If he *gave up* every time you guys said one of his initiatives was dead, he would have *gone home* a long time ago. (informational as well as modality; from CSPAE)
      - Mayor Bloomberg [of New York City] is trying to get New Jersey and neighboring states to go ahead and *jump on this bandwagon*... (informational as well as evaluative; from CSAME)
      - Since Prime Minister Hosokawa left, we have not heard back from the Japanese government on the framework talks. *The ball is in their court*... (from CSPAE)
   b) Evaluative:
      - The military can carry it out, but it will not be *a cakewalk*... (from CSAME)
      - ... they're *in the driver's seat* in these negotiations. (from CSAME)
      - The report she's given on the status of those discussions *is right on the money*, that there's still a lot hard work left on this subject and part of that hard work is reflected in the correspondence the President [Clinton] exchanged with President Yeltsin. (from CSPAE)

2. *Interpersonal:*
   a) Interactions
      - But right now, in particular, we're talking about the whole idea of homosexual men in the priesthood. *What's your take on this?* (from CSAME)
      - Explain to me, David? *What were you up to there?* (from CSAME)
      - I'm Paula Zahn. Thanks so much for being with us and be sure to join me every weekday for "American Morning" right here on CNN. *So long.* (from CSAME)
      - Mike, *let me jump in* for a moment quickly. And we need to begin to *wrap this up*. But can you *put a little bit of bones on* the reference I made earlier...
        ... *Could I jump in* here. I've been on the Intelligence Committee as well... (from CSAME)
      - *Knock it off*, will ya? You're drowning out my big drum solo.

        Malzberg: But these parents are despicable. These parents did not protect that child. And if they are doing the same thing now, they are not protecting the children that they have left.

IDIOM USE   **31**

   How dare they let strangers come in their house and then not . . .
   (interrupted by Bouley, an opposing discussant)
   Malzberg: Hey, I didn't interrupt you. And then not check on the
      children after they see a door open in the middle of the night?
      That's irresponsible. They [the authority] should take the kids
      that are with them away.
   Bouley: In the 70s, these parents would have been considered good
      neighbors. OK.
   Malzberg: Oh, *cut it out.*
   . . . (from CSAME]
   • Tucker Carlson, "Crossfire" host: Maybe he [President G. W.
      Bush] is going to talk about corporate greed. I remember in the
      Clinton years, unbridled greed was known as growth. The decade
      of greed in the 90s.
   Begala: That's sort of like, on Wall Street, Mr. Inside Trading
      speaking out
   Carlson: *I beg your pardon.*
   . . . (from CSAME)

   b) Modality or adverbial adjuncts of qualifications
   • Our soldiers? Well, our soldiers are not in the line of fire, *so to
      speak*, over in the region. They are not at risk in the state of Israel,
      if that's what you are suggesting. (from CSPAE)
   • But *by and large*, when you look at the magnitude of what has to
      take place based on the Dayton Agreement by the 19th of January
      that I showed you on the earlier chart, I think the NATO
      commanders would tell you they are very pleased with the activity
      on both sides. (from CSPAE)

3. *Textual:*
   • Barbara Walters: The two teenagers have pleaded not guilty to the
      koala caper. They'll have their day in court later this month. *By the
      way*, koalas are not bears at all. They are marsupials. They are cousin
      to the kangaroo, which is certainly not a bear.
      OK, well, listen, *you know what?* I want to *switch gears* for a second and
      go from America to the Middle East. I know you've spoken on that
      issue, that crisis before. (both from CSAME)
   • There's no basis at all for them having that perception. We've given
      them no indication that this kind of conduct will be tolerated; *on the
      contrary*, we've given them every indication that they will be held to
      the high standards of international law. (from CSPAE)

- There are no clear studies yet showing whether vouchers actually improved the learning of kids who use them. All three of the voucher programs in Cleveland, Milwaukee, and in Florida are being challenged in court *on the grounds that* the programs do not adequately meet the requirement of the separation of church and state. (from CSAME)

Of course, these general functions can break down further into some very specific speech acts, such as expressing complaints and disagreement, and some specific textual moves like terminating and summarizing a topic or shifting in topic in conversation (Dew & Holt, 1988, 1995).

Distribution of Types of Idioms in the Three Functions

One may notice from the above examples that idioms used in the ideational function category are primarily verb or noun phrases, such as *give in, jump on the bandwagon, drop the ball, a cakewalk,* and *the bottom line*. These are the prototype idioms in the traditional sense of the term "idiom" (Fernando, 1996), or "lexemic" idioms by Makkai's (1972) definition. They form the majority of the idioms in the English language. It is no wonder that, according to Moon (1998), informational and evaluative uses (both ideational) account for 79 percent of all the idiom uses in her corpus data. Interpersonal idioms, on the other hand, are primarily formulaic sayings, such as *What's up, Would you mind –ing/if. . .?*, and *I've got to run* (I have to leave immediately), although they include some idiomatic adjuncts (adverbials) such as *by and large* and *so to speak*. Overall, they are mostly what Makkai (1972) calls "sememic" idioms and are usually complete clauses used to signify greetings, requests, evaluations, and so on. They constitute 15 percent of the idiomatic expressions in Moon's data. As for textual idioms, they are often prepositional and infinitive phrases, such as *by the same token, in short/summary, to sum up,* and *to switch gears*. They account for 6 percent of idioms in Moon's data. Another interesting point that Moon (1998) observes in her data is that while metaphorical and formulaic idioms (e.g. *dropped the ball* and *Someone got more than he/she bargained for*) are "typically evaluative," anomalous ones (e.g. *stay put* and *beg the question*) are "typically informational" (p. 221). Of course, the functions of the two types of idioms are not exclusive. Instead, metaphorical idioms may sometimes be used to convey information and, conversely, anomalous idioms may be used for expressing evaluations.

Performing Multiple and Cross Functions

As has previously been mentioned, an idiom does not always perform just one function. In fact, an idiom may often perform different functions in different contexts. It may even perform multiple functions simultaneously. For example, the idiom *chicken out* in "Tom *chickened out*" is not only informational (that is, conveying the information that Tom did not do what he promised) but also evaluative (that is, indicating that in the speaker's view Tom's action was cowardly). According to Moon's analysis (1998), nearly 47 percent of all idioms in her database "are classified as having two or more text functions: that is, they contribute to their texts in two or more ways," leading her to the conclusion that "as with other kinds of grammatical and linguistic categories, [idioms] operate on different levels at the same time" (p. 239).

Besides multiple functions, idioms, according to Moon (1998), may be used across functions. A cross-function use refers to a speaker or writer using idioms "in functions other than their canonical ones, thereby foregrounding or thematizing the selection" (p. 241). The following examples cited by Moon (1998) may help illustrate such uses. During a discussion of political scandals on a TV show, a TV reporter asks the discussant:

> Are there any *skeletons left in the cupboard* to come out? Has *the last cat in the bag been let out?* (p. 242)

In general, the idioms *skeletons in the cupboard* ["closet" in American English] and *let the cat out of the bag* are canonically evaluative but here they are used as a preface or a signal device. In other words, the two idioms were used to guide the discussants to the issue deemed important and worth discussing.

Functional Differences between High-Frequency and Low-Frequency Idioms

An interesting finding made by Moon (1998) about the use patterns of idioms is that in terms of proportion, more high-frequency idioms are used for modalizing and textual functions, while more low-frequency idioms are evaluative. The phrase "in terms of proportion" is important, because it stresses that it is just in proportion, not in absolute number, that more high-frequency idioms are used for modalizing and textual functions. In fact, in terms of absolute number, low-frequency idioms account for the majority of all idiom uses in all categories. As mentioned earlier, ideational (informational and evaluative) uses constitute the majority of all idioms used (79 percent in Moon's data), and these uses involve mostly low-frequency and highly marked idioms such as *drop the ball, jump on the bandwagon,* and *right on the money.* Interpersonal (including modality) and textual uses, on the other hand, make up only 15 percent and 6 percent of the total number of idiom uses respectively. The idioms used in the latter two functions are often high-frequency idioms such as *all in all*, *by the way*, and *so to speak*, but low-frequency idioms sometimes do show up in these functions, for instance *call it a day* and *switch gears*. In short, high-frequency idioms account for only a small portion of the total number of idioms used but proportionally they are used more often than low-frequency idioms in modalizing and textual functions.

Functional Differences between Single Words and Idioms

As is shown above, idioms may be used for many different functions. In terms of ideational functions, idioms can perform all roles that single words can, such as giving information, offering evaluation, and expressing attitudes. For example, the information-giving single word "died" in "He died" can be substituted by idioms like *passed away* or *kicked the bucket*, depending on the context. Similarly, the evaluative word "caviling" in "He is caviling" can be replaced by the idiom *hair-splitting*. Then are there any differences between single words and idioms in these ideational functions? The answer is yes, according to Fernando (1996): "While the functions of single words and idioms are broadly the same, there are points of difference which may partly account for why idioms of the ideational sort exist" (p. 99). The difference lies largely in the packaging of the information. Fernando identifies four areas of such packaging differences between single words and idioms:

1. While single words can be general (*cars*, *drive*) and specific (*sedan*, *speed* as a verb), ideational idioms are usually specific (*backseat driver*, *team player*, *spinning wheels*, *walk a tightrope*).
2. Whereas single words can be both non-imaginist (*quarrel*) or imaginist (*river*), ideational idioms are generally imaginist (*stumbling block*, *hair-splitting*, and *put one's foot in one's mouth*).
3. While single words can be both literal (e.g. the word "snake" meaning a reptile) and non-literal (the word "snake" meaning a cunning person), idioms are, more often than not, non-literal (compare the examples in 2).
4. Whereas single words can be both neutral (*child*, *police*) and attitudinal (*brat*, *cop*), idioms are typically attitudinal (*backseat driver*, *rug rats*). In fact, idioms are used much more often to express negative emotions and evaluations than to express the positive.

The last point is aptly supported by Moon's corpus analysis (1998, p. 247). Only 34 percent of all the idioms found in her data were positive; in contrast, roughly 66 percent—that is, two-thirds of them—convey negative meanings.

One difference between individual words and idioms that Fernando fails to mention is that ideational idioms are generally more colorful than single words. Few can miss the vividness of the following idioms in conveying their messages: *put one's foot in one's mouth* for saying the wrong thing, *dropping the ball* for making a serious mistake, and *backseat driver* for a person who doesn't do anything but likes to give orders. Another difference is that idioms are in general more informal than single words. This is especially true in the case of phrasal verb idioms as against single-word verbs.

When and Where Not to Use Idioms

Although idioms are used extensively and for a variety of functions, there are situations where they may need to be avoided, considering especially the fact that idioms are proportionally more negative than positive, and that idioms are often more informal than single words. Strässler (1982, p. 119) proposes two general rules on this issue: (1) "Do not use an idiom if you believe you are in a social situation which does not allow such use," and (2) "do not use idioms if you are not sure about the present social situation." To follow the first rule, one has to know what types of situations generally do not allow the use of idioms. There are several such situations. First, because of the rather informal nature of idioms, very formal situations are in general not appropriate for the use of idioms. For example, phrasal verb idioms are not suitable for formal writing such as legal documents. It will look much more appropriate in a court document to say that "the fire was *extinguished* at approximately 11:25" than to say "the fire was *put out* at about 11:25." Second, because idioms frequently convey negative attitudes and sometimes have a comic effect, serious situations and topics will not be very proper contexts for the use of some idioms. For instance, *kick the bucket* is not a good choice of expression when referring to the death of a friend or a colleague, nor is *shake a leg* a good one for a police officer telling another officer to hurry to an accident scene. Third, due to the often informal, negative, and comic nature of many idioms, one may need to avoid idioms when interacting with individuals of a higher social status or much older age. The second rule—not using idioms when one is not sure about the social situation—is especially important but also extremely challenging for L2 learners, because how to interact in a social situation sometimes varies from culture to culture and because non-native speakers are often uncertain about the nature of a social situation in L2. This challenge creates a dilemma for them. On the one hand, they need opportunities to learn and use idioms, yet on the other hand they are not supposed to use idioms inappropriately, because inappropriate idiom use may have serious consequences.

VARIATION

One important defining feature of idioms is their invariance or restricted variance. Yet some studies (Fernando, 1996; Liu, 2003; Moon, 1998) have shown that in actual use, many idioms do show some variations.[4] Via a close corpus analysis, Moon finds that approximately 40 percent of idioms contain lexical variations or strongly institutionalized transformations, and about 14 percent possess variations on their canonical forms (1998, p. 120). She also identifies many different types of variations such as "lexical variations," "systematic variations," and "variations within frames." The most noticeable type is lexical variation. The following are some major types of lexical variations that Moon identifies (adapted from pp. 124–132).

Type	Examples
Verb variation	*set/start the ball rolling* and *up/raise the ante*
Noun variation	*a skeleton in the closet/cupboard* and *the calm/lull before the storm*
Adjective/modifier variation	*a bad/rotten apple* and *a level/even playing field*
Particle variation	*in/at full throttle* and *with/in regard to*
Conjunction variation	*hit and miss/hit or miss* and *when/if push comes to shove*
Addition	*pass the hat (around)* and *turn (over) in one's grave*
Truncation (abbreviation)	*a bird in hand (is worth two in the bush)* and *make hay (while the sun shines)*
Reversal	*day and night* vs. *night and day/You can't have your cake and eat it* vs. *you can't eat your cake and have it, too.*
Variations between English varieties	*flog a dead horse* (British) vs. *beat a dead horse* (American) / *let off steam* (British) vs. *blow off steam* (American)

Systematic variations refer to those with regularity. Examples include *get a raw deal/ have a raw deal*, *stick one's neck out/with one's neck stuck out*, and *know the ropes/learn the ropes/show someone the ropes*. Systematic variation is also often found in **truncated idioms** like *a bird in hand (is worth two in the bush)* and *birds of a feather (flock together)*. An idiom is **truncated** when a part of it (words or a phrase in it) is omitted. Such truncated idioms have become systematic thanks to the fact that their original forms are well known and also rather long. In other words, the familiarity and length of the original forms make the truncation functional and necessary. Not all truncated idioms are systematic. In fact, some are *ad hoc*, made possible solely because of the context, as shown in the following example reported by Liu (2003). At a White House press briefing, a spokesperson made the following remark:

> So this is to bring him [President Clinton] up to speed on all the details of the schedule. Certainly he's got a number of bilaterals, he's got a number of multilateral meetings to prepare him for the substance of these meetings so he can have thoughtful, meaningful conversations just to continue to *bring him up* [italics added]. (p. 682)

The truncation of the second *to bring him up to speed* to *to bring him up* will not be interpreted as *to rear him* (a meaning that the phrase *bring up someone* often conveys), because the context makes such an interpretation impossible.

Variations within frames are those that occur within "fixed frames" and they "share single or common structures, but the realizations of one constituent vary relatively widely, though usually still within the bounds of a single lexical set," as is shown in the cluster of *down the chute/down the drain/down the pan/down the toilet/down the tube* (Moon, 1998, pp. 145–146).

While in many cases the variations in form of an idiom have no semantic implications and the choice of which form to use is largely a matter of personal preference, in some cases the variations are meaning-motivated and hence rather systematic. For example, Liu's (2003) study reveals that the alternative use of the words *run* and *term* in the idiom *in the long/short run/term* is not random. The word *run* is used far more often than *term* (by a ratio of three to one) when the adjective preceding it is *long* (e.g. *in the long run*) but when the adjective becomes *short*, the word *term* is preferred (e.g. *in the short term*). This suggests that to most Americans, a *run* appears longer than a *term*. Similarly, Moon (1998) demonstrates that the verb variation in some idioms is also meaning-dependent: *get the cold shoulder* versus *give someone the cold shoulder*, and *learn the ropes* versus *know the ropes*. In each of the two pairs, which verb to use (*get* versus *give* and *learn* versus *know*) depends on the meaning— that is, whether the subject is the agent or the experiencer (as shown in the first pair) or whether the subject is still in the learning process or already in possession of skills (as demonstrated in the second pair).

Besides context-motivated, *ad hoc* truncations, there are also some creative *ad hoc* variations, or what Moon calls idiom "exploitations," that individuals resort to for achieving stylistic effects in communication. Such variations usually involve the manipulation of the lexis as well as the semantics of idioms such as alteration or replacement of a word or words in the idiom. Examples include *burn the candle at five* (two) *ends* and *pull another highway* (a rabbit) *out of the hat*. According to Moon, such creative variations are often used to produce humor or to achieve discourse cohesiveness. The idiom variant *pull another highway out of the hat*, cited by Liu (2003), may serve as an example of this type of variation. It came from an ABC news report concerning U.S. Congressmen's practice of doling out federal money for local projects, known as "pork projects," for the purpose of reelection. The report mentioned that Arkansas Congressman Jay Dickey managed to obtain some federal funds for highway construction in his state in the previous election, and this time for his reelection he again secured $100 million in federal money for highway construction. So the report goes, "Now he's pulled another highway out of the hat just in time for this election." The comment sarcastically pokes fun at what the Congressman did. As for using creative *ad hoc* variations to achieve discourse cohesiveness, an example can be found in the passages cited by Moon (1998). The passages were from an article in the *Guardian* discussing clothing color fashion changes:

> Riftat Ozbeck, whose spring collection includes some brilliantly coloured Turkish jackets, believes that the tide may be turning. "I think that black will continue, but it won't be as strong. It'll lose that fashion victim thing that it's had for the last three years. We'll be mixing it with colour and not wearing it in the black-on-black, high techy sort of way any more."
> The signs are that *the worm may indeed be on the turn*. Fashion people are at last expressing boredom with their dour wardrobes and seeing something of the silly side of their obsession with black. (p. 215)

As Moon points out, in the first sentence of the second paragraph the author changed the usual form of the idiom *the worm is turning* to *the worm may indeed be on the turn* to attain "cohesion with *the tide may be turning* in the previous paragraph, since *on the turn* typically collocates with *tide*, not *worm*" (p. 215).

Finally, there are also language variety-based variations. While *beat a dead horse* is what Americans like to say, *flog a dead horse* is the choice in British English. Similarly, the American idiom *fall through the cracks* becomes *fall through the net* in British English. A related issue is that, in addition to variations in form, there are variations in the types of idioms used in different varieties of English. For example, many popular baseball idioms in American English are not found in British English, e.g. *out in the left field* and *three strikes and you're out*. Furthermore, idiom use also varies from region to region in the same country. An example in point is that the idiom *wouldn't hit a lick at a snake* (meaning being lazy) used in the southeast of the United States is unknown in many other parts of the country.

In conclusion, idioms show some considerable variation in use. However, despite variations, there is a certain degree of fixedness in each idiom that makes them idiomatic. As Moon (1998) states on the issue, "even in extreme cases there still remains some kind of fixedness, symmetry, or integrity [in the idioms in question]: it is just that it is not always *lexical* fixedness" (p. 122). In short, idioms do not allow unlimited variations.

FREQUENCY

Two different approaches have been employed in examining the issue of idiom use frequency. One is to look at how frequently specific individual idioms are used in a corpus—that is, how many times a given idiom is used in the data; the other is to determine how frequently idioms are used in a given corpus by calculating how many idioms are used per minute or per number of words in the data. According to the first approach, the frequency of the use of a given idiom is not very high. For example, Biber et al.'s (1999) analysis of the *Longman Spoken and Written English Corpus*, which boasts over 40 million words, finds that on average an idiom has a use frequency of fewer than 5 tokens per million words. Moon's (1998) study of the 18-million-word Oxford Hector Pilot Corpus (OHPC) yields similar findings. Many of the idioms she examined had a low use frequency, with fewer than 1 token per million words. This is especially true of pure idioms, or what Makkai calls "tournures," such as *kick the bucket* and *pull someone's leg*. Yet Moon's findings do show that about 30 percent of the idioms enjoyed a medium use frequency of 2 to 50 tokens per million words. Similar findings are also reported in Liu's (2003) study of three spoken American English corpora consisting of 6 million words.

However, when the second approach (the number of idioms used per minute or per number of words) is used, the frequency of idiom use has been found to be very high. Pollio et al. (1977) examined the use of idioms in 200,000 words made up of a variety of speeches, including political debates and psychotherapy sessions. Their analysis indicates that speakers in their sample used 4.08 idioms per minute. Cooper's (1998) study of taped TV soap operas yielded similar findings: approximately 3 idioms per minute. With a 4 idioms per minute rate, the number of idioms a speaker uses a day, as Cooper figures, would be very high. Assuming people speak for about four hours a day, the number of idioms a person uses comes to 980 a day (Cooper, 1998, p. 255). Liu's (2000a) study of fourteen college instructors' instructional language also found a high frequency of idiom use. He recorded and transcribed a total of twenty-eight classes taught by the participating instructors (two classes per instructor), whose areas of teaching varied considerably, covering most of the typical academic subjects taught in college including humanities, sciences, and business. Using the x number of idioms per 100 words method, he found that the instructors used on average approximately 3 idioms per 100 words.

Besides the computation methods involving the x number of idioms per minute or per number of words, some scholars have used other means of calculating idiom use frequency, such as the percentage of utterances containing idioms. They too have reported a high frequency of idiom use. For example, Larzar et al. (1989) examined the use of multiple-meaning expressions including idioms and metaphors in the instructional language of twenty-one kindergarten to eighth-grade teachers. They audiotaped and transcribed a full day of instruction for every teacher. Every single utterance was coded by type of expression. The analysis results showed that 11.5 percent of the teachers' total utterances contained idioms—that is, more than one out of ten utterances involved idioms—and that idioms were the only type of multiple-meaning expressions that increased with grade levels. If even kindergarten and elementary school teachers use such a high amount of idioms in their instructional language, then we would expect the frequency of idiom use by the general public to be much higher. This is because adults, including teachers, generally are rather conservative in their use of idioms when communicating with young children. The high frequency of idiom use in language, including even instructional language, clearly shows the importance of understanding and learning idioms, especially for L2 students.

REGISTER

Concerning the issue of register, all existing studies show that idiom use is highly register-sensitive (Biber et al., 1999; Liu, 2003; Moon, 1998). In general, idioms are more common in informal discourse, such as fiction and conversation, than in other, more formal registers. Idiom use frequency even varies quite significantly from fiction to conversation, with a great deal more idioms occurring in fiction than in actual conversation. According to Biber et al. (1999), idiomatic expressions for social interaction (what Makkai would call sememic idioms and what Fernando would classify as interpersonal idioms) are used frequently in fiction to "represent stereotyped dialogue" (p. 1025). In addition, not all idioms feature more prominently in conversation and informal settings. Some idioms occur more frequently in writing. For example, Moon notices that pure idioms are more likely to appear in written discourse (1998, p. 72). There is also register variation among individual idioms—that is, some idioms are more formal than others, and some idioms are used more often in certain registers than in others. For example, according to Liu's (2003) examination of three spoken American English corpora, the idiom *hang out (with)* is very informal, as it occurred mostly in the four least formal genres in the MICASE corpus—School Tours, Study Groups, Labs, and Office Hours—and it had no occurrence in the seven more formal categories such as Presentations, Interviews, and Colloquia. Liu also finds *come up with* to be more common in the spoken academic register than in the spoken media register, while the opposite is true of *come up*. The high frequency of *come up with* in the spoken academic register is due to the fact that instructors often use the expression to ask their students to develop or find answers to their questions.

CULTURE AND IDIOM USE

Idioms are found in all languages. Yet some types of idioms are more prominent in one language than in another, and they may be culture-specific (Boers, 2000a, 2003; Boers & Demecheleer, 1997, 2001; Boers et al., 2004b; Charteris-Black, 2002; Deignan, 2003; Emanatian, 1999; Gibbs, 1994, 1999; Holme, 2004; Kövecses, 1999, 2002; Liu, 2002; Yu, 1995, 2000). Thus, culture should not be neglected in the discussion of the use of idioms. Research has shown that most figurative idioms (arguably the largest type of idioms) are metaphorically based and conceptually motivated.[5] For example, the use of sports idioms in politics, business, and other aspects of life such as *hit a home run* and *strike out* is motivated by the metaphorical concept that life is a competitive sport. A metaphorical concept that is noticeable in one culture may, however, be relatively inconspicuous in another, due to cultural differences. Such a disparity may sometimes result in some metaphorical concept-motivated idioms featuring prominently in one language but not in another. Liu (2002) demonstrates this phenomenon in his comparative study of dominant metaphorical idioms in American English and those in the Chinese language.

Via an exploration of the different values and beliefs prevalent in the two cultures, and through a close analysis of extensive public discourse including the media, Liu (2002) argues that for unique historical reasons, sports, business, and driving have played a uniquely important role in American life, whereas eating, the family, and Chinese opera have occupied an unusually important place in the Chinese psyche. Consequently, while sports, business, and driving have been three dominant metaphorical concepts for idioms in American English, eating, the family, and drama have been three major metaphorical concepts for Chinese idioms. As a result, the two languages sometimes use very different metaphorically motivated idioms to depict the same activities. For instance, while political elections are mostly reported using sports metaphors in English, they are frequently described in military metaphorical idioms in Taiwan, due perhaps to the fact that governmental successions in Chinese history have always been achieved by force (military fighting). Similarly, personal interactions or relationships are often portrayed using sports and business metaphors in American English but the same relationships are typically depicted via family and eating metaphorical idioms in Chinese. Examples in point: when not accepting or agreeing with another person's explanation or view, or behavior, Americans like to say, "I don't *buy it*," but Chinese will often utter the phrase, "wo bu chi nei tao" ["I don't *eat that*"]; in asking who is in charge in a place or organization, Americans often use the expression "Who is *calling the shots* here?" while Chinese prefer the saying "zhe er shui dangjia" ["Who *is managing the family* here?"]. These are just a few examples showing that the use of idioms is sometimes culture-bound. The comparisons and contrasts between English and French in the use of some idioms conducted by Boers and Demecheleer (2001) and Boers et al. (2004b) also demonstrate cross-cultural differences in the relative salience in idiom source domains.

SUMMARY

Language works on two complementary principles: the **open choice principle** and the **idiom principle**. Both principles are needed to account for human language use. While language users do have some freedom in word choice, they are often constrained by the topic, context, and register of their conversation or writing, and need to resort to prefabricated or semi-prefabricated phrases. Hence, idioms are ubiquitous. Like other linguistic items or units, idioms perform a variety of functions, including **ideational** (offering information and evaluation), **interpersonal** (serving to facilitate and maintain meaningful and effective interaction), and **textual** (providing cohesion in discourse) functions. While idioms are used widely and often, there are some contexts in which idioms may not be appropriate such as marked situations. Despite their notoriety as fixed expressions, idioms do show some variation in use due to a variety of reasons, including language use creativity. Corpus data also show that idioms are used very frequently, especially in speech and fiction, although individual idioms do not usually have a high frequency of occurrence. Furthermore, idiom use is highly register-sensitive. Finally, some idioms are culture-specific, especially metaphorical idioms, because the latter idioms are motivated by concepts and beliefs that may be prominent in one culture but not in others.

Questions for Study or Discussion

1. Do you find Sinclair's "idiom principle" convincing? Select a passage, preferably from a speech, and explore and explain how the wording in the passage supports or contradicts the "idiom principle."
2. Idioms may perform a variety of functions such as ideational (informative and evaluative), interpersonal (interactions and modality or adverbial adjuncts of qualifications), and textual. Sometimes an idiom carries out just one function. In other instances, one idiom may fulfill multiple functions simultaneously.
    A: read the following sentences or short exchanges, paying close attention to the idioms (italicized phases), and then decide what their functions are (keep in mind that an idiom sometimes may perform more than one function).

IDIOM USE

1) a) What did you think of the mid term? b) Oh, it was *a piece of cake*.
2) We've done our part. Now *the ball is in your court*.
3) a) We can certainly get this done in a week. b) Really, I hope *you put your money where your mouth is*.
4) a) We've made a lot of progress on the project. b) Good, could you please *fill me in* on what you've done so far?
5) All the suggestions you guys made about the project proposal make good sense. Yet *it all boils down to* whether we can get any funding for it from the government.

B: Select a text (either spoken or written) that interests you, identify the idioms used in it, and then determine their functions,

3. Idiom use is register-sensitive—that is, some idioms are used primarily in informal speech while other idioms may be found in formal writing. Give some examples to support this point.
4. Corpus data show that idioms are not always fixed expressions. There are many reasons why idioms may vary in form. What are some of the major reasons? Give a few examples of idiom variation to support your answer.

PART II

IDIOM COMPREHENSION

Chapter **3**

L1 Idiom Processing and Comprehension

INTRODUCTION

As was mentioned in Chapter 1, most idioms are non-literal or semi-literal in meaning and invariant or variance-restricted in structure. Thus, how speakers process and understand this unique group of expressions has been a topic of great importance and interest for many scholars and language educators. This chapter examines the major theories concerning L1 idiom comprehension.

There have been numerous studies on L1 idiom comprehension, and they have led to many different theories regarding how idioms are processed and understood. These different theories boil down to the following five major hypotheses, sequenced in the chronological order of their appearance: (1) *the literal first* (also known as *idiom list*) hypothesis, (2) the *simultaneous processing* (also known as *lexical representation*) hypothesis, (3) the *figurative first* (also known as *direct access*) hypothesis, (4) the *compositional analysis* hypothesis, and (5) the *dual idiom representation* model. Besides the five major idiom processing models, there are two other interesting hypotheses concerning idiom comprehension that deserve scrutiny in this chapter: the "syntactic and semantic disassociation" theory and the "idiom key" concept and its role in idiom comprehension. Although they are not complete idiom processing models, the latter two hypotheses render some insightful understanding of the idiom comprehension process. Before we discuss the processing models and the two theoretical issues, it is important to note that some factors, such as the degree of an idiom's familiarity and the degree of its compositionality, may affect how a specific idiom is processed. While we will touch on the effects of a few such factors in discussing the five major theories, an extensive discussion of all the relevant factors and their effects on idiom comprehension will be given in Chapter 5.

FIVE MAJOR PROCESSING MODELS

The Literal First or Idiom List Hypothesis

The *literal first*, or *idiom list*, hypothesis, proposed by Bobrow and Bell (1973), posits that upon encountering an idiom, a language user first processes it literally, but when the context does not allow a literal interpretation, the person accesses the meaning of the idiom in a special idiom list that is not part of the normal mental lexicon. The latter process differs from that used for processing literal expressions, where "each word is perceived, its meanings discovered, and then mapped into a semantic whole" (p. 343). The notion of the existence of a special idiom list, first developed by Weinreich (1969), suggests that a person's mental lexicon contains a list of idioms in addition to the usual lexical items. The entry of a normal lexical item in the lexicon consists of phonological, syntactic, and morphonemic features, and a meaning description. The entry of an idiom item, on the other hand, includes a string of morphemes of various lengths plus its unique meaning. Bobrow and Bell's (1973) hypothesis was based on the results of a study they conducted. In the study, they first presented to each of their subjects either a set of four literal but ambiguous sentences (for example, "Mary fed her dog biscuits," a sentence that can either mean "Mary gave biscuits to her dog" or "Mary gave dog biscuits to a female person") or a set of four idiom-containing ambiguous sentences (for example, "John and Mary buried the hatchet," which can be interpreted either literally or idiomatically). Then, following the set, they gave the subject an ambiguous idiomatic test sentence (that is, one that can be interpreted either literally or idiomatically) and asked them to report which meaning came to mind first. In general, the subjects reported idiomatic interpretations of these sentences if they had just been given an idiomatic set of sentences but literal understandings after they had been presented with a literal set. Because the set conditions used in the study (literal versus idiomatic sets) were not grammatical or semantic cues, Bobrow and Bell concluded that the observed results could have arisen only from different processing modes: the literal and the idiomatic (i.e. the idiom list access) modes. The idiom processing mode is triggered when the literal processing of an idiom fails.

This hypothesis has been rejected by later studies that investigated the speed at which participants understood the meanings of idioms (Gibbs, 1980; 1984; McElree & Nordie, 1999; Ortony et al. 1978). On the basis of Bobrow and Bell's (1973) hypothesis, literal meanings must always be understood more quickly than idiomatic ones. Yet in these later studies, no subjects were found to interpret idioms' literal meanings more quickly than their figurative ones. For example, in Gibbs' (1980) study he presented to his subjects on a computer display expressions that could be literal or figurative in meaning depending on the story context. An example of such sentences is *He is singing a different tune*, because it can mean either literally that "He is singing a different song" or figuratively that "He has now changed his mind" depending on the context in which it is used. He presented all these expressions in four different conditions: (1) a literal context (that is, the story permits only a literal interpretation), (2) an idiomatic context, (3) a literal meaning with no context, and (4) an idiomatic meaning with no context. After showing each of the expressions, he presented the subjects with a paraphrase (either a literal or an idiomatic one). The subjects had to decide whether the paraphrase was correct, and their response time was measured. The results showed that the subjects took much less time to understand the idiomatic uses of the expressions than their literal ones. Ortony et al.'s (1978) study yielded similar findings: when presented in the same context—that is, with the same amount of contextual information—idioms did not take longer to comprehend than literal expressions. In fact, they seemed to be processed slightly faster than the latter. McElree & Nordie's (1999) experiment showed that literal and figurative interpretations are computed in equal time, a finding further refuting, though indirectly, the *literal first* theory.

The Simultaneous Processing or Lexical Representation Hypothesis

Put forward by Swinney and Cutler (1979), the *simultaneous processing*, or *lexical representation* idiom processing model postulates that idioms reside in the mental lexicon as long words side by side with all the other ordinary words—that is, there is not a separate list of idioms as suggested by the *literal first hypothesis*. When encountering an idiom, speakers process it both literally and figuratively at the same time until they decide on the appropriate interpretation based on the context in which the idiom is used. According to this hypothesis, lexical access takes place as part of the normal linguistic processing. Idioms such as *so to speak* and *pull someone's leg* coexist, as long lexical items, with individual words like *so, to, speak, pull, one*, etc. Thus, the process of understanding an idiomatic expression entails a race between linguistic processing and idiom access. Whether a person understands its literal or idiomatic meaning first depends on the time needed for the completion of full linguistic processing and lexical/idiom access and on the discoursal and contextual information provided. The idiomatic meaning has a processing advantage in terms of speed because it is fixed, with the whole phrase treated as a single unit. Swinney and Cutler derived this hypothesis from the findings of a study in which the subjects were directed to read on a computer display 152 strings of words and to judge whether they were meaningful English expressions.

Of the 152 strings, 23 were meaningful grammatical idioms (e.g. *break the ice*), 23 matched control items where one word in each of the idiomatic strings was replaced by a word of the same length, same part of speech, and equal or higher frequency (e.g. "break the *cup*"), 30 grammatical but non-idiomatic phrases, and 76 ungrammatical strings (e.g. "stranger is during"). Also, all the 23 meaningful idiomatic strings had been shown in a pre-test to be equally biased toward their literal and idiomatic interpretations—that is, they had an equal chance of being interpreted literally or idiomatically. After the display of each of the strings for 2 seconds, the subjects were asked to decide whether the string was a meaningful expression in English by pressing the "yes" or "no" button. Their response time was recorded. The subjects were found to be much faster in recognizing idioms than the control strings. This finding led Swinney and Cutler to conclude that idioms were stored as fixed units together with non-idiom phrases and the former were processed faster because the comprehension of the latter required full linguistic processing, including lexical, syntactic, and semantic analysis. This hypothesis differs from the *idiom list* model in that it rejects the notion of a special idiom list/lexicon and refutes the literal first processing sequence. This simultaneous processing hypothesis was later supported by a few other studies, including that of Cronk and Schweigert (1992). It is necessary, though, to point out that while Cronk and Schweigert support the simultaneous processing mode, they believe the simultaneous dual processing is conducted by a unique processor, a phrase processor. They propose the following as the idiom comprehension process:

> When a phrase is encountered while reading, the phrase processor starts two subprocesses: one that looks for the phrase as a single lexical unit, and another that analyzes the meaning of the words one at a time in an attempt to construct a meaning for the phrase (p. 140).

The Figurative First or Direct Access Hypothesis

Introduced by Gibbs (1980, 1984), the *figurative first*, or *direct access*, model is a radical extension of the *lexical representation* or *simultaneous processing* hypothesis. It asserts that native speakers rarely attempt literal comprehension of an idiom because they can often recognize an idiom when seeing one, and therefore they access its idiomatic meaning directly, completely bypassing linguistic processing. This is because, as pointed out previously, accessing an idiom is usually much quicker than figuring out the meaning of an expression through linguistic processing. This "direct access" hypothesis was based on a series of experimental studies Gibbs conducted in the early 1980s (1980, 1983, 1984), especially two experiments reported in 1984. As in his 1980 study, the subjects in the first 1984 experiment were presented with a series of brief stories or dialogues that all ended with an idiomatic expression that could be interpreted either literally or figuratively depending on the story context in which it appeared. For example, the expression *keep something under one's hat* may mean "keep something secret" in a non-literal story context or "place and keep something literally under one's hat." Then the subjects were asked to decide the meaning of the expression by selecting one of the three provided paraphrase responses (literal, figurative, and not related), and their response time was recorded. The results were the same as those reported in his 1980 study because they showed that the subjects took significantly less time to process and comprehend idiomatic sentences than literal ones.

The finding that the subjects took more time to respond to the literal story context sentences prompted the hypothesis that the subjects perhaps interpreted the literal expressions figuratively (idiomatically) first and then literally after they had determined that the figurative interpretation did not work. To test the hypothesis in the second experiment, Gibbs used the same procedures and stories he used in experiment 1, except that he made changes in the concluding sentence in every one of the literal stories so that the sentence no longer contained the idiom-like expression. For example, he changed *Please don't rock the boat* in one of the literal stories to "Stop making the boat tip." This time the results showed no significant difference between the subjects' response time to the figurative sentences and their response time to the literal sentences. Such a finding supported his hypothesis that people tended to interpret idiomatic expressions figuratively, even when these expressions were used literally, because in the second experiment, when the idiomatic expressions in the literal stories were changed to non-idiomatic ones, the subjects' response time decreased significantly.

The Compositional Analysis Hypothesis

Espoused by Cacciari and Levorato (1989), Gibbs et al. (1989), and Flores d'Arcais (1993), the *compositional analysis* hypothesis, a more recent theory, asserts that idiom comprehension uses normal language processing together with a pragmatic interpretation of the use of the idiom in its discourse context. In other words, idiom comprehension does not require a special mode. Gibbs et al. (1989) first formed this hypothesis on the basis of a series of experiments on subjects' response time in deciding whether a word string presented was a meaningful English expression. In addition to some control items, the idiomatic strings used in the study consisted roughly of two major types: semantically decomposable idioms and non-decomposable idioms. A semantically decomposable idiom is one whose constituting parts have either literal or figurative meanings that contribute independently to the string's overall idiomatic meaning, as can be seen in the examples of *get* (understand) *the picture* (situation) and *spill* (reveal) *the beans* (secret). A non-decomposable idiom, on the other hand, is one whose individual components do not contribute at all to the phrase's figurative meaning. That is, its idiomatic meaning cannot be obtained via an analysis of the meanings of the composing words, as in the cases of *kick the bucket* or *shoot the breeze*. The results of the study indicate that the subjects took significantly less time to process decomposable idioms than non-decomposable ones. Such a finding suggests that in processing idioms, people first attempt some decompositional analysis. If an idiom is decomposable, people process the individual word meanings and then easily decide how these meaningful parts work together to form the overall figurative meaning of the string. Yet if an idiom is not semantically decomposable, people will have difficulty interpreting it, because the analysis of the meanings of the individual parts and their combination offers no assistance in their effort. In fact, the compositional analysis will usually result in a conflict between the syntactic structure and the lexical meanings of the individual words because the normal sum of meanings of the individual parts offers no clue to the idiomatic meaning in question, hence significantly slowing down the interpretation process.

The results of Flores d'Arcais' (1993) five experimental studies also provide support for the compositional analysis hypothesis. For example, in one of the experiments the subjects were presented, on a computer display, one at a time, with 24 sentences containing idioms (12 of which were highly familiar and 12 of which were unfamiliar) together with 60 control (filler) sentences. Half the presented sentences each had a grammatical error. The subjects were asked to decide whether each of the sentences was grammatically correct. The subjects successfully detected about 30 percent of the idioms that contained an error (31 percent of the highly familiar ones and 28 percent of the unfamiliar ones). The results indicated that the subjects did indeed engage in syntactical and lexical analysis in processing the idioms, including even the highly familiar ones. In another experiment, one that studied the time subjects needed to process sentences containing an idiom and those without one, the subjects were asked to read sentences one word at a time on a computer display—that is, a subject had to press a key for the next word in the sentence to appear. A total of 96 sentences were used in the study, with 24 being idiom-containing sentences (12 familiar and 12 unfamiliar) and the remaining 72 being control items with no idioms. Twenty-four of the 72 control sentences matched the 24 idiom-containing sentences in syntactic structure and content. The time that the subjects took to inspect or process the *key* word (the word in an idiom string at which the string is recognized as an idiom, a concept that will be discussed in detail below) and its immediate following word was measured. In a matched control sentence, inspection time of the counterpart words (i.e. words that matched the idiom *key* word and its following words) was recorded. The results showed no significant difference between the average amount of time the subjects took to inspect the words in the familiar idioms and the time they used for the words in the control sentences, but there was a significant difference between the average time for inspecting the words in the familiar idioms and those in the unfamiliar ones. These findings led Flores d'Arcais to the conclusion that while idiom processing is no different from processing normal language items, unfamiliar idioms may require more time and effort to process and comprehend.

In explaining how the compositional analysis model works, Flores d'Arcais (1993) hypothesizes that, as in normal language processing, the idiom comprehension process consists of three components: syntactic parsing, lexical processing, and semantic analysis. When we encounter an idiom, our *syntactic parser* dissects its grammatical structure, the *lexical processor* accesses its lexical items in the mental lexicon and obtains the individual words' meanings, and then a semantic analysis is conducted using the information obtained from the syntactic parsing and the lexical processing. Of course, the first two components work like a "modular, with the lexical processor feeding to the parser the results of its analysis" (Flores d'Arcais, 1993, p. 85). Finally, the processing results from all the three components will be integrated and assessed at the *message* level or the *thematic interpretation unit* level. This *thematic interpretation unit*, also known as the *thematic processor*, operates by collecting, comparing, and interpreting all the information from the linguistic components available.

In summary, according to the compositional analysis view, the process of idiom comprehension may go as follows:

> [T]he syntactic parser and the lexical processor would work "normally" throughout the process of analyzing the input, the parser yielding a syntactic structure upon which the appropriate lexical representations computed by the lexical processor would be inserted. At the point of idiom identification, the lexical processor should retrieve the unique lexical representation of the idiom and its corresponding meaning. Thus, some conflict could arise at this point, in principle but not necessarily, between the syntactic processor and the lexical processor. The interpretation available so far to the message or thematic interpretation unit could become inconsistent with the new information sent by the lexical processor. This inconsistency may result in some processing difficulty. It is likely that such difficulty is only present with nonfamiliar idioms. Highly familiar ones would become immediately available even at the lexical level and would not constitute any problem. Because most metaphors are understood without many difficulties, unfamiliar idioms also should present no problems for understanding. (Flores d'Arcais, 1993, pp. 85–86)

Of course, the degree of an idiom's familiarity is not the only factor that may pose difficulty in our idiom comprehension process. There are many other factors, such as the degree of an idiom's compositionality, the context in which the idiom is used, and the language user's background knowledge. How these factors can affect our idiom comprehension will be discussed in detail in Chapter 5.

The compositional analysis hypothesis has also been indirectly supported by both neuro- and psycholinguistic studies. Papagno et al. (2006) examined idiom processing by two groups of brain-damaged individuals, one with damage to their left brains and the other with damage to their right brains. Their data analysis showed that both groups had great difficulty understanding idioms. On the basis of this finding and the fact that the left hemisphere of the brain is in charge of linguistic processing and the right deals with extra-linguistic (contextual) information, Papagno et al. conclude that idiom comprehension "requires all the lexical and extra-lexical skills involved in the comprehension of literal discourse" (ibid., p. 605). Using psycholinguistic analysis, Honeck and Temple (1994) investigated the comprehension of proverbs and found that their subjects used various problem-solving strategies in interpreting proverbs and that their comprehension process was effortful and controlled, rather than automatic (that is, rather than an easy retrieval of meaning from the mental lexicon, as the *direct access* hypothesis suggests). Bulut and Çelik-Yazici (2004) and Cooper (1999) reported similar results in their studies. Because their subjects were ESL learners, their research will be discussed in detail in L2 idiom comprehension in the next chapter. The findings of these studies demonstrate clearly the use of compositional analysis, pragmatic knowledge, and contextual information in idiom processing.

The Dual Idiom Representation Model

The *dual idiom representation* model is the most recent theory, first proposed by Titone and Connine (1994, 1999) and enhanced by Abel (2003). This hypothesis takes into account idiom differences explicitly in its postulation about idiom processing.[1] Building on all four earlier hypotheses, this model theorizes that idiom comprehension involves both normal linguistic processing (the essence of the *compositional analysis* hypothesis) and direct memory retrieval (the gist of all the first three hypotheses). Specifically, it agrees with the *compositional analysis* hypothesis that idiom comprehension involves normal linguistic processing where both literal and figurative meanings may be activated but it also believes that during the comprehension process, two alternative representations may ensue depending on whether the idiom is decomposable or non-decomposable. A decomposable idiom, whose constituents contribute to its total idiomatic meaning, usually will be first processed as a "constituent entry" like all normal, non-idiomatic phrases, but it can become an idiom entry (a direct retrieval item) if the idiomatic expression is repeatedly encountered as an idiom. On the other hand, a non-decomposable idiom, whose constituents do not contribute at all to its idiomatic meaning, will need to be understood and represented as an idiom entry. Furthermore, in comprehending decomposable idioms that lack an idiom entry at the lexical level, conceptual representations are accessed together with pragmatic knowledge and contextual information.[2]

This dual idiom representation model is based on the combined findings from a study by Abel (2003) and one by Titone and Connine (1994). In the latter study, Titone and Connine gave their subjects (fifty-six native speakers of English) 169 idioms and had them judge whether the idioms were each decomposable or non-decomposable. They also had the subjects rate the familiarity of the idioms using a seven-point scale. Abel (2003) used Titone and Connine's instruments and basically the same procedure in his study, but his subjects were non-native speakers of English (169 German college students). Abel compared the results of his study with those of Titone and Connine and found that the percentage of the idioms judged to be decomposable by native speakers was much lower than that by non-native speakers. This finding suggests that native speakers do not decompose idioms as often as non-native speakers. Abel believes the reason for this is that many more idioms have become idiom entries in the native speaker's lexicon than in the non-native speaker's. The more familiar an idiom is (that is, the more frequently it is encountered as an "idiomatic configuration"), "the more probable is the development of an idiom entry, independently of whether the idiom is decomposable or nondecomposable" (2003, p. 334). This hypothesis is further supported in the study by the finding that non-native speakers who had more exposure to English idioms also judged more idioms to be non-decomposable than did those who had less exposure. Based on these findings, the dual idiom representation model posits that in idiom comprehension, normal linguistic processing with conceptual representation competes with direct memory retrieval from idiom entries, and which of the two is activated depends on the decomposability and familiarity of the idiom.

One weakness of the model is that the findings on which it is based are not direct evidence showing how the two competing representations actually work in idiom processing. Another problem with the model lies with Abel's claim that "nondecomposable, i.e. noncompositional idioms require an idiom entry" (2003, pp. 342–343). In fact, when a person first encounters such an idiom (e.g. *kick the bucket*) there is no idiom entry, so the person, as the *compositional analysis hypothesis* suggests, will initially approach it using normal linguistic processing; when it does not lead to a sensible meaningful interpretation, the person will resort to conceptual representation by using contextual information and pragmatic knowledge, or knowledge of the world. In other words, initially a non-decomposable idiom does not have an idiom representation. Such a representation exists only after it has been learned as an idiom.[3]

As we conclude our discussion of the five major idiom processing models, it is important to note that some scholars (e.g. Glucksberg, 1993) believe that the first three hypotheses (the *literal first* or *idiom list* hypothesis, the *simultaneous processing* or *lexical representation* hypothesis, and the *figurative first* or *direct access* hypothesis) could be grouped together as one "direct look-up" model because, in essence, they are all based on the assumption that the idioms are understood via direct memory retrieval instead of linguistic processing. They contrast with the *compositional processing* hypothesis because the latter insists that idiom comprehension is not different from the comprehension of other expressions, as it involves normal linguistic and discourse processing. The *dual idiom representation* model, on the other hand, incorporates both normal linguistic processing and direct look-up in idiom comprehension. Viewed in this light, there are only three major idiom processing models. Now let us turn to two theoretical issues related to idiom processing: the "syntactic and semantic processing disassociation" hypothesis proposed by Peterson and Burgess (1993) and the "idiom key" proposition put forward by Cacciari and Tabbossi (1988), Flores d'Arcais (1993), and Tabossi and Zardon (1993, 1995). Although the two hypotheses are not idiom comprehension models per se, they offer unique insights into how we process idioms.

THE "SYNTACTIC AND SEMANTIC PROCESSING DISASSOCIATION" HYPOTHESIS

On the basis of a series of experimental studies, Peterson and Burgess (1993) first proposed the theory that there is a disassociation between the syntactic and the semantic processors in idiom comprehension. They reaffirmed it later in a study they conducted with their associates (Peterson et al. 2001). In developing this hypothesis, Peterson and Burgess provided some neurolinguistic support for the *compositional analysis* idiom processing model. According to Peterson and Burgess, the various idiom processing hypotheses may be grouped into three major models: the *syntactic-dominance* model, the *semantic-dominance* model, and the *syntactic-semantic autonomy* model (a model built on the syntactic and semantic disassociation theory). Both the *literal first* (*idiom list*) hypothesis and the *dual processing* (*lexical representation*) hypothesis belong to the *syntactic-dominant* model because they both hold that idiom comprehension always involves a literal processing—that is, a bottom-up syntactic processing of the idiomatic string (although idiomatic processing is usually faster than literal processing, according to the *lexical representation* hypothesis). The premise of the *syntactic-dominant* model is that "output of the syntactic processor automatically guides the operation of the semantic processor; that is, the semantic processor is obligatorily responsive to structural input" (Peterson & Burgess, 1993, p. 204).

The *figurative first* or *direct access* hypothesis, on the other hand, constitutes a *semantic-dominant* model because it postulates that the figurative meanings of idioms can be accessed directly, without any literal or syntactic analysis. On this model, people always assess the figurative meaning of an idiom first and they will process its literal meaning only if the figurative meaning turns out to be inappropriate in the context. In other words, the semantic processor plays the leading role in the idiom comprehension process, relegating literal or syntactic processing to the role of a secondary function. Peterson and Burgess find this model inadequate, arguing that for such a processing model to work, the semantic processor needs to terminate the literal processing once a language user encounters the first word of an idiom, but such instant termination is not likely in most cases. Take, for example, the processing of the sentence "The man *kicked the bucket.*" According to the *direct access* model, when encountering the first word of the idiom, "kicked," a language user has to stop literal processing of the idiom and understand the remaining verb phrase idiomatically. Yet often there is no contextual clue to suggest that the remaining sentence will end idiomatically. In fact, the string "The man kicked . . ." in most cases will end in a literal statement such as "The man kicked a ball." While Peterson and Burgess question the chances of the immediate termination of literal processing, they do believe that during the process of an idiom comprehension, the semantic processor may be able to suspend literal processing when sufficient contextual information indicates the expression is an idiom. That is, the semantic processor may abort the literal processing, including the syntactic processing, of an idiom in a figuratively biasing context. Yet such a suspension often may not be feasible due to the time constraints in language processing.

According to Peterson and Burgess, the *compositional analysis* hypothesis, which posits that the syntactic and lexical processor work normally throughout the idiom comprehension process, forms the basis of the *syntactic-semantic autonomy* model. This model shares the *semantic-dominance* model's position that the semantic processor may be able to terminate the literal processing of an idiom but differs from the latter model in a very important way: "[I]n this model there is no feedback from the semantic to the syntactic processor, hence the termination of the literal analysis does not inhibit further [syntactic] processing" (1993, p. 206). In other words, a full syntactic analysis of an idiom is always conducted, although no complete literal interpretation will be generated. The first half of the hypothesis—that is, the

TABLE 3.1
Empirical Predictions Made by the Three Models

Empirical Question	Syntactic-Dominance Model	Semantic-Dominance Model	Syntactic-Semantic Autonomy Model
Does an idiom undergo a full syntactic analysis?	YES	NO	YES
Is the literal meaning of an idiom computed?	YES	NO	NO

From Peterson and Burgess (1993, p. 210). Reprinted by permission of the publisher, Lawrence Erlbaum.

proposition that a complete syntactic analysis is always involved in idiom processing—is in fact shared by the *syntactic-dominance* model, but the second half of the hypothesis—the suggestion that no complete literal interpretation is conducted—differentiates the *syntactic-semantic autonomy* model from the *syntactic-dominant* model because the latter insists on the engagement of a full literal analysis of an idiom. Table 3.1 from Peterson and Burgess (1993, p. 211) shows the similarities and differences among the three models.

Peterson and Burgess support their syntactic and semantic disassociation theory with the results of three experiments they and their associates conducted. In the first experiment, they read their subjects sentences that ended with an incomplete idiom such as *kick the*... Some of the sentences were biased for a literal noun completion such as "The soccer player slipped when trying to *kick the* (ball)"; others were biased for a figurative noun completion such as "The man was old and feeble, and it was believed that he would soon *kick the* (bucket)." After the subjects heard each of the incomplete sentences, they were given a target word (either a noun or a verb, e.g. "grown" or "town") on a computer screen and were told to name the word as quickly as possible. The subjects' response times (latencies) were recorded and examined for a possible syntactic priming effect. According to previous studies, subjects respond to syntactically appropriate words much faster than to inappropriate ones. Therefore, if a complete syntactic analysis of an idiom is indeed always conducted in idiom processing, the subjects' response time to a syntactically inappropriate word (in this case, a verb) would be much slower than that to an appropriate word (a noun). The results of the experiment supported this hypothesis, for the subjects' response time to the target words of verbs was much longer than to those of nouns in both literally and figuratively (idiomatically) biased sentences. In response to the possible criticism that the faster response time to the nouns could have been due to the fact that the nouns were more semantically related to the general meaning of the sentences than the verbs, Peterson and Burgess with their associates conducted another experiment where every procedure and condition was the same as the first one except that the target words were not real words but made-up nouns (e.g. "glatter" and "ditter") and verbs (e.g. "glatted" and "ditted"). The same results were obtained in this experiment, further supporting the hypothesis of an obligatory full syntactic analysis in idiom processing.

To test whether a full literal interpretation of an idiom is always involved in idiom comprehension, Peterson and Burgess carried out with their associates a third experiment in which the conceptual priming effect, rather than the syntactic priming effect, was studied. The experiment was identical to the previous ones except that the types of target words were not nouns and verbs but concrete ones versus abstract ones. The incomplete sentences were all biased for a concrete noun completion. If a complete literal interpretation of an idiom is always conducted, the subjects' time in responding to an abstract target word would be much slower than to a concrete word. Yet the results of the experiment did not support this hypothesis. While the subjects' response time to abstract words in the literally biased sentences was indeed much slower than to concrete words, their response time to abstract words in the figuratively biased sentences was actually slightly faster than to concrete words, suggesting that "the literal meaning of an idiomatic phrase is computed only in literally biased contexts," and in an idiomatic-interpretation-biased context, "literal analysis appears to be terminated before the final word of the phrase" (1993, p. 216). In explaining how the syntactic and semantic disassociation works in idiom comprehension, Peterson and Burgess cite new developments in neurolinguistics regarding modularity which show that the right hemisphere is involved in some aspects of language processing. While the left hemisphere is largely responsible for syntactic processing, the right hemisphere plays a role in interpretation of meaning, especially figurative meanings. In other words, the left hemisphere typically interprets a sentence mostly through syntactic parsing, often giving it a literal interpretation, but the right hemisphere usually approaches a sentence from its discourse context, and is often quicker at uncovering a figurative meaning. The two hemispheres often engage in a horse race in interpreting an expression, enabling a disassociation between the two.

THE "IDIOM KEY" HYPOTHESIS

Another important concept related to idiom comprehension process that deserves our attention is the *idiom key* hypothesis proposed by a group of scholars (Cacciari & Tabossi, 1988; Flores d'Arcais, 1993; Tabossi & Zardon, 1993, 1995). This hypothesis, which has also been called *point of idiom uniqueness* or *point of idiom recognition* (Flores d'Arcais, 1993), suggests that the processing of an idiomatic string begins literally until sufficient information in the string makes it recognizable as an idiom. The *idiom key* thus refers to the point in an idiomatic string at which people can identify the string as an idiom. While some scholars (e.g. Abel, 2003) have classified the idiom key hypothesis as a separate idiom processing model—the "configuration model"—most, including those who proposed it, do not view it as a complete processing model because the hypothesis does not involve a different processing mode. Instead, it uses a model similar to the *compositional analysis*, and it only deals with the exact point in the comprehension process at which the idiom meaning is activated. Cacciari and Tabbossi (1988) first operationalized the hypothesis in an experimental study in which the subjects were given an increasingly longer idiom fragment and were asked to complete the idiom. For example, for the idiom *to be in seventh heaven*, they were first given the phrase "to be in," and then the fragment "to be in seventh." The point at which the majority of the subjects completed the fragment idiomatically was identified as its *key*. In the example of *to be in seventh heaven*, the word "seventh" was found to be the idiom's *key*. Cacciari and Tabossi highlight the importance of the key by hypothesizing that "in the absence of a context which could anticipate the recognition of an idiom . . . , the recognition of the idiomatic configuration cannot take place until after the key has been accessed" (1988, p. 679).

The concept of idiom key has been compared to the uniqueness or the recognition point of a lexical item (Tabossi & Zardon, 1993) and to the point at which an ambiguous sentence is disambiguated (Flores d'Arcais, 1993). According to Tabossi and Zardon (1993), the uniqueness point of a word in a language depends on the lexicon of the language. For instance, in English, *pow* may be an initial fragment of several words such as *powder, power*, or *powwow, powd* can only be a part of one word: *powder*. Therefore, the letter *d* is the uniqueness or recognition point of the word *powder* because no other existing English words begin with the *powd* letter string. The similarity between the idiom key and the uniqueness point of a word lies in the fact that they both refer to the point where a language user is able to decide the meaning of the item in question, be it an idiom or a word. However, as Tabossi and Zardon point out, the concept of idiom key also differs from the uniqueness point as well as the recognition point of a lexical item in two aspects. First, while the uniqueness point of a word serves as a point after which only one word or meaning is possible, as in the case of *powd*, the idiom key does not set such a constraint because even after the key of an idiom, a literal completion of the string may still be possible. Tabossi and Zardan illustrate the point with the example *to be in seventh heaven*, an idiom whose key has been identified as *seventh*. Yet this does not mean that the string cannot be completed as "to be in seventh place." The second difference between the key of an idiom and the uniqueness point of a word is that a word can be recognized before its uniqueness point because contextual information may work along with perceptual data to help a language user identify a word. Yet the key of an idiom is not context dependent, because studies show that language users tend to interpret a string with an idiom structure idiomatically even in contexts where a literal interpretation is also possible. For example, in Cacciari and Tabossi's (1988) study, the subjects were asked to complete partial strings of Italian expressions in context and they were found to prefer idiomatic completions even when literal ones were equally legitimate. For instance, many opted for *seventh heaven* when the context seventh place was also a correct choice. Tabossi and Zardon thus conclude that the key of an idiom does not mean exactly the same as either the uniqueness or the recognition point of a lexical item, and hence its function in idiom processing cannot be identical to that of either concept in word recognition.

According to Flores d'Arcais (1993), understanding idioms is very similar to understanding ambiguous sentences, because many idiomatic phrases can be treated as ambiguous structures that are open to two alternative interpretations. Thus, the point where a word string is recognized as an idiomatic expression is almost tantamount to the point where an ambiguous sentence is disambiguated. What happens in both cases is that sufficient linguistic and contextual information is now available to trigger the clarification and identification of the meaning of the structure in question. Of course, a fundamental difference exists between ambiguous sentences and idioms: disambiguating an ambiguous sentence usually entails two alternative parsing undertakings that result in two different grammatical structures, but no such alternative parsing operations are involved in understanding the two interpretations of an idiom (a literal one and an idiomatic or figurative one when both are possible). Furthermore, unlike in an ambiguous sentence where the two alternative meanings are incongruous, the two meanings of an idiom are often related, with the idiomatic meaning being a metaphorical extension of the literal one, as can be seen in the examples of *being in hot water* (whose idiomatic meaning of "being in trouble" is derived from its literal one) and *spinning wheels* (whose idiomatic meaning of "wasting effort" is a figurative extension of its literal one).

In short, while the key of an idiom resembles the point of uniqueness or the point of recognition of a lexical item and the point at which an ambiguous sentence is disambiguated, it differs from each of them in some important ways. It is thus a concept peculiar to idioms. As Tabossi and Zardon (1993) point out, the key of an idiom has no formal property and no special syntactic function. It can be a content word or a functional word such as a preposition and it may be made up of more than one word (Cacciari & Tabossi, 1988). It does not constitute a point in a word string after which no other than idiomatic completion is possible. Nor does it signify a syntactic ambiguity or aberration. Instead, it merely indicates a point after which a word string is most likely to be completed as an idiom, although a literal completion may still be possible. The idiom key does, however, claim one more important feature: it is the most essential part of an idiom. As has been widely noted, not all segments in an idiom are equally important in its constitution as an idiom. While some words in an idiom are substitutable (e.g. *develop/have cold feet*), others are not (e.g. *have cold ankles?*).

Another question concerning the idiom key concept is where the key is usually located in an idiomatic expression. Because the idiom key refers to a point where sufficient information becomes available for identifying a string as an idiom, the key is unlikely to be in the first one or two words in the expression. Instead, it is most likely to be in the second half of the word string. Yet where in the latter half is it usually located? The question may be difficult to answer, given the aforementioned fact that the idiom key does not have any formal property or any special syntactic role, a fact which may suggest the key's location may vary from idiom to idiom. Although no studies seem to have been conducted on the question exclusively, a few have looked at it indirectly or as a subissue in a larger investigation (Flores d'Arcais, 1993; Tabossi & Zardon, 1993). The results of these studies appear to show that the location may be determined by the types and/or structure patterns of idioms. For example, in one of Tabossi and Zardon's (1993) experiments, fifteen native speakers of Italian were invited as judges to complete increasingly longer segments of idiomatic Italian strings that were all made up of the syntactic structure of Verb (Noun Phrase) (Prepositional Phrase), where at least one of the two parenthetical constitutes is present. In the case of the idiom *tirava acqua al suo milino* (*pulled water to her mill*, meaning "pursued her interest"), the fifteen judges would be asked to complete the idiomatic expression, first after being presented only with the verb *pulled*, then after being presented with the words *pulled water*, and so on. The results indicate that in some of the idiomatic strings, 90 percent of the judges were able to complete the string as an idiom after the first content word following the verb, and in many others, 90 percent of them had to wait until the second noun to complete the string idiomatically. Thus, it could be assumed that in idioms with a V (NP) (PP) syntactic structure, the key is most likely either the first or the second content word after the verb. The results of another experiment by Tabossi and Zardon also indirectly supported the assumption. In this experiment, the subjects were presented with sentences containing the aforementioned idioms one word at a time and asked to indicate their recognition of the idiomatic meaning. It was found that with the idiomatic strings whose key was believed to be the first content word after the verb, the subjects were all able to recognize their idiomatic meanings after the first content word, and with those strings whose key was supposed to be the second content word, the subjects' activation of the idiomatic meanings occurred with the second content word.

SUMMARY

Many different theories have been proposed regarding idiom comprehension, and they boil down to five major hypotheses: (1) *the literal first* or *idiom-list* hypothesis, (2) the *dual processing* or *lexical representation* hypothesis, (3) the *direct access* hypothesis, (4) the *compositional analysis* hypothesis, and (5) the *dual idiom representation* model. Of the five, the last two, especially the *dual idiom representation* model, appear to offer a more complete picture of idiom processing. Two other interesting and important theoretical issues related to idiom comprehension are "syntactic and semantic processing disassociation" and "the idiom key," each of which offers an interesting and thought-provoking insight. An examination of these various theories indicates that idiom comprehension is a very complex process and a very challenging research issue for linguists and applied linguists alike.

Questions for Study or Discussion

1. Without referring to any of the hypotheses regarding idiom processing mentioned in the chapter, say how you comprehend idioms (both familiar and unknown ones). Then decide whether the process you use conforms to any of the hypotheses and explain why.
2. Compare and contrast the five hypotheses regarding idiom comprehension.
   Based on your comparison and contrast,
   - develop a list of the similarities and differences among them;
   - explain which one of the hypotheses you find most convincing and why.
3. The *literal first* (or *idiom list*) hypothesis posits a separate idiom list in our mental lexicon, and the *lexical representation* model, while denying a separate list, also postulates idioms exist in the lexicon as "long word" lexical items, basically also acknowledging the existence of idioms as unique items distinctive from other regular lexical items. Similarly, the *direct access* and the *dual idiom representation* models indicate, directly or indirectly, the existence of idiom entries in our lexicon. On the basis of your experience and understanding, do you think there are idiom entries in a speaker's lexicon? Why?
4. The *dual idiom representation* model postulates that two alternative processes compete in idiom comprehension: normal linguistic processing (involving conceptual representation) and direct memory retrieval from idiom entries. The model also proposes that which of the two processes is activated depends on the decomposability and the

familiarity of the idiom. The hypothesis is based on indirect evidence. Can you think of a way to test this model empirically in a direct manner?

5. Peterson and Burgess's "syntactic and semantic processing dissociation" hypothesis presupposes the existence of a syntactic as well as a semantic processor in idiom processing. On the basis of your experience and/or your reading of neuro- or psycholinguistics, do you agree with this separate processor theory? Why, or why not?

6. According to Tabossi and Zardon (1993), the *idiom key* in idioms with a verb plus noun(s) (i.e. the complement of the verb) is usually the first or the second content word after the verb. Test the theory by following the procedure they used in their study to examine four English idioms that conform to the verb plus noun(s) structure such as *jump the gun* and *tie up loose ends*.

Chapter 4

L2 Idiom Processing and Comprehension

INTRODUCTION

How do L2 learners process and understand idioms? What strategies do they employ? What are the differences between L2 and L1 idiom processing? These are some of the questions that will be addressed in this chapter. While, as was shown in the last chapter, there has been an enormous amount of research on idiom processing in L1, the number of studies on L2 idiom comprehension has been rather small. Fortunately, despite a lack of adequate research on L2 idiom processing, the few studies that do exist (Abdullah & Jackson, 1998; Abel, 2003; Boers, 2000b; Bulut & Çelik-Yazici, 2004; Charteris-Black, 2002; Cooper, 1999; Galka & Flahive, 2005; Irujo, 1986a; Kövecses & Szabó, 1996; Littlemore, 2001) have yielded some very informative findings about L2 idiom comprehension. Although these studies, with the exception of that of Cooper (1999), did not make a specific attempt at identifying a unique L2 idiom comprehension model, their findings about the common strategies L2 learners use in processing idioms do offer good glimpses into the L2 idiom comprehension process. To help the reader understand this process, we shall first discuss the major strategies that L2 learners use and then explore the development of an L2 idiom comprehension model based on those proposed by Abel (2003) and Cooper (1999).

MAJOR STRATEGIES USED IN L2 IDIOM COMPREHENSION

Use of Contextual Information

Using contextual information is a major strategy that L2 learners use in processing idioms. Such use is found in all the studies that have examined L2 learners' understanding of idiom in context (e.g. Bulut & Çelik-Yazici, 2004; Cooper, 1999).[1] In fact, according to both Cooper (1999) and Bulut and Çelik-Yazici (2004), guessing from contextual information is the most frequently used and also the most effective strategy. Using the "think aloud" technique, Cooper (1999) examined eighteen college ESL students' use of strategies in idiom comprehension. He identified eight key strategies the subjects employed. Of the total number of strategies the subjects employed, using contextual information accounted for 28 percent, the highest percentage. Of the other strategies, only "discussing and analyzing" (24 percent) and "using literal meaning" (19 percent) made up more than single-digit percentages. In terms of the accuracy rate of each of the strategies in figuring out the meaning of idioms, the use of contextual information surpasses the other strategies by an even larger margin. It accounted for 57 percent of the total number of correctly guessed idioms, while the other seven strategies accounted for only 43 percent. In Bulut and Çelik-Yazici's study, the statistical analysis of the subjects' (eighteen Turkish teachers of English) use of strategies in the interpretation of twenty idioms (all borrowed from Cooper's study) yielded similar findings. That is, "guessing from context" was not only the most frequently used strategy but also the most successful one. Of course, as can be inferred from the findings, the use of contextual information, effective as it is, does not always lead to correct understanding of an idiom.

Use of L1: Aid or Interference?

One of the first questions that researchers examine in dealing with L2 idiom comprehension is perhaps how learners' L1 may assist or hinder their understanding. The influence of L1 on L2 language acquisition has been extensively examined and well documented, although the extent of the influence is debatable (Gass & Selinker, 1983; Kellerman, 1977, 1979; Odlin, 1989, 2005). It is thus no accident that the impact of L1 on L2 idiom comprehension has also been a focus of study in L2 idiom comprehension and learning. Almost all studies that examined idiom comprehension and learning in L2 have looked at the issue of L1 influence (Abdullah & Jackson, 1998; Charteris-Black, 2002; Cooper, 1999; Irujo, 1986a; Littlemore, 2001). The findings of the studies all indicate some L1 influence. While some studies show that looking for L1 equivalents is usually the first strategy L2 learners employ in dealing with a new idiom, the extent of the influence of L1 has been shown to vary depending on whether the L2 idiom has a comparable counterpart in L1 and on the degree of its similarity to or difference from the counterpart.

For example, in one of the early studies on L2 idiom comprehension and use, Irujo (1986a) investigated advanced Venezuelan ESL learners' comprehension, recall, and production of idioms. To test the subjects' recognition and comprehension of English idioms, Irujo selected 45 idioms, 15 of which were identical in form and meaning to their Spanish equivalents, 15 similar to their Spanish equivalents, and 15 were completely different. She created 45 multiple-choice questions with each question containing one of the 45 idioms. The students were asked to select from four choices an answer that correctly defined the meaning of the idiom in question. The four choices included a correct paraphrase, a statement related to the correct paraphrase, a literal interpretation, and an irrelevant statement. After the multiple-choice test, the subjects were asked to write a definition of each of the idioms in either English or Spanish. Statistical analyses of the subjects' performance on the tests reveal that the subjects performed significantly better on the idioms identical and similar to their Spanish equivalents than on those different from their Spanish counterparts, suggesting that, in understanding L2 idioms, "subjects were able to generalize from the meaning in their first language to the meaning in the second language if the form was identical or similar; slight differences in form did not affect this process" (ibid., p. 294). In other words, L1 knowledge may assist L2 learners in their comprehension of L2 idioms that are identical or similar to L1 equivalents. By the same token, idioms that have no similar or identical L1 equivalents pose greater challenges for L2 learners.

Abdullah and Jackson (1998) also report that idioms that are identical in both L1 and L2 are the easiest for L2 learners to understand. Yet their findings about those L2 idioms that have similar but not identical L1 equivalents are quite different. They examined 120 Syrian college seniors' comprehension and production of English idioms. In measuring the subjects' comprehension of idioms, they first gave the subjects an 80-item multiple-choice comprehension test with each item containing an idiom. The subjects were asked to tell the meaning of the idiom by selecting the correct definition from the multiple choices given. Of the 80 English idioms, 20 were identical to Syrian idioms both in form and meaning (e.g. *to play with fire*, an idiomatic saying that occurs in both languages and has exactly the same meaning: "court trouble"), 20 were similar in structure but different in meaning (e.g. *to bite the dust*, an idiom that means "to die" or "be finished" in English but "to be very poor/miserable" in Syrian Arabic), 20 were different in form but had the same meanings or pragmatic functions (e.g. the English idiom *to add insult to injury* and the Syrian idiom *to make clay wetter*, though different in form, have the same meaning of "making a bad situation worse), and 20 were completely different both in form and meaning. In addition to the multiple choice test, the researchers asked the subjects to translate each of the idioms into Syrian to double-check their comprehension. In the production part of the study the subjects were told to translate into English 80 Syrian idioms, 60 of which were counterparts of the first 60 on the English idiom comprehension test used in the first part of the study: 20 identical, 20 similar in form but different in meaning, and 20 different in form but similar in meaning. The other 20 Syrian idioms had no English equivalents. In the third part of the study the researchers interviewed the subjects to ascertain the strategies the subjects used in their comprehension and production of the idioms.

The results of the study reveal that the subjects used their L1 in both the comprehension and the production tests and exhibited both positive transfer and negative transfer in the process. The subjects scored much higher in both the comprehension and production of identical (or cognate) idioms thanks to positive transfer, and they scored significantly lower on idioms that were identical in form but different in meaning (i.e. false cognate idioms), due to negative transfer. They also noticed a surprising phenomenon with regard to the identical idioms. The subjects' scores on the comprehension of the identical idioms were significantly higher than their scores on the production of these idioms (i.e. translating Syrian counterpart idioms into English). Many of the subjects did not translate the identical Syrian idioms into English (e.g. not translating *play with fire* from Syrian into English), fearing that no such identical idioms existed in English. This contrasts with the fact that the subjects had no problem translating the English *play with fire* into Syrian verbatim. This leads Abdullah and Jackson to the hypothesis that L2 students often entertain the erroneous assumption that idioms are always language or culture specific, an assumption that causes them, in turn, to avoid direct translation of identical idioms from their L1 into the target language.

In a study examining thirty-six Malay speakers' comprehension and production of English metaphorical idioms, Charteris-Black (2002) obtained some similar findings regarding L2 speakers' use of L1 or the influence of L1 in L2 idiom comprehension. Bulut and Çelik-Yazici (2004) and Cooper (1999) also identified some use of L1 in their studies, although such use was found to be rather minimal. Of course, it is very difficult to decide the exact extent of the use of L1 strategies. The difficulty is further compounded by the fact that sometimes the distinction between L1 and L2 strategies is a very close judgment call (Irujo, 1986a, 1993). Viewed as a whole, the findings from the various studies suggest that while idioms identical in L1 and L2 pose no challenges for L2 learners, the jury is still out on the level of difficulty of idioms that are similar but not identical either in form or in meaning between

L1 and L2. For example, Irujo (1986a) found that similar idioms, like those identical ones, were fairly easy for L2 learners to comprehend, but Abdullah and Jackson (1998) and Charteris-Black (2002) discovered that such idioms were more difficult than those that were totally different between the two languages or absent in learners' L1. The latter finding is similar to those obtained in the studies about L1 influence on L2 acquisition of grammatical structures and lexical items in general (Schacter, 1974; Laufer, 1991). For instance, in Schacter's study (1974) on L2 learners' use of English relative clauses it was found that students whose native languages boasted relative clauses similar to those in English in structure (e.g. Arabic and Persian) made more errors in using English relative clauses in writing than those students whose native language possessed relative clauses that are significantly different (e.g. Chinese and Japanese). Of course, one explanation for the smaller number of errors the latter group of students made is that they used substantially fewer relative clauses in English (that is, they used the avoidance strategy) because of the differences between English relative clauses and those in their native language.

Use of Pragmatic Knowledge or Knowledge of the World

Many studies on L2 idiom comprehension show that L2 learners make heavy use of pragmatic knowledge, or knowledge of the world (Abdullah & Jackson, 1998; Bulut & Çelik-Yazici, 2004; Charteris-Black, 2002; Cooper, 1999). Before I elaborate on this issue, it is necessary to mention that the use of pragmatic knowledge often overlaps with the use of the literal meaning of an idiom to work out its figurative meaning, and sometimes scholars classify such use exclusively as the latter (Bulut & Çelik-Yazici, 2004; Cooper, 1999). For example, Bulut and Çelik-Yazici cited the following excerpt from a subject's think-aloud transcription as an example of the strategy of "using the literal meaning of the idiom as a key" to figure out the meaning of *to stir up a hornet's net*:

> *To stir up a hornet's nest* . . . I don't know the meaning of hornet, but I think it is a kind bird or maybe bee. When I see this idiom, I think of a person who is stirring up a nest, he is causing trouble. Uh . . . Nest symbolises peace and this person destroys the peace by stirring up, so I think it means making others angry.
>
> (2004, p. 110)

While, indeed, the subject was making use of the literal meaning here, he or she was simultaneously using common world knowledge about bird or bee nests and the negative consequence that disturbing such a nest would incur to decipher the idiom's meaning. In fact, the person even extended such pragmatic knowledge to make metaphorical associations in saying, "Nest symbolises peace." Similarly, Cooper's example of the use of literal meaning below also demonstrates the employment of world knowledge: in figuring out the meaning of *burning the candle at both ends*, his subject was quoted as saying, "the wax [of the candle burning at both ends] would be melting quicker . . . working too much" (1999, 249). Here, like the subject in Bulut and Çelik-Yazici's study, this student also made a metaphorical association, one between "burning too quickly" and working too hard.

The use of pragmatic knowledge, as well as metaphorical association, was explicitly identified in Abdullah and Jackson's study (1998). For example, with the idiom *to give someone the cold shoulder*, the subjects reportedly inferred that the word "cold" could metaphorically suggest "unwelcome" because "cold" meant the opposite of "warm," hence the meaning unwelcome. For the idiom *to skate on thin ice*, the subjects understood, on the basis of their knowledge of the world, the danger of skating on thin ice and associated it with doing something very risky. In fact, in processing idioms that were different in form but similar in meaning and function and those that were completely different between the English and Syrian, the subjects relied completely on "pragmatic knowledge" and "metaphorical association"—that is, they did not use their L1 at all. According to Winner (1988), adequate world knowledge is crucial in the understanding of metaphorical idioms. Yet because many metaphorical idioms are culturally bound (e.g. *white elephant* and *carry coals to Newcastle*), L2 learners often do not have the cultural knowledge needed to comprehend these idioms, a point that will be addressed later. Note, however, that the use of pragmatic knowledge may not always lead to the correct interpretation of idioms. Furthermore, not all idioms are metaphorical. Hence, metaphorical association and world knowledge may not be beneficial in helping learners to understand non-metaphorical or non-decomposable idioms, especially those that violate semantic rules (*rain cats and dogs*) or are ill-formed—that is, those that violate syntactic rules (*by and large, trip the light fantastic*) (Abdullah & Jackson, 1998, p. 104).

Use or Interference of L1 Cultural Knowledge

Research demonstrates that the use of many idioms, especially those based on metaphors, is motivated by our conceptual system (Boers & Demecheleer, 1997, 2001; Boers et al., 2004b; Kövecses & Szabó, 1996; Nayak & Gibb, 1990). These idioms are made meaningful by the conceptual structures underlying them. For example, it is the conceptual (metaphorical) structure of "life/work being sport" that has allowed the baseball idiom *hit a home run* in American English to mean "achieved a great success in something" outside sports. Furthermore, a series of experiments that Gibbs and his associates conducted exhibit that conceptual knowledge is usually activated in the comprehension of metaphorical idioms (Gibbs, 1990, 1992, 1995; Gibbs et al., 1997; Gibbs & O'Brien, 1990; Nayak & Gibbs, 1990).[2] Nayak and Gibbs' (1990) findings from six experiments also demonstrate that human "understanding of idioms is often constrained by their conceptual knowledge of the domains to which idioms refer" (p. 328), and it is this conceptual knowledge of the metaphorical connection between the source and target domains that makes our understanding of metaphorical idioms possible.

It is necessary to add that conceptual knowledge is sometimes culture-specific because some conceptual metaphoric links have been found to be shaped by specific cultures (Boers & Demecheleer, 1997, 2001; Johnson & Rosano, 1993; Liu, 2002). Boers and Demecheleer's corpus research (1997) indicates, for example, that sailing is a relatively prominent source of metaphorical idioms in English while food and cooking are a more productive source in French. Johnson & Rosano's study (1993) also provides empirical evidence. In their study, native English-speaking subjects and ESL subjects (mostly from the Far East) were asked to interpret some metaphors. The two groups' interpretations of the metaphor were found to be very different. Regarding the metaphor "My sister was a butterfly," the native English-speaking subjects' interpretations focus on the sister's physical diminutiveness, fragility, timidity, innocence, vulnerability, and tenderness, while the ESL subjects' center on the sister's pretty and colorful appearance and mobility. It is clear that in the East, "butterfly" carries metaphorical images very different from those found in the West. Similarly, Liu (2002) also demonstrates how the knowledge of some of our conceptual and metaphorical links is culture-specific via an extensive comparison between dominant American and Chinese metaphorical idioms. For instance, he finds that in numerous instances, Americans use sports and business metaphorical idioms but Chinese employ eating and family metaphors in expressing the same meaning.

Furthermore, lack of culture-specific conceptual knowledge has been found to cause idiom comprehension problems in L2 (Boers & Demecheleer, 2001; Boers et al., 2004b; Charteris-Black, 2002; Littlemore, 2001). Boers and Demecheleer (2001) had French college ESL students guess the meaning of metaphorical idioms in English that had no equivalents in French but whose source domains varied. Some of the source domains were also prominent in French (e.g. food) and some were not (e.g. sailing). The results revealed that the students had significantly more difficulty in inferring the meaning of English idioms whose source domains were not productive in French. Charteris-Black's study of Malay students' understanding of forty English metaphorical idioms also shows the importance of culture-specific conceptual knowledge. Charteris-Black divided the idioms into six types according to their similarities to and differences from the Malay idioms in meaning and structure. Type 1 were those with "equivalent conceptual basis and equivalent linguistic form" (e.g. *change hand* in both English and Malay). Type 2 were those sharing "similar linguistic form and equivalent conceptual basis" (*big mouth* in English and *mouth big jar* in Malay). Type 3 were those having "equivalent linguistic form but different conceptual basis" (e.g. *eat your heart out* in English but *eat liver* in Malay). Type 4 were those with "different linguistic form but equivalent conceptual basis" (e.g. *poke your nose into something* in English but *mix hand* in Malay). Type 5 were those having "different linguistic form and different conceptual basis" with transparent meaning (e.g. *turn a blind eye to* in English but *transport foot* in Malay). Type 6 were those with "different conceptual basis and different linguistic form" with opaque meaning (e.g. *turn the other cheek* in English but *thin eared* in Malay). The results of the study show that the subjects performed best in comprehending Types 1 and 2 idioms followed by Type 4 (different linguistic form but equivalent conceptual basis). They did worst on Type 3 (equivalent linguistic form but different conceptual basis), worse even than on Types 5 and 6 (no similarity either in form or concept basis). The subjects' special difficulty with Type 3 idioms suggests that equivalent linguistic forms may lead learners to resort to their first language conceptual basis and result in a misinterpretation of idioms. The fact the subjects had more difficulty with Type 3 than Type 4 idioms also indicates that L1 conceptual transfer causes more serious problems than L1 linguistic form transfer.

Like Charteris-Black, Littlemore (2001) also finds in her study the interference of L1 cultural background knowledge on L2 learners' idiom comprehension. The subjects in her study were twenty Bangladeshi students attending civil service reform courses at a British university. They listened to a recorded lecture extract that contained ten metaphorical idioms such as *add a new chapter to something* and *hand-picked*. These expressions were used primarily for evaluative purposes—that is, for gauging the speaker's opinion of or attitude toward various new civil service policies that the British government had just implemented. After finishing listening, the students were asked to write down their interpretations of the ten metaphorical expressions and explain how they had arrived at the meaning—that is, via "context, guessing, knowing it before . . ." Then they were requested to answer, in writing, questions such as what they believed to be the speaker's opinion toward the subject under discussion. The results show that the metaphorical idioms did present special challenges for many of the subjects because these students often resorted to their L1 cultural background knowledge. From these findings, Littlemore (2001) concludes that "cultural background and expectations play a large part in determining the interpretations that students make [regarding metaphorical idioms]" (p. 345). It is thus important to caution L2 learners about the use of L1 culture-specific conceptual structure to interpret idioms.

In short, the discussion in this section shows a strong need for L2 speakers to possess knowledge of the concepts that motivate metaphorical idioms in the target language in order to understand such idioms.

HEURISTIC APPROACH: A DISTINCTIVE L2 IDIOM PROCESSING MODEL?

Of the four aforementioned strategies, the use of native language and native cultural knowledge is peculiar to L2 idiom processing. The use of contextual information and conceptual knowledge, on the other hand, is found in L1 idiom processing as well. Yet even though the latter strategy is also used in L1, the frequency of its use is expected to be much higher in L2. The reason is that the chances of L2 speakers encountering unknown idioms are much higher than for L1 speakers, and comprehending unknown idioms is a much slower and more complex process than understanding known ones. As Abel's (2003) dual idiom representation model indicates, when one encounters a known idiom it often prompts an idiom representation (that is, a direct memory retrieval), but when one comes across an unknown idiom it activates a much slower and more complex conceptual representation. Given all the above information, it is safe to say that L2 learners use more strategies, in terms of both type and frequency, than native speakers in processing idioms. What does this fact say about L2 idiom processing? Does it make L2 idiom comprehension a unique process different from L1 idiom processing? Cooper (1999) and Bulut and Çelik-Yazici (2004) appear to believe so.

On the basis of his scrutiny of his ESL subjects' use of strategies, Cooper (1999) concludes that L2 idiom processing does not completely follow any of the four well-known L1 idiom processing models: (1) *literal first*, (2) *idiom-list*, (3) *direct access*, and (4) *compositional analysis*. Instead, L2 speakers use a *heuristic* approach, one that involves a greater variety of strategies than any one of the L1 models encompasses. By the term *heuristic*, Cooper means "both a procedure and a learning method" (ibid., p. 254). In such a procedure, an L2 learner approaches an idiom as a problem and tries to solve it on a trial and error basis by using a variety of strategies, including guessing, using pragmatic knowledge, and experimentation. Cooper's conclusion is later supported by Bulut and Çelik-Yazici's (2004) study of the idiom processing strategies employed by eighteen Turkish teachers of English. Bulut and Çelik-Yazici's (2004) data analysis shows that their subjects, like Cooper's, also used a heuristic approach in their interpretation. An additional finding by Bulut and Çelik-Yazici is that "guessing from context" always seems to be the first strategy used in the *heuristic* model. They hypothesize that L2 learners usually will not resort to other strategies until the use of contextual information fails to lead to a meaningful interpretation.

While this *heuristic* model makes good sense for dealing with unknown idioms, this does not appear to be the case with known idioms. When an L2 speaker encounters a known idiom, a compositional analysis may or may not be activated, but even when it is, it may soon lead to direct memory retrieval (an idiom representation) as is often the case in L1 idiom comprehension. Therefore, a dual processing model like Abel's (2003) is needed to account for L2 idiom comprehension: a *heuristic* approach to unknown idioms and a direct memory retrieval (an idiom representation) for known idioms in most cases. Of course, this dual processing model is very similar to Abel's *dual idiom representation* model but it does differ in that the *heuristic* approach, as Cooper (1999) and Bulut and Çelik-Yazici (2004) contend, is a more complex and slower process than the conceptual representation activation used among native speakers' idiom processing. Furthermore, given the fact that there are significantly fewer known idioms (or idiom entries) in an L2 learner's lexicon than in a native speaker's, the use of direct memory retrieval will be much less among L2 learners.

SUMMARY

L2 idiom comprehension appears to be a slower and much more complex process than that for L1. It involves the use of more strategies in terms of both type and quantity. The process does not seem to conform to any of the major L1 idiom comprehension models mentioned in the previous chapter. Instead, it takes the form of a *heuristic* approach, a process in which L2 learners approach an unknown idiom as a problem and try to solve it on a trial and error basis by using a variety of strategies. Yet this *heuristic* approach does not seem to apply to known idioms, for when a person, be it a native speaker or L2 speaker, encounters a known idiom, a normal linguistic analysis may not be activated or may soon lead to a direct memory retrieval. Thus, a complete L2 idiom comprehension model needs to be a dual-process one, with the *heuristic* approach in charge of unknown idioms and direct memory retrieval being used for known idioms in most cases.

Questions for Study or Discussion

1. What are the major similarities and differences between L2 and L1 idiom processing and comprehension? Give examples to support your answer.
2. Research suggests that L2 learners use a variety of strategies in processing idioms and they use more strategies than L1 speakers do. Why do you think that is the case?

3. Of the various strategies L2 learners use in processing idioms, which one or two do you think play the most important role, on the basis of your experience?
4. Discuss and explain with examples how L1 can facilitate and interfere with L2 idiom comprehension.
5. Some research findings show that L2 idioms that have L1 counterparts similar in linguistic form but different in meaning or conceptual structure pose great difficulty for L2 learners, more than those L2 idioms that are entirely different or absent in L1. From your experience, do you find that surprising? If you don't, what do you think are the reasons for the difficulty of such idioms?
6. Of the three English idioms *it's a piece of cake*, *step up to the plate* (a baseball idiom), and *switch gears* (a driving idiom), which one's conceptual/metaphorical basis is perhaps the easiest and which one the most difficult for ESL students to understand and why? (Hint: think in terms of how culture-specific the conceptual bases or cultural practices or knowledge underpinning each of the idioms is.)

Chapter 5

Factors that Affect Idiom Comprehension

INTRODUCTION

In exploring the theoretical models of idiom comprehension in both L1 and L2, research has also shown that there are many factors that affect our comprehension process. These factors fall into two major categories: (1) those on the part of the idiom and its use, and (2) those on the part of the language user. Factors in the former category include an idiom's frequency of use (familiarity), its transparency, its analyzability, and the context in which it is used. Factors on the part of the language user consist of age, cognitive styles, and knowledge about idioms' sources. Each of these factors and its effect on idiom comprehension will be discussed in this chapter. With a few exceptions, most of the factors apply to both L1 and L2 idiom comprehension.

FACTORS RELATING TO IDIOMS AND THEIR USE

Familiarity (Use Frequency)

Before we address the influence of familiarity on idiom comprehension, a discussion of terminology is in order. Very often, idiom familiarity and frequency are used interchangeably. Although closely related, they are really two different concepts. Idiom use frequency refers to how often an idiom is used. It can be and is often now measured objectively, with the availability of corpus programs. Idiom familiarity, on the other hand, concerns how familiar an idiom is to a given language user or a given language community. The measurement of an idiom's familiarity is usually obtained through a survey of language users, an undertaking that, unlike the frequency measurement, is rather subjective. That said, most scholars would argue that the two concepts are closely related, because a frequently used idiom will generally be more familiar than a seldom used one. For that reason, we treat the two terms synonymously in this discussion and we will, following most of the studies, use the term "familiarity."

Research shows that familiar idioms are processed much faster and more accurately than unfamiliar ones (Cronk & Schweigert, 1992; Forrester, 1995; Moon, 1998; Schweigert, 1986; Schweigert & Moates, 1988) and that they are more likely to be stored in the lexicon as idiom entries than unfamiliar ones (Abel, 2003). These findings suggest that the degree of an idiom's familiarity does affect its processing and comprehension.

In one of the first few studies on the issue, Schweigert (1986) examined the amount of time it took to process both familiar and unfamiliar idioms. She presented her subjects with 12 familiar idioms and 12 unfamiliar ones in three different sentence types or three different contexts. The first type favored a figurative interpretation, the second was biased toward a literal understanding, and the third was unbiased. She recorded the time it took the individual subjects to respond to each of the idiom presentations. She found that the subjects read the familiar idioms much faster than they did the unfamiliar ones in both the figurative and literal contexts. Forrester (1995) investigated the same question with a slightly different research design. Instead of using three contexts for his idiom presentation, he included only two contexts: figurative and literal (that is, no unbiased context was involved). Furthermore, in addition to familiar and unfamiliar idioms, Forrester included a group of what he called "semantic equivalent expressions." Specifically, for each of the 6 familiar and 6 unfamiliar idioms, he created a "semantic equivalent expression"—that is, one that, compared with the idiom, was synonymous in meaning but different in lexicon and structure. For example, "a smudge on the sheepskin" is a "semantic equivalent expression" for the idiom *a fly in the ointment*. Thus, in total, Forrester presented the subjects with 24 expressions consisting of 12 idioms and 12 semantic equivalent expressions. The results show that the subjects processed the familiar idioms and their semantic equivalent expressions much faster than their unfamiliar counterparts. Cronk and Schweigert's (1992) study yielded similar findings but the study and its results will be presented in the next section (the factor of idiom transparency) because their focus in the study was not the effect of idiom familiarity but the effect of an idiom's degree of transparency (literalness) and the interaction effects of idiom familiarity and idiom transparency.

Given that it is more difficult and takes more time to process unfamiliar idioms, one naturally wonders what people do in trying to understand them. Research on the issue, as reported in the previous chapter, suggests that L2 speakers tend to employ a heuristic approach using a variety of strategies (Bulut and Çelik-Yazici, 2004; Cooper, 1999). Similarly, native speakers typically use contextual information and pragmatic knowledge. When no contextual information is available, they rely primarily on analogy and lexical skills. In a mini-study examining how fifteen Britons interpreted the American idiom *on the bubble* (an idiom not found in British English) presented out of context, Moon (1998) found that, in guessing its meaning, most subjects tried to compare the idiom to other idioms similar in form. For example, quite a few thought that the idiom *on the bubble* (meaning to be in an uncertain situation, in danger of failing to get something or being defeated) meant "in an intense state of activity" because of its similarity in structure and lexical items to such idioms as *on the boil* and *bubbling along*.

Transparency in Meaning and Semantic Analyzability (Decomposability)

The reason that the effects of idioms' transparency and their semantic analyzability are discussed together is that the two factors are closely related. An idiom's transparency refers to its semantic clarity or, as it has often been called, its "literalness," for it is well known that the more literal an idiom is, the easier it will be to discern its meaning. An idiom's semantic analyzability relates to the extent to which its individual lexical parts contribute independently to its overall figurative meaning. The more the meanings of an idiom's individual parts contribute to its overall figurative meaning, the more semantically decomposable the idiom is. Therefore, an idiom's transparency and semantic analyzability (or decomposability) refer basically to the same thing.

According to Gibbs (1987, 1991, 1993), idioms fall into three groups according to their degree of semantic analyzability: (1) decomposable or "normally decomposable", (2) abnormally decomposable, and (3) non-decomposable. A normally decomposable idiom is one whose individual lexical components contribute to the overall figurative meaning of the idiom such as *be in the dark about something* and *button one's lips*. The figurative meanings of these idioms can be discerned relatively easily because the individual words' normal meanings do contribute to the idiom's overall figurative meaning. For instance, *be in the dark* suggests that a person cannot see anything and does not know what is going on. Therefore, one can easily interpret the expression as meaning not knowing anything. Abnormally decomposable idioms lie between the normally decomposable and the non-decomposable ones. *Carry a torch* and *give the green light* are two examples. As is the case with the normally analyzable idioms, the individual components of an idiom in this middle group do make a contribution to the overall figurative meaning but they do so indirectly. For example, to identify the figurative meaning of *carry a torch*, one has to know that "torch" has the meaning of being the symbol of a cause or a large effort. Similarly, to understand the figurative meaning of *giving the green light*, one has to possess the knowledge that "green light," in traffic regulations, means permission to move. In both cases, it is not the normal semantic meanings of the individual words that are tapped to arrive at the idiom's figurative meaning. Such a fact makes these idioms different from the normally decomposable ones where the conventional meaning of the individual parts is put to work. For example, in *button your lips*, the usual meanings of "button" as an action of "closing" and "lips" as the faculty for speech are at work. In contrast with the first two types, a non-decomposable idiom is one whose individual parts do not contribute to its overall figurative meaning at all. Examples of this type of idioms include *kick the bucket* and *shoot the breeze* because there is basically no way to arrive at these idioms' figurative meanings by analyzing and synthesizing the meanings of their individual components. It is thus clear that the more semantically decomposable an idiom is, the more transparent its meaning is, hence the close connection between an idiom's semantic decomposability and its transparency.

Now let us turn to the effects of semantic transparency/decomposability on idiom comprehension. Quite a few studies have been conducted on the issue and the results indicate that semantic transparency/decomposability can significantly affect both the accuracy and the speed of idiom comprehension (Cronk & Schweigert, 1992; Gibbs, 1987; Gibbs et al., 1989; Levorato & Cacciari, 1999). In terms of accuracy, in an experimental study involving kindergarteners and first-, third-, and fourth-graders, Gibbs (1987) presented his subjects with transparent and opaque idioms in two environments: in context (i.e. in a short story) and out of context.[1] The subjects were asked to explain verbally the meanings of the idioms and then to choose, out of two interpretations provided, which they believed to be the correct one. The subjects performed significantly better on the semantically transparent idioms than on the opaque ones in context, although there was no significant difference between their performances on the two types of idioms out of context. In other words, semantically transparent idioms are easier to understand than opaque ones when they are placed in context. A similar study by Levorato and Cacciari (1999) showed a slightly different result because their subjects performed better on analyzable idioms both with and without context. Gibbs et al. (1989) examined the time it took to respond to the three types of idioms in terms of semantic decomposability: normally decomposable, abnormally decomposable, and non-decomposable. They had a group of undergraduate students read 72 word strings on a computer screen, 18 of which were idioms, 18 were non-idiomatic but grammatically correct and meaningful strings used as literal control items (e.g. "use the hatchet" for *bury the hatchet*), and the remaining 36 of which were unacceptable and meaningless strings serving as control items (e.g. "no sleep it floor out" and "wish out the table to"). The subjects were told to decide as quickly as possible whether each of the strings was a meaningful phrase in English. Their response time for each string was recorded. A comparison of the amount of time it took for the subjects to respond to each type of string reveals that the subjects were significantly faster in responding to both types of semantically analyzable idioms than to those non-analyzable ones. Cronk and Schweigert's (1992) study produced similar results.

Syntactic Analyzability

Syntactic analyzability differs from semantic analyzability in that while the latter deals with the extent to which an idiom's individual components contribute to its overall figurative meaning, the former relates to the degree to which the formation of an idiom follows the usual syntactic rules in the language. On the basis of the syntactic rules involved, syntactic analyzability may be divided into two subcategories: syntactic frozenness and syntactic abnormality. Syntactic frozenness deals with the extent of transformation and variation an idiom may undergo.[2] For instance, while *roll out the red carpet* and *pass the buck* are not syntactically frozen because they both can be used in the passive voice, *kick the bucket* and *beat about the bush* are syntactically frozen because neither can be used in the passive voice. Syntactic abnormality, on the other hand, refers to the degree to which the formation of an idiom violates established syntactic rules. *By and large, happy-go-lucky,* and *of late* are a few examples of syntactically abnormal idioms, for each of them has violated a grammatical rule. For instance, the words "*by*" and "*large*" belong to different parts of speech but they are used in parallel in the idiom.[3] The differentiation between syntactic frozenness and syntactic normality is important because a syntactically frozen idiom may not be syntactically abnormal. For example, *kick the bucket* is syntactically frozen but not syntactically abnormal because it is grammatically sound.

If we look at the above examples of both syntactically frozen and syntactically abnormal idioms, we should not fail to notice that these idioms are often semantically opaque—that is, semantically non-decomposable. Thus, these idioms are usually difficult to comprehend because they cannot be processed compositionally. In other words, other factors being constant, these idioms generally take more time to comprehend than syntactically unfrozen or normal idioms. It is necessary to mention, though, that although syntactically frozen and abnormal idioms are usually opaque, not all syntactically unfrozen or syntactically normal idioms are transparent in meaning. For instance, *pass the buck* is not syntactically frozen but it is not semantically transparent either. Similarly, *put one's foot in one's mouth* is not syntactically abnormal, yet its meaning is not transparent either. In short, the above examples demonstrate that an idiom's syntactic analyzability is not highly correlated with its semantic transparency, although a syntactically frozen or abnormal idiom is often semantically opaque.

Context of Use

The context in which an idiom appears plays a very important role in its comprehension. As research has shown, both L1 and L2 speakers use contextual information to figure out the meaning of an unknown idiom. Furthermore, it has been reported that both the amount and the types of contextual information can significantly affect an idiom's understandability (Cacciari & Levorato, 1989; Gibbs, 1980; Levorato & Cacciari, 1999; Nippold & Martin, 1989; Nippold & Rudzinski, 1993; Nippold & Taylor, 1995; Ortony et al., 1978; Schweigert & Moates, 1988).

In one of the first studies that examined the effect of context on idiom comprehension, Ortony et al. (1978) had their subjects read and process target idiomatic as well as literal expressions in two different conditions: after a short text (limited context) as compared with after a long text (full context). They recorded the time it took the subjects to process the expressions. Here is an example of a target idiom after a long text:

> *Metaphorical context*
> The children continued to annoy their babysitter. She told the little boys she would not tolerate any more bad behavior. Climbing all over the furniture was not allowed. She threatened to spank them if they continued to stomp, run, and scream around the room. The children knew that her spanking hurt.
>
> *Target*
> Regardless of the danger, *the troops marched on.*
> (Ortony et al., 1978, p. 467)

In contrast, in the condition of a short text, there was only one sentence preceding the "target": "The children continued to annoy their babysitter." The results showed that in the short text condition it took the subjects a longer time to process the idioms than the literal equivalent expressions, but in the long text condition the subjects processed the idioms as fast as they did the literal expressions. The findings clearly suggest that context plays an important role in idiom comprehension.

Similarly, Gibbs' (1980) study also shows the importance of context in idiom comprehension. Gibbs compared the idiom processing speed and the number of errors made by subjects who were presented idioms in context (two types of context: literal context and idiomatic context) with the speed and the number of errors made by students who were given idioms without

FACTORS THAT AFFECT IDIOM COMPREHENSION

context. The results show that it generally took subjects more time to process an idiom without a context than with a context, and subjects given idioms without a context generally made more errors than for those presented with context.

Three very interesting and revealing studies concerning the importance of context in idiom comprehension are those by Cacciari and Levorato (1989), Levorato and Cacciari (1999), and Nippold and Martin (1989). These studies examined not only the role of context but also the effect of subjects' age and idioms' semantic analyzability in idiom comprehension. As we address the issue of age and idiom analyzability in other sections, we will focus on the effect of context here. Cacciari and Levorato (1989) conducted multiple experiments in their study involving both elementary and middle school students. They first presented their subjects a series of idioms in three conditions: (1) in an idiomatic context—that is, in stories biased towards an idiomatic interpretation of the idiom; (2) in a literal context—that is, in stories favoring a literal interpretation of the idiom; and (3) without context —that is, no stories given. The subjects were randomly placed into the three conditions. After the presentation of each idiom, the subjects were asked to interpret the meaning of the idiom by doing a multiple-choice test with three options: an idiomatic interpretation, a literal one, and an associate answer, one that differed from both 1 and 2 but plausible in the context. The following contains an example of an idiomatic context and an example of a literal context with the multiple-choice test.

> A little boy named Paul moved house. It was winter so he had to go to a new school. His mother suggested that he should try and get to know his new schoolmates. Once at school, he lent them his box of crayons and so he broke the ice. [*idiomatic context*]
> What did Paul do when he broke the ice?
> (a) he made friends with his schoolmates;
> (b) he broke a piece of ice;
> (c) he told his mummy everything.
>
> One winter, a little boy named Paul went to the mountains with his parents. They were staying at a hotel. The first day his mother told him that there were other children in the hotel and that he should try and meet them. He went to play on a frozen lake where there were other children, and he broke the ice. [*literal context*]
> (From Caccari & Levorato, 1992, pp. 392, 395)

The results of the students' multiple-choice test performance indicates that the children gave significantly more idiomatic answers in both context-given situations than in the no-context setting, thus suggesting that context aids idiom comprehension. Similar findings about the role of context were reported in a later study they conducted (Levorato & Cacciari, 1999).

Nippold and Martin's study (1989) also shows the important role that context plays. They presented twenty idioms to 475 subjects between the ages of 14 and 17. Half of the idioms were presented in isolation (e.g. "What does it mean to *take a back seat?*") and the other half were each shown in a two-sentence mini-story (e.g. "Billy often gets into fights with other kids at school. His mother says he has a chip on his shoulder. What does it mean to have a *chip on one's shoulder?*"). The subjects were asked to answer the questions in writing. Their responses were rated as correct and incorrect (the latter type was then further classified as "literal," "unrelated," "no response," etc.). The accuracy of the subjects' performance on the idioms given in context was significantly higher than their accuracy on the idioms in isolation, showing context to be an important factor again. The results of the study were affirmed by Nippold and Rudzinski (1993) and Nippold and Taylor (1995).

FACTORS RELATING TO LANGUAGE USERS

Age and Cognitive Ability

Research in general shows that age and cognitive ability are important factors in children's comprehension of idioms (Cacciari & Levorato, 1989; Johnson, 1989, 1991; Levorato & Cacciari, 1995, 1999; Nippold & Taylor, 1995; Nippold & Duthie, 2003). Cacciari and Levorato's (1989) three experimental studies on this issue are very informative. Their first two experiments each involved a group of first-graders (7 years of age) and a group of fourth-graders (9 to 10 years of age), plus some college students (who served only in the control group). The subjects were asked to interpret idioms in three different contexts: literal, idiomatic, and no context. In the first experiment, the subjects were given eight idioms one at a time, and after each idiom was given, they were asked to select an interpretation of the idiom from three choices: (1) an idiomatic interpretation, (2) a literal one, and (3) an "associate" answer, one that differed from both (1) and (2) but plausible in the context. The use of multiple-choice mode to assess children's understanding of idiom was wise, because studies have shown that due to their limited language ability, children show their understanding of idioms better when responding to multiple-choice questions or enacting metaphoric meaning than when responding to verbal interpretation questions.

For half of Cacciari and Levorato's (1989) subjects, the idioms were given without any contextual information. For the other half, the idioms were each presented at the end of a brief story that was biased for an idiomatic interpretation. In other words, the idioms were presented in an idiomatic context. In the second experiment, the procedure was basically the same as that of the first, except that for the half of the subjects who were given the idioms in

TABLE 5.1
Percentage of Idiomatic Answers by Age Groups and Context

Age Group	Idiomatic Context	Literal Context	No Context
7	59.1	52.5	21.2
9	87.5	72.5	51.3
College	–	–	97.6

Adapted from Cacciari and Levorato's (1989) Table 1 and Table 2 by combining the two; used by permission of the publisher, Cambridge University Press.

context, the context was biased for a literal interpretation of the idiom. In other words, the idioms were given to them in a literal context. The college students were only given the idioms without any context. The results from the two experiments (shown in Table 5.1) show that in all three contexts (literal, idiomatic, and no context), the percentages of idiomatic responses increased with the subjects' age, as the percentage of idiomatic interpretations for the college students was the highest, followed by that of the fourth-graders and then the first-graders. More importantly, the fourth-graders' percentage was significantly higher than that of the first-graders, illustrating clearly that age is a factor in children's comprehension of idioms, a point that will be discussed in more detail below.

While multiple-choice questions allow children to exhibit their idiom understanding better, such a response mode does have the potential of overestimating their ability in this regard, because there is a good chance for students to select the correct answer simply by guessing. To make sure that the multiple-choice test format had not overestimated the children's real ability to understand idioms, Cacciari and Levorato conducted a third experiment where a group of second-graders (8 years of age) and a group of fifth-graders (11 years of age) were given the same stories as were used in the first experiment but, unlike in the first experiment, the idiom in each story in this study was incomplete. The students were asked to complete it.

The students' answers fell into three major types: (1) idiomatic completion where the targeted idiom was used with the exact wording, for example *break the ice*; (2) literal completion where the student usually used an object mentioned in the story, for example "break the crayon," to form an answer that, though incorrect semantically, did make some sense; and (3) figurative completion, where the student provided a phrase that expresses a meaning that is close to that of the idiom or the action in question but it is not the targeted idiom, for example "break the shyness" instead of *break the ice*. Similar to the results of the previous two studies, in this experiment the older children (the 11-year-olds) gave many more idiomatic completions and far fewer literal completions than the younger ones (see Table 5.2).

TABLE 5.2
Percentage of Completion Answer Types by Two Age Groups

Age Group	Idiomatic	Figurative	Literal
8	13.9	39.2	41.2
10	40	26.9	26.2

From Cacciari and Levorato's (1989) Table 3. Reprinted by permission of the publisher, Cambridge University Press.

The fact that the younger children are much more likely to interpret idioms literally suggests that in processing an idiom, they resort largely to a literal strategy—that is, they employ only lexical and morphosyntactic competence in their analysis because such a literal strategy is the only strategy available to them. In other words, they do not have the cognitive and linguistic competence that a figurative processing strategy would require, a competence that goes beyond lexical and morphosyntactic competence.

Many of the other studies on the age factor in relation to idiom comprehension produced similar results (Levorato & Cacciari, 1995, 1999; Nippold & Rudzinski, 1993; Nippold & Taylor, 1995). It is found that, in general, before the age of 6, children possess limited cognitive ability and thus often interpret idioms literally, even though, as a few studies (Vosniadou & Ortony, 1983; Winner, 1988) suggest, they may have some rudimentary competence in understanding language figuratively.

Learner Cognitive Style

Johnson (1989) and Johnson and Rosano (1993) looked at the relationship between cognitive styles (as well as language proficiency) and the ability to interpret idioms. Their subjects included both native English speakers and ESL speakers. They assessed the subjects' cognitive style (analytical or field independent versus field dependent), English language proficiency, and metaphor fluency (measured by the subjects' ability to produce appropriate interpretations of metaphors). A statistical analysis of the correlations among the variables shows that the native English speaker subjects' metaphor proficiency is significantly correlated with an analytic/field-independent cognitive style, suggesting that an analytical cognitive style is more conducive to idiom comprehension. Yet no such significant correlation was found for the ESL subjects. In fact, the ESL subjects' metaphor proficiency appeared to be related to a field-dependent cognitive style, a style characterized by a holistic approach to learning instead of the active analytic one that dominates the field-independent style. This finding is puzzling, especially considering the fact that other research findings suggest that L2 learners use primarily a *heuristic* approach—that is, a problem-solving approach that uses analytical skills extensively (Bulut & Çelik-Yazici, 2004; Cooper, 1999). Johnson and Rosano (1993) suggest that their unusual finding may be attributed to the uniqueness and size of the samples, and problems with the measurement instruments used in their study.

Knowledge of the Metaphorical Links between the Source and the Target Domains

As was shown in Chapters 2 and 4, many idioms are metaphorical expressions, such as *have two strikes against someone, The bottom line is . . .*, and *running on all cylinders*. Knowing the links between the source and the target domains will greatly assist the comprehension of such idioms. Take the *have two strikes against someone* as an example. Knowing the "three strikes and you're out" baseball rule will enable one to understand that *having two strikes against someone* would mean someone is placed in a disadvantageous position. Lacking knowledge of this metaphorical link between the source and the target domains surely would make understanding this idiom very difficult, if not entirely impossible. That is why Gibbs (1993) contends that such knowledge "provides the basis for the appropriate use and interpretation of idioms in particular discourse situations" (p. 70). Yet L2 learners often lack this knowledge, due to the fact that some source domains of L2 idioms are unknown or inconspicuous in their native culture. For example, while baseball is very popular in the United States, it is not so in many other countries. Thus, it is important for L2 learners to develop knowledge of such culture-specific source domains.

FACTORS AFFECTING L2 IDIOM COMPREHENSION ONLY

As the following factors were explored to various degrees in the previous chapter, only a summary discussion is presented here.

L1

While the L2 learner's native language (L1) has been found to have an impact on their idiom comprehension, the extent of its effect often varies according to the difference of L2 idioms from, or their similarity to, L1 idioms. L2 idioms that are identical to those in L1, in both form and meaning, pose little difficulty for L2 learners because L2 learners can easily transfer their understanding of such idioms from L1 into L2 (Abdullah & Jackson,

1998; Irurjo, 1986a). Yet while such idioms' identicalness or close similarity to those in L1 seems to facilitate L2 learners' comprehension of these idioms, it often makes L2 learners hesitant to use them in production for fear that these idioms actually differ in meaning from those in L1 despite their surface identicalness or similarity. In fact, several studies have found that L2 learners often commit such avoidance errors in L2 idiom production (Hulstijin & Marchnas, 1989; Irujo, 1986a, 1993; Jordens, 1977; Kellerman, 1977; Laufer, 2000).

L2 Proficiency

As was mentioned earlier in this chapter, children's comprehension of idioms in L1 is tied closely to the development of their cognitive ability and linguistic skills; therefore, L1 proficiency is a very important factor in children's understanding of idioms. The effect of L2 proficiency on L2 idiom comprehension is, however, a more complex issue. While one study (Trosborg, 1985) indicates that L2 students' ability to understand and use metaphorical idiomatic expressions is correlated with their language proficiency, research by Johnson (Johnson, 1989, 1991; Johnson & Rosano, 1993) shows that L2 proficiency plays a limited role in metaphor or idiom comprehension. There are two likely explanations for Johnson's finding, though. First, the subjects in the studies all had some English proficiency, and the difference between their proficiency levels was not significant. Thus, the limited effect could be due to the fact that the subjects had all passed a threshold English proficiency level. In other words, the role of L2 proficiency decreases after a threshold proficiency level. Second, the subjects had all achieved a level of proficiency in their L1. In certain language functions, an L2 speaker's L1 proficiency can be a facilitating factor. For example, research (Cummins, 1979, 1991) indicates that a learner's cognitive academic language proficiency (CALP) is transferable. A good L1 CALP may lead to a good L2 CALP after the L2 learner has developed a threshold proficiency in L2. The same may be true for L2 students' ability in L1 idiom comprehension: it may be transferable into their L2 idiom comprehension. Thus, it is possible that students with a high figurative language competence in L1 but a relatively low L2 proficiency may actually perform better in the comprehension of metaphorical idioms than those who have a lower L1 figurative competence but a higher L2 proficiency.

SUMMARY

Many factors may affect idiom comprehension. They generally fall into two major categories: those on the part of idioms and those on the part of learners.

Key factors on the part of idioms include **transparency in meaning, semantic analyzability, syntactic analyzability,** and **context of use**. Major factors on the part of the language user are **age and cognitive ability, cognitive style, conceptual knowledge, L1 transfer and interference,** and **L2 proficiency** (the last two for L2 users only). Knowing these factors and their effect will help teachers better understand the difficulties different students may have in understanding different types of idioms and, in turn, to allow teachers to develop ways to assist students accordingly.

Questions for Study or Discussion

1. Quite a few factors on the part of idioms may affect idiom comprehension such as transparency in meaning and syntactic complexity. How should teachers take these factors into consideration in selecting idioms for instruction and in determining the sequence of their instruction?
2. Ill-formed idioms include two subcategories: those that are syntactically ill-formed (that is, they violate syntactic rules) and those that are not syntactically ill-formed but violate usual collocation patterns and semantic restrictions. Determine to which of the two categories each of the following idioms belongs:

   All of a sudden   *jump down someone's throat*
   face the music   *long time no see*
   Beg the question   *take after someone*
   go ballistic   *under the weather*

3. Research has found that the context in which an idiom is used has a significant influence on people's understanding of it. What do you think are the pedagogical implications of this finding?
4. It has been argued that cognitive styles may affect our understanding of idioms. Try first to support the argument with evidence from your reading as well as from your experience. Then discuss what teachers can do to help students with different cognitive styles to acquire idioms more effectively. There are two areas in which teachers may work to help: (1) adjustments teachers can make and techniques teachers can use in presenting idioms to students, and (2) activities that may help students capitalize on and/or adapt their cognitive styles to better understand idioms.
5. Conceptual knowledge has been found to play a key role in understanding conceptually motivated idioms such as metaphorical idioms.

Furthermore, some metaphorical idioms are based on culture-specific domains. What are the pedagogical implications of these findings—that is, what can teachers do to help students develop and use conceptual and culture-specific knowledge in L2 idiom comprehension?

PART **III**

IDIOM ACQUISITION AND PEDAGOGY

Chapter 6

Idiom Acquisition and Its Importance in Language Development

INTRODUCTION

How are idioms acquired? Why is idiom acquisition necessary for language development? These are the two main questions this chapter explores. Before we address these questions, it is important to point out that, while there have been numerous studies on idiom comprehension, research on idiom acquisition per se has been quite limited. A reason for this disparity is that idiom comprehension is in itself an acquisition issue because the comprehension of an idiom is a prerequisite for its acquisition. In fact, many studies on idiom acquisition approached the topic by examining, in part, their subjects' level(s) of understanding or lack of understanding of idioms (Douglas & Peel, 1979; Levorato, 1993; Levorato & Cacciari, 1992; Lodge & Leach, 1975; Nippold & Taylor, 1995; Nippold & Duthie, 2003; Prinz, 1983; Vosniado & Ortony, 1983; Winner, 1988). Of course, the issue of idiom acquisition goes beyond how people process and understand idioms. It also deals with, among other things, how people learn to use idioms in their own language production. This chapter will address all the important questions about idiom acquisition, including issues such as knowledge and skills needed for acquiring idioms, models of development of figurative competence for acquiring metaphorical idioms, and unique problems related to L2 idiom acquisition. It will conclude with a discussion of the importance of grasping idioms in language development.

KNOWLEDGE AND SKILLS REQUIRED FOR IDIOM ACQUISITION

Research on idiom acquisition has focused almost exclusively on children. The major questions examined so far include: Do children have to reach a certain level of cognitive and linguistic ability before they can understand and acquire idioms, given that most idioms are figurative in meaning? Do people rely primarily on general cognitive and linguistic skills to grasp idioms or can they acquire idioms simply by rote learning (that is, by treating an idiom as a long word form and associating it with its meaning)?[1] What types of cognitive and linguistic skills are needed? So far, research results seem to suggest that children's acquisition of idioms is tied closely to their general cognitive and linguistic development, because children's ability to understand idioms has been shown to increase significantly with age (Cacciari & Levorato, 1989; Douglas & Peel, 1979; Levorato, 1993; Levorato & Cacciari, 1992, 1999; Lodge & Leach, 1975; Nippold & Taylor, 1995; Nippold & Duthie, 2003; Prinz, 1983; Vosniado & Ortony, 1983; Winner, 1988). As is the case with their ability to understand idioms, children's ability to produce idioms is also correlated with their development in cognitive and general linguistic skills (Caccari & Levorato, 1989; Larzar et al., 1989; Levorato, 1993; Levorato & Cacciari, 1992, 1999). In general, it is found that a cognitive-based figurative competence is required for acquiring figurative idioms. As is the case with L1, this figurative competence in L2 correlates, to a degree, with learners' proficiency in the target language (Trosborg, 1985). For figurative competence to be functional in L2, a threshold language proficiency level is required.

Models for the Development of Figurative Competence for Idiom Acquisition

If a cognition-based figurative competence is needed for the understanding of most idioms, then how is it developed, or what is the process or model for its development? To answer this question, a clarification of terminology is in order, because various terms have been used to refer to the cognitive and linguistic ability needed for idiom acquisition. The list of such terms includes "figurative competence" (Levorato, 1993), "figurative proficiency" (Charteris-Black, 2002), and "metaphorical competence" (Winner, 1988). For the purposes of consistency and simplicity, the term "figurative competence" will be used in the discussion here. Concerning the development of figurative competence, while several studies have touched on the issue (Cacciari & Levorato, 1989; Levorato & Cacciari, 1999; Gibbs, 1987; Lodge & Leach, 1975; Nippold & Martin, 1989; Prinz, 1983), only Levorato (1993) and

Winner (1988) have addressed the question directly and systematically. On the basis of a series of studies that they each conducted either independently or with their associates, Levorato (1993) and Winner (1988) have proposed models for figurative competence development.

Winner's (1988) model focuses on the understanding of metaphorical idioms. In her analysis, children's understanding of metaphors falls into four categories: literal, metonymic, primitive metaphoric, and genuine metaphoric. These four types of interpretation may represent four developmental levels of metaphorical idiom understanding. In a literal interpretation, a child interprets a metaphorical idiom completely literally, showing no figurative ability at all. In a metonymic understanding, the child, though still unable to understand the idiom's figurative meaning, no longer interprets it completely literally; instead, the child renders an interpretation based on what Winner calls "associative relationship"—that is, a relationship the child finds between the words in the metaphorical idiom and what the child may associate them with. For example, for the utterance "Tom is *a wolf in sheep's clothing,*" a child with metonymic understanding will not entertain a complete literal understanding of the sentence such as viewing Tom as a wolf wearing sheep's clothing; instead, the child may interpret the sentence as meaning "Tom is playing wolf with sheep's clothing" or "Tom is wearing sheep's clothing."

Compared with metonymic understanding, pre-metaphoric understanding is one step closer to metaphoric comprehension. Such an understanding of a metaphor is already at the figurative level, but it is still incorrect in meaning because it is based on the wrong type of (often a surface-level) relationship between its topic (the intended unconventional referent or target domain) and vehicle (the conventional referent or the source domain). Research indicates that metaphors often work on two types of relationships between the topic and the vehicle: a sensory (physical) one and a non-sensory (psychological) one. A metaphor may work on either one or both types. For example, while the metaphorical meaning of "John is a tiger" rests largely on a sensory relationship (a physical similarity between John and a tiger: both have a strong body and physical strength), the meaning of "John is a snake" hinges on a non-sensory relationship (a psychological similarity between John and a snake: both are slippery in nature). In the case of the expression "Tom is a *wolf in sheep's clothing,*" its metaphorical meaning is built on a non-sensory psychological similarity between the target and the vehicle: the falsehood of both Tom and the wolf in sheep's clothing. A child with only pre-metaphorical understanding of the idiom will fail to understand this relationship and will, instead, focus on some physical similarities between Tom and a wolf such as their hairiness, thus (mis)interpreting the expression to be something like "Tom is like a wolf or sheep with a lot of hair." Unlike pre-metaphorical understanding, genuine metaphorical comprehension accurately identifies the underlying topic–vehicle relationship of an idiom and offers a correct interpretation.

Thus, according to Winner (1988) there are four steps or levels of understanding of metaphorical idioms, no understanding or literal understanding being 0, metonymic 1, pre-metaphoric 2, and genuine metaphoric 3. Metonymic understanding is classified as a level higher than literal because its interpretation is based on an "association" that a child makes, a process more advanced than literal comprehension—the lowest level of understanding. Pre-metaphoric represents a higher level than metonymic because its understanding is grounded in a similarity between a metaphor's topic and vehicle rather than in an association that a child randomly makes. Pre-metaphoric understanding is, however, succeeded by genuine metaphoric comprehension as the latter surpasses the former in identifying the correct topic–vehicle similarity in an idiom. Children's understanding of metaphorical idioms evolves along the four steps. At the age of 6, children's comprehension in this area is primarily literal, metonymic, and pre-metaphoric. The percentage of such understandings decreases and the proportion of genuine metaphoric comprehension increases as children grow older. Between 8 and 10 years old, children will all have developed basic genuine metaphoric comprehension ability.

Unlike Winner (1988), Levorato (1993) proposed a six-phase (0 through 5) model for children's development of figurative competence. In phase 0 or the "nominal realist phase" (p. 119), a child very young in age does not see language as signification but views it as reality. To the child, the names of objects are intrinsic to the objects—that is, the name of an object has the same properties as the object it represents, and changing the name of the object will change the properties of the object as well. In phase 1, the child abandons "nominal realism" and begins to appreciate the symbolic nature of language. This new understanding is accompanied by the development of a conceptual system. Yet this conceptual development is only in the burgeoning stage. Thus, in this phase the child still tends to process language literally. According to Levorato, this tendency to process language literally is exhibited by four concrete tendencies the child uses in language processing: "(a) a tendency to conceive of meaning as the mere sum of the meanings of the component words, (b) a tendency to submit the linguistic information to shallow processing, (c) a tendency to be misled by the imaginative contents of figures of speech, and (d) a tendency to consider only the concrete elements of an expression" (1993, p. 120).

At level 2, or the "suspended literalness" phase, the child, usually age 7 or 8, no longer uses only literal strategies in language processing and no longer considers language use merely referential and literal. The child now understands the importance of context in language use and resorts more to interpretive strategies (than literal strategies) in language processing. Level

3 is marked by the new understanding that language is arbitrary in nature. Normally, children attain this level at the age of 9 or 10. At this level, the child has learned that to understand the true meaning of an expression or a text, one often has to go beyond the surface linguistic forms. With this understanding, the child is able to acquire figurative language, including idioms, metaphors, and proverbs. Level 4 extends beyond level 3 in that the child now is beginning to develop familiarity with idiomatic expressions. Yet at this level the child's idiom acquisition is limited, because the child tends to understand and use idioms as fixed units or formulae that can never be modified or varied according to context. Level 5 marks the attainment of complete figurative competence. In this phase, the child is able to use language figuratively.

Levorato (1993) acknowledges, however, that the development sequence in the model is not invariable. There may be some inversions in the sequence, especially the sequence between levels 3 and 4, because of differences among individuals' learning experiences, cognitive maturity, and knowledge. Furthermore, there is also the possibility that "a child may be at different levels at the same time according to the extent of his or her knowledge relating to a particular semantic domain and the linguistic expressions connected with it" (p. 124). For example, a child who plays baseball will understand baseball idioms better than one who does not, due to the former child's knowledge of the sport. In fact, the six phases can be condensed into just two major phrases: first, the pre-figurative competence phase, which includes phases 0 and 1; and then the figurative competence development phase, which covers phases 2 through 5. The first major phase, which lasts until the age of 7 in most children, is marked by literal understanding of language. In contrast, during the next major phase—that is, the figurative competence development phase—children, by now with more developed cognitive and linguistic skills, are better able to process the information available to arrive at an appropriate and coherent interpretation of figurative expressions. At the end of this phase, typically around the age of 13, children will have acquired figurative competence completely.

Overall, despite the differences in the terminology and classification systems they use, the researchers on idiom acquisition appear to have a consensus on the major phases of the development of figurative competence. Their discussions all seem to suggest that the development of figurative competence begins at about the age of 7 (that is, before this age, children in general tend to understand language literally), a basic competence is acquired at approximately the age of 9, and a full competence is attained between the ages of 13 and 15. Of course, in L2 idiom acquisition this competence needs to be complemented by a basic proficiency in the language.

THE ROLE OF ROTE LEARNING IN IDIOM ACQUISITION

It is clear that the development of figurative competence is essential in idiom acquisition. What role does rote learning play, then? Given the fact that idioms are fixed in structure and unique in meaning, many would be tempted to wonder whether idioms are learned primarily by rote learning. Quite a few scholars have examined the issue empirically. Levorato and Cacciari (1992), for example, conducted two experimental studies, one involving idiom comprehension and one idiom production. The first study examined the effects of children's age and the familiarity of idioms on their comprehension of idioms. The hypothesis was that if the development of general cognitive and linguistic abilities was a prerequisite for idiom understanding, then age or cognitive and linguistic maturity would play a much more important role than the familiarity of an idiom in children's process of identifying an idiom's meaning. In other words, an idiom's familiarity (defined in terms of the frequency of the idiom) would not have a significant impact on the process of identifying the idiomatic meaning. On the basis of the results of a survey about the use frequency of some idioms, Levorato and Cacciari first selected five very common idioms and five uncommon idioms, and then created, for each idiom, two stories, both of which had the idiom as the concluding statement. The first of the two stories offered an idiomatic context, setting up the idiomatic interpretation of the idiom as the only logical and semantically appropriate answer; the second story provided a literal context that permitted a literal interpretation although the idiomatic interpretation was still the more appropriate. The reason for including the two linguistic contexts was to further test whether contextual information would affect students' idiom comprehension. The subjects of the study were in two age groups (first-graders and fourth-graders). They first listened to the stories and then were asked to interpret the meaning of the idiom by answering a multiple-choice test question with the following three options: (1) idiomatic interpretation, (2) literal interpretation, and (3) associate response, an answer that differed from the first two but was plausible in the context. A comparison of the two groups' answers to the familiar idioms and the unfamiliar idioms in the two different linguistic contexts showed a significant difference between the two groups' responses in the two contexts, and a significant difference between the two contexts, but no significant difference between the two types of idioms, thus suggesting that age and context were significant factors in idiom comprehension but the familiarity of an idiom was not a significant one.

In the second experiment they tested the effects of age and the familiarity of idioms on children's idiom production. The subjects were a group of second-graders and a group of fifth-graders. In this study the subjects listened to the same stories (that is, those containing the five familiar and five unfamiliar idioms) but with the concluding idioms being incomplete (for example, with only "broke . . ." instead of *broke the ice*). The children were asked to complete the idioms on the basis of the stories. The students' completion responses fell into three categories: (1) idiomatic, (2) literal, and (3) figurative—a type of figurative interpretation that is not the complete and correct idiom (e.g. "broke the silence" instead of *broke the ice*). Concerning the responses to the stories with familiar idioms, percentage-wise, most of the responses for both groups were idiomatic (62 percent for second-graders and 82 percent for fifth-graders), although the fifth-graders' percentage was significantly higher than that of the second-graders. Concerning the responses to the stories with unfamiliar idioms, the results were very different. Very few (3 percent) were idiomatic for either group; the highest percentage for the second-graders was literal (65 percent) but the highest for the fifth-graders was figurative (50 percent). The results suggest that the younger children produced many more literal completions than the older children in the cases of both familiar and unfamiliar idioms, but especially so in the latter case. It was also shown that children were more likely to produce figurative completions in the case of unfamiliar idioms than in the case of familiar idioms. This is especially true of the older children, for they produced significantly more figurative completions than the younger children in this case. Such results show again that children's ability to comprehend and use idioms depends largely on their age or the development of their overall cognitive and linguistic skills.

Using the results of the two experiments, Levorato (1993) argues that idioms are not acquired simply by rote learning: "the acquisition of idioms by children is far from a simple matter of passively learning conventional expressions, but is, on the contrary, a process involving complex linguistic and cognitive skills" (p. 119). In other words, in their initial encounter with an idiom, children generally do not approach it as a non-decomposable long word and simply memorize it. This proposition of idiom acquisition being dependent on the adequate development of cognitive and linguistic ability is, in fact, supported by the most current idiom processing theories discussed in Chapter 3, especially the compositional analysis model, which posits that idiom comprehension involves a compositional analysis as well as the use of various problem-solving strategies. If idioms are indeed processed using compositional analysis and problem-solving strategies, their acquisition will definitely call for the development of adequate cognitive and linguistic skills, because these are the skills that make compositional analysis and problem solving possible. Weinert (1995), on the basis of an examination of the role or function of idioms (formulaic expressions) in language learning, also questions the value of rote learning not only in idiom acquisition but also in language acquisition in general.

However, while it is clear that the development of adequate general cognitive and linguistic ability is an essential requirement for idiom acquisition, this does not mean that rote learning plays no role in idiom learning. As was reported in Part II of the book, research has found that familiar idioms are processed faster than unknown ones. Such a finding supports the idiom representation (direct idiom retrieval) theory for comprehending familiar idioms (Abel, 2003; Titone & Connine, 1999). This theory posits that after the initial compositional analysis and understanding, an idiom is then memorized, consciously or unconsciously, and stored in the lexicon as an idiom entry for future retrieval when encountered again.

In fact, the second experiment of Levorato and Cacciari's just-mentioned study (1992) also demonstrates the role of memory in idiom acquisition. The results of the experiment indicate that the idiom completion (or production) performance by the subjects of both age groups was better on the familiar idioms than on the unfamiliar ones, suggesting the effect of memory. In other words, the results imply that the familiar idioms had found their way into a learner's memory (that is, becoming idiom entries) and were thus more readily available for access and use in production. This finding from Levorato and Cacciari is of unique importance because while the other studies of the effect of familiar idioms focused on comprehension, theirs looked at the effect of familiarity on idiom production. Like language acquisition in general, idiom acquisition entails not only comprehension but also production. To fully acquire an idiom, one needs not only to understand it but also to produce it correctly. As idiom familiarity facilitates both idiom comprehension and production, the role of memory in idiom acquisition is thus important.

Furthermore, various studies (Boers, 2001; Boers et al., 2004a; Boers & Lindstromberg, 2005; Lindstromberg & Boers, 2005; Wray, 2004) have also shown that using various mnemonic strategies significantly enhances L2 students' retention of idioms. The importance of memorization plays an even more important role in the learning of those idioms that are non-compositional and non-figurative in meaning, such as *by and large* and *pull someone's leg*. According to Grant and Nation (2006), these idioms, or what they call "core idioms," must be learned as whole units, and, as such, memorization is the best route. Rote learning should also be a very useful strategy for grasping "sememic" or "interpersonal" idioms, such as "*So long*" and "*What's up?*"

In summary, we can posit that idiom acquisition (with the exception of core idioms) may consist of two phases: the processing and comprehension phase and the memorization and storage phase. In the first phase, cognitive and linguistic skills are instrumental and there is perhaps no role for rote learning. Yet in the second phase, the memorization and storage phase, rote learning plays a crucial role. For core idioms, only memorization is involved. Of course, the development of an adequate cognitive and linguistic ability is the first and most important condition for idiom acquisition to take place. Rote learning is secondary not only in sequence but also in importance.

THE EFFECT OF DIFFERENT TYPES OF IDIOMS, AND SEQUENCE OF IDIOM ACQUISITION

Research also indicates that different types of idioms may present different levels of difficulty and may not be acquired at the same time or stage. For example, it has been found that metaphorical idioms are usually understood and acquired before proverb-type idioms (Douglas & Peel, 1979). There are two likely reasons for the special difficulty of proverbs. First, proverbs are usually complete sentences and are thus much longer and more complex than the other types of idioms, most of which are phrases. Second, proverbs are generally culture-specific—that is, a proverb usually is rooted deeply in the beliefs of a culture, at least more so than other idioms. For that reason, proverbs may not be easily understood by people unfamiliar with the culture. In general, idioms that are transparent in meaning and simple in structure are likely grasped before those that are opaque in meaning and complex in structure, because the latter often require higher cognitive ability or culture-specific knowledge to be understood. Then there are also those completely opaque idioms, or what Grant and Bauer (2004) call **core idioms**. These idioms are generally more difficult to understand than the others because they cannot be understood using compositional analysis, either literally or figuratively. They are best learned and memorized as complete individual lexical units (Grant and Nation, 2006). Most of them are thus not acquired early; however, a few rather common expressions such as *by and large* and *so long* may be among the first group of idioms grasped by some ESL students. Furthermore, Gibbs (1987) suggests that in L1 child language acquisition, idioms that do not allow word substitution or passive form are easier to learn and also learned earlier than those that do, because the former are acquired as whole units.

Comprehension before Production

Research suggests that idiom acquisition follows the same "comprehension before production" development pattern as does language acquisition in general. In several studies (Cacciari & Levorato, 1989; Levorato & Cacciari, 1992), children were asked to show their ability to understand and use the same idioms. Their comprehension was measured by a multiple-choice test and their productive ability was assessed via an idiom completion test. In all the studies the students performed better on the comprehension test than on the completion test, suggesting clearly that "comprehension before production" also holds true for idiom acquisition. Also, many studies have shown that children begin to develop a figurative competence and understand some idioms at the age of 7. Yet their ability to produce figurative language, including idioms, does not seem to start at the same age. According to a study by Pollio and Pollio (1974), children are able to produce figurative idioms at the age of around 9, about two years later than when they begin to understand some figurative idioms.

Idiom Production and the Avoidance Error in L2 Idiom Acquisition

The comprehension before production principle is perhaps even more evident in L2 idiom acquisition than in L1. Research has shown that using idioms in production poses a much greater challenge for L2 learners than idiom comprehension, for L2 learners, even very advanced ones, often tend to avoid using idioms for fear of making mistakes (Abdullah & Jackson, 1998; Charteris-Black, 2002; Irujo, 1986a; 1993; Hulstijn & Marchena, 1989; Jordens, 1977; Kellerman, 1979; Laufer, 2000). Such a practice of avoidance, often known as **avoidance error**, is, of course, common in L2 acquisition in general. However, avoidance in L2 idiom production is very different from avoidance in other areas of L2 use, such as the use of grammatical structure. Unlike avoidance in the use of grammatical structures, where learners normally avoid structures or items that are either absent or different from those in their L1, in terms of idiom use L2 learners seem to avoid idioms that are similar or even identical to those in their native language.

For example, Jordens (1977) and Kellerman (1979) both found in their experimental studies that L2 learners had the tendency to consider L2 idioms that had equivalents in their L1 to be ungrammatical. In Hulstijin and Marchena's (1989) study of Dutch learners' use of English phrasal verb idioms, the subjects tended to avoid phrasal verbs with Dutch equivalents having identical meanings. Similar findings are also reported in Abdullah and Jackson's study (1998). When asked to translate Syrian sentences with idioms into English, their subjects often avoided translating verbatim Syrian idioms that had identical counterparts in English because they were afraid that such idioms were absent in English. Such avoidance is very understandable, though, for two rather obvious reasons. First, given the uniqueness of idioms in structure and meaning, it is natural for L2 learners to believe it unlikely that an idiom in their native language also exists in the target language. Second, the multiple-word nature and the rigid structure of idioms make it difficult for learners to use them correctly, for the learner has to remember the exact wording of an idiom in addition to its unique meaning. When given the choice between a non-idiom expression and an idiom, an L2 learner will very likely, and understandably, use the former, because it is simpler in structure and more straightforward in meaning. Furthermore, in many cases the meaning of an idiom can be expressed by a non-idiom word or phrase.

Acculturation

As shown in the two previous chapters, many idioms are culture-bound. A solid understanding of the L2 culture should assist a learner in understanding and acquiring these idioms. The study by Dörnyei et al. (2004) shows that the degree of acculturation or active participation in the L2 social community is significantly correlated with the learner's level of success in acquiring formulaic sequences (a fairly large number of which are idioms).

THE IMPORTANCE OF IDIOM ACQUISITION IN LANGUAGE DEVELOPMENT

As has been shown, idioms are a very difficult aspect of language for L2 learners to acquire. Why then should L2 learners spend the time and effort needed to acquire them? The following is a list of the main reasons. The first two relate to the importance of idioms in language use and have been discussed in more detail in Chapter 2. The last five pertain especially to language learning and development.

1. According to Sinclair (1987), language use is governed by two operating principles: the **open choice principle** and the **idiom choice principle**. The two principles are complementary in ensuring successful language production. The **idiom principle** posits that word choices or combinations are not random, and speakers use a large number of preconstructed phrases including idioms in their communication. Although the term "idiom" in Sinclair's "idiom principle" refers to idiomatic use of language, rather than what we call idioms, it is undeniable that idioms are an important class of preconstructed phrases. They are ubiquitous in language and many of them have a very high-frequency use.
2. Research demonstrates that, because of their vividness and appeal to our senses and imagination, idioms are especially useful and effective in performing informative and evaluative functions (Fernando, 1996; Moon, 1998; also consult Chapter 2 for an in-depth discussion of this issue). Sometimes idioms can help speakers convey their messages in a way non-idiom expressions are unable to.
3. Formulaic expressions including idioms (especially figurative idioms) not only may allow L2 speakers to communicate more effectively but might also assist L2 learning by offering learners language input that can be segmented and analyzed (Bardovi-Harlig, 2002; D. Wood, 2002; Wray, 2000). D. Wood (2002) renders an excellent explanation of the possible dual role of formulaic expressions in L2 acquisition:

They are acquired and retained in and of themselves, linked to pragmatic competence and expanded as this aspect of communicative ability and awareness develops. At the same time, they are segmented and analyzed, broken down, and combined.... Both the original formulas and pieces and rules that come from analysis are retained. (p. 5)

Some colorful idioms, such as *kill two birds with one stone* and *go the extra mile to* . . ., are especially suitable for such double learning functions.

4. Idioms in a language contain rich, unique features of the language and culture. Many idioms are culture- or language-specific. Learning these idioms provides L2 learners with a good opportunity to understand and acquire information about L2 cultural beliefs and customs as well as the second language's linguistic features. For example, in terms of cultural learning, acquiring popular sports idioms in American English such as *step up to the plate* and *go the whole nine yards* will help L2 learners understand Americans' tendency (often an unconscious one) to view life as a sport (their staunch belief in free competition). With regard to the unique linguistic features of the target language, learning the ubiquitous phrasal verb idioms in English will allow L2 learners to appreciate the extremely important role phrasal verbs play in the language, especially in speaking.

5. Idioms, especially colloquial ones, are very frequently used in conversations between friends or peers. Encouraging students to learn and use such idioms creates more language input and practice opportunities.

6. The extent of an L2 learner's grasp of idioms is a good indicator of his or her language proficiency level (Yorio, 1989). Research indicates that the number of idioms (and formulaic sequences at large) acquired is positively correlated with the degree of success on communicative tasks, suggesting a close connection between idiom acquisition and communicative ability (Duquette, 1995; Schuster-Webb, 1980; Weinert, 1995; Wray, 1999, 2002; Schmitt, 2004).

7. Many L2 learners, especially intermediate and advanced students, yearn to learn idioms. These learners, with a good exposure to the target language, have learned to appreciate the value and the importance of idioms, including their vividness and effectiveness in communication. The students also begin to understand that the extent of an L2 learner's use of idioms is a good indicator of the person's language proficiency. This love for L2 idioms also often works as a strong motivator for learners in striving for continuing improvement in the target language.

A CAVEAT

While we are discussing the importance of idiom acquisition in language development, it is necessary to take note that there is also the danger that language learners and educators may overemphasize idioms in language learning. In fact, in a blind drive to grasp as many idioms as possible, some learners suffer from what Richards (1996) calls "**idiomatosis**," an unhealthy condition marked by "an urge to force as many idiomatic expressions into a sentence as one can" (p. 32). Such a disease results in speeches filled with inappropriate and rarely used idioms. Richards attributes this malady partially to an overexposure to commercial idiom teaching materials such as idiom dictionaries. These teaching materials often contain many idioms of low use frequency and provide no adequate usage information, such as the appropriate context(s) for the use of a given idiom. Learners and teachers alike need to be cautious about the instructional value of these materials and should guard against an overzealous impulse to use indiscriminately all the idioms they encounter or learn.

SUMMARY

To acquire idioms, a person needs to develop adequate cognitive and linguistic skills. A special cognition-related ability required for acquisition of metaphorical idioms is figurative competence. The development of such a competence goes through several phases, marked by age. These phases, described using different terms by different scholars, may boil down to two major ones: a pre-figurative competence phase and a figurative competence development phase. The acquisition of metaphorical idioms is made possible mostly by such a competence and the application of other cognitive and linguistic skills. The majority of idioms are thus not acquired mostly by rote learning, although memorization does play a role. Idiom acquisition also follows the "comprehension before production" sequence found in language learning in general. Idiom types also may affect idiom acquisition sequence and rate. Finally, idioms are very important for language learners to acquire because of their ubiquity, the unique and sometimes indispensable role they play in communication, and the cultural information they carry. A good command of idioms is often synonymous with a high degree of proficiency in the language. Idiom acquisition is thus very important for L2 learners. Yet when we emphasize the need to acquire idioms, we should also guard against **idiomatosis**, the malady of blind and excessive use of idioms, or their inappropriate use.

Questions for Study and Discussion

1. Suppose there are two groups of ESL learners, one consisting of children aged from 4 to 7 and one composed of college students, and both groups exhibit difficulty in understanding and grasping some English idioms such as *put one's foot in one's mouth* and *kick the bucket*. Is the major cause of the problem the same for both groups? If not, then what is it for each group, and why?
2. Both cognitive/linguistic ability and rote learning appear to play important roles in idiom acquisition. Explain what role or roles each plays?
3. Why do L2 learners avoid using idioms in their language production, especially those that look very similar to those in their native language? What can teachers do to help students overcome this problem?
4. Besides the points mentioned in the chapter about the importance of idiom acquisition, think of a few others.
5. The following quotation is part of an introduction given by a tour guide speaking English as a foreign language cited in Richards (1996, p. 32). Do you see any problem(s) with the expressions the tour guide used? If you do, explain the problem(s).

> We are going to start our tour in the city center, which is far and away the best place to begin. You'll feast your eyes on some of our historic buildings. I hope I know my stuff and can answer all of your questions. I think you'll find the city tour today really hits the nail on the head.

Chapter 7

Selection and Organization of Idioms for Learning and Instruction

INTRODUCTION

Given the enormous number of idioms in a language and the great difficulty involved in L2 idiom learning, teachers have to be selective in including idioms for students to learn. They will often need to decide not only which idioms to include but also in what order the idioms will be introduced, because selecting the right idioms is crucial for effective instruction. Furthermore, teachers should also consider what usage information to provide regarding the selected idioms. Idiom usage information is very important for learners, because idioms vary in terms of function, formality, register, and connotation. Some idioms are used only in informal contexts and some are found primarily in only one register. Learners need such information about the idioms they are learning in order to use them appropriately. This chapter explores various issues related to idiom selection for instruction, including criteria and useful practices for determining which idioms to include, the types of information that should be provided regarding the idioms, the sources available for idiom selection, and some methods of idiom classification or organization that may aid idiom learning and teaching.

SELECTION CRITERIA AND USEFUL SELECTION PRACTICES

Often, what idioms should be included for instruction depends on various factors such as students' learning objectives and language proficiency level. There are, however, some general selection criteria that apply in most learning situations. We shall now discuss these criteria and some specific techniques that can be used in idiom selection. The criteria are given in order of importance.

Students' Needs

What students need to learn constitutes arguably the most important criterion. Idioms chosen for instruction should be those that students need the most in terms of their learning goals—that is, those that students have to grasp immediately in order to successfully perform the communicative tasks they are engaged in. In other words, the idioms must possess the "urgency of applicability" (Yorio, 1980, p. 439). For example, for immigrants, survival English items such as *What's up?* and *hold on* (meaning "wait") should be high on the list of the idioms they need to grasp. Of course, determining what idioms one's students need to learn is not an easy task in most cases. There are, however, several practices that can be used to help accomplish the task. One is to survey students and their prospective employers regarding the types of idiomatic expressions the students will need to use. Another approach is to conduct searches of a corpus or corpora consisting of language data that represent the type (register) of language the students will learn to use. Register is a very important factor to consider, because idiom use is extremely register-sensitive. One more useful practice is to have students generate a list of idioms that they either are interested in learning or believe to be useful for their current or future employment. Obviously students will not be able to provide specific idioms, for they do not know them. What they can do is to write down the types of idioms they want to learn, such as "idioms expressing moods" (which may include *on cloud nine, bummed out,* and *down in the dumps*) or "idioms expressing a great accomplishment" (which may cover *hit a home run/a grand slam* and *score a touchdown*). Therefore, instead of asking students for idioms, the teacher should ask what types of idioms students wish to learn, what functions they want to use them for, and when and where they want to use them. Finally, students' needs may also help determine the sequence of idioms to be taught. For example, idioms used in daily social interactions (e.g. *What's up?* and *So long*) will probably need to be taught early.

Usefulness/Frequency

The usefulness of an idiom should also be an important selection factor because it is a waste of valuable instructional time to teach idioms that students may never use (Liu, 2003). While this criterion may in some cases overlap with the first one, it is not the same, because the usefulness of an idiom in general terms is determined by its frequency, not by a student's particular learning needs. Thus, an idiom useful for a particular group of learners may not be useful for the general public. For example, *go around* and *have numbers* are two very useful idioms for pilots and air traffic controllers (the former is used by controllers to instruct a pilot to abandon an approach or landing and the latter is used by pilots to indicate they have received runway, wind, and altimeter information) but not for other people—or, as in the case of *go around*, at least not with the same meaning. As a rule of thumb, high-frequency idioms should generally be taught before low-frequency idioms unless there is a compelling reason to the contrary. An example of the latter case will be an idiom that is of low frequency but high on the students' needs list. Thus, a caveat is in order: it is not prudent to exclude all low-frequency idioms because sometimes an idiom of low frequency may be a rather useful one, especially for students learning English for special purposes. As Cornell (1999) correctly points out, sometimes an idiom that is generally of low frequency may be used often in a particular context or community in which a learner works or lives.

How do we determine the usefulness or the frequency of an idiom? In the past, teachers, and writers of idiom teaching material, relied mostly on intuition. With the ever-increasing accessibility of corpora and the ever-improving corpus search engines, corpus research has become the most effective method of ascertaining the use frequency of idioms. It enables researchers and teachers alike to determine the frequency of very large numbers of idioms within a relatively short period of time. Some fruitful work has been conducted in this regard, including that by Biber et al. (1999), Grant (2005), and Liu (2003). A very important characteristic of these studies is that they were register-specific and, in some cases, language variety-specific (Liu, 2003). Their findings are, therefore, of special value to language learners and teachers because, as explained in the idiom register section in Chapter 2, idiom use is extremely register-sensitive and language variety-specific. For example, for learners who are interested in idioms in American spoken English in public discourse, Liu's (2003) list of the 302 most frequently used Spoken American English idioms is very helpful. The list is compiled on the basis of his frequency searches of approximately 10,000 idioms in three spoken American English corpora with a total of 6 million words. The idioms in the lists are grouped into three bands according to their frequency. Band 1 consists of those that occur 50 times or more (i.e. more than 50 tokens) per million; Band 2 contains those that have a use frequency of between 11 and 49 times per million words; and Band 3 includes those with a frequency of 2 to 10 times per million. Furthermore, the list also includes three sublists based on the three corpora used for the study: Academic (MICAS), Media (CSAME), and Professional (CSPAE). The creation of the sublists allows

English learners in any of the three specific fields to know what the most frequently used idioms in their field are and, in turn, to focus on them, making idiom learning much more effective.

An important issue that a teacher needs to consider when conducting corpus-based research of idiom frequency is that the corpus must be representative in terms of its content and size. If a teacher wants to compile a list of the most frequently used idioms used in medicine, then the corpus must be a medical one of an adequate size. On the basis of Kennedy's (1998) suggestion regarding the number of words in a corpus necessary for ensuring the data's descriptive adequacy for lexical items, and according to my own experience, a corpus needs to contain a minimum of 2 million words to allow a meaningful and reliable frequency study of common idioms (that is, not enough for a study of rarely used idioms).[1] Similarly, a list of the most useful academic idioms must be based on corpora consisting of language used in the various functions of school such as lectures, classroom question and answer exchanges, and discussions. There are now many corpora designed for specific professions and purposes. They will be ideal for studying the frequency of the idioms used in the profession in which one is interested.

The following is a list of corpora available to the public (some require a fee for purchase or use): the British National Corpus (BNC), with over 100,000,000 words and a condensed version called BNC Baby with approximately 4,000,000 words that boasts more and better search functions designed primarily for language learning; the Brown Corpus, with 1,000,000 American English words; the Michigan Corpus of Academic Spoken English (MICASE), with approximately 2,000,000 words; and the Corpus of Spoken Professional American English (CSPAE), also with 2,000,000 words. MICASE is accessible free online at http://micase.umdl.umich.edu/m/micase. The BNC may also be accessed free of charge online via an interface at http://corpus.byu.edu/bnc, a web page for BNC designed by Mark Davies at Brigham Young University.

Finally, it is important for teachers to know that searching for idioms in a corpus is sometimes a laborious and complex task that requires some skills. This is because some searches will result in many irrelevant hits (e.g. the search for the idiom *come by* meaning "acquire" will produce many instances of "come by + a place" meaning "visit" a place). Another reason for the complexity is that many idioms are not frozen—that is, they sometimes vary in form. A transitive phrasal verb idiom may vary because its particle may be placed either before or after the verb (i.e. *turn down* an offer or *turn* an offer *down*). Some idioms have established noun or verb variations (e.g. *set* or *start the ball rolling*; *bite the cannonball* instead of *the bullet*). Then, the tense or aspect of a verb in an idiom may change. Just conducting a straight-out search will miss out many examples of an idiom. To avoid the problem, one needs to make sure to search for all possible variations of an idiom. A technique that is especially effective is the use of the wild card (usually *). For example, by entering *turn* * down*, one will be able to find all the *turn something* down examples, including those with the verb in the form of *turn, turns, turned,* or *turning.*

Appropriateness

Whether an idiom is appropriate for students to use for their age, their language register, etc. is one more important determining factor. For example, generally speaking, teachers should not teach idioms deemed vulgar or offensive in public such as (*kiss my xxx* and *piss someone off*). If such idioms are taught, for whatever reason, students should understand their offensive nature. Some scholars (Irujo, 1986b) even suggest excluding colloquial idioms (*you bet your boots*) or slang expressions (*don't sweat it*), although others would disagree. Whether to include colloquial or slang idiomatic expressions will depend, again, on students' learning needs. For immigrants these idioms are certainly appropriate, but perhaps not so for international students pursuing academic degrees in college, and definitely not for EFL students. Determining the appropriateness of an idiom is a challenging task, too, because there are really two appropriateness issues: (1) appropriate for context, and (2) appropriate for the speaker/learner. An idiom that is appropriate for a context or register may not be appropriate for a particular group of students to use. For example, some informal slang idiomatic expressions are appropriate for close adult friends to use in private but they are certainly not proper for teenage school students to use. Corpora are, again, a very good source and tool for ascertaining the context and speaker-appropriateness of idioms. For example, from corpus data we can find out in what contexts an idiom is used most often and by what type of people. When there does not appear to be a clear-cut decision as to whether an idiom is appropriate for adult students, the teacher may leave the decision to the students, because they are the learners and they know what they need. Yet before the students make a decision, the teacher needs to help them understand the idiom's register, level of formality, connotation, etc. so they can make an informed decision. In general, in choosing appropriate idioms we should bear in mind that they must be appropriate to the students' needs—that is, they will be helpful for the students in performing their communication tasks successfully.

Easiness to Learn

How easy an idiom is for learners to grasp should be another important selection criterion. Moving from easy or simple items or rules to more difficult and complex ones is a long-cherished principle of successful learning. It thus makes good sense to teach easy and simple idioms first and then move slowly to more difficult and complex ones. The level of an idiom's easiness to learn may be determined by several factors, such as its transparency (in meaning), de-compositionality, simplicity (in vocabulary and structure), and level of similarity to its counterpart in the learners' L1 if there is one. The following is an elaboration of these factors.

1. Transparency (in meaning) and de-compositionality: the two criteria are grouped together because they are closely related and overlap to a certain degree. Generally, an idiom that is decomposable such as *bite off more than one can chew* is simultaneously transparent in meaning. Such idioms are easier to understand than those that are opaque and non-decomposable.
2. Simplicity in vocabulary and syntax: idioms whose vocabulary components and syntactical structure are simpler usually pose less difficulty for students than those with complex vocabulary and structure. For example, the idiom *a piece of cake* should be easier for students to understand than *a needle in a haystack* because the word "haystack" is not a common word that many ESL students are likely to know. Similarly, *hit a home run* is syntactically easier to process than *have two strikes against someone*.
3. Similarity to idioms in L1: idioms that are identical or similar to L1 idioms both in meaning and structure pose little difficulty for students to understand and they are generally easy to remember. For this reason, both Cooper (1999) and Irujo (1986b) suggest that these idioms should be among the first to be introduced (**not learned**, because students in fact already know them in their L1). Even though students know these idioms in their L1, an introduction of these idioms in L2 is necessary because learners should be made aware of the existence of these idioms in the target language. Otherwise, as studies (Abdullah & Jackson, 1998; Irujo, 1986a) show, many students will question whether these idioms exist in the L2 and refuse to use them, fearing they are false friends. Of course, this criterion works only for classes with a homogeneous L1.

A factor that needs to be taken into consideration in determining the level of easiness or difficulty of idioms is learners' age. As Douglas and Peel's (1979) study demonstrates, metaphorical idioms are difficult for young children and are not appropriate for those under the age of 6. Proverb-type idioms are even more difficult because they are challenging even for 10- or 11-year old children.

It is important to take note that in applying the above criteria in selecting idioms, one may notice that sometimes the criteria may contradict one another. For instance, an idiom that students need or want to grasp may not be one of high frequency and may not be easy to learn, either. In such a situation, a teacher should weigh the conflicting criteria to determine which is the most important when all the relevant factors are taken into consideration.

TYPES OF IDIOM INFORMATION THAT NEED TO BE PROVIDED

After idioms have been selected, a teacher should look for and include the necessary information that will help students grasp them, including the typical functions the idioms perform and the contexts in which they are usually used. Such information will enable students to learn how to use the idioms appropriately. The following addresses the types of information that will need to be provided.

Formality, Register, and Language Variety

How formal an idiom is and what register and language variety it is used in constitute perhaps the most important information for language learners in order for them to use it appropriately. Some idiom dictionaries and teaching materials published within the past decade provide this type of information, including the *Cambridge International Dictionary of Idioms* (1998) and the *Oxford Idioms Dictionary for English Learners* (2001). There is also some established information on this issue. For example, phrasal verb idioms are, in general, not very formal and are more common in speaking than in writing. They are not appropriate for highly marked formal registers such as legal documents. When an application is rejected, people usually say it has been *turned down*, but in a legal document the one-word verb "rejected" is the preferred choice. In the event that no known information about an idiom's formality is available and no such information can be found in reference and teaching materials, a teacher may conduct a corpus search to find it. BNC, BNC Baby, and MICASE are especially helpful because they each consist of searchable register-specific subcorpora. The BNC (via the aforementioned Mark Davies's interface web page) and BNC Baby contain, among other registers, Written Academic Prose, Written Fiction, and Spoken subcorpora. MICASE includes Lectures, Group Discussions, Colloquia, Advising Sessions, etc. It can also be searched by academic discipline such as biological and health sciences, humanities/arts, and physical sciences and engineering. By searching an idiom in the different subcorpora one can quickly find the idiom's register information. For example, a quick search of the idiom *get rid of* in the BNC Baby's Spoken and the Written Academic Prose will show that while it is used only six times in the Academic Prose subcorpus, it has a use frequency of 66 in the Spoken subcorpus. In other words, it is used eleven times more in speaking than in academic writing. Such register information is very important for ESL learners in learning to use the idiom in the right context and discourse.

Function and Connotation

For language learners to use an idiom appropriately and effectively, they will also need to know what function or functions the idiom may perform and what connotation it carries. This is because some idioms are primarily evaluative (e.g. *chicken out* and *a cakewalk*), some are informational in nature (e.g. *come by something* and *call it a day*), some are textual (e.g. *by the same token* and *by the way*), some express modality such as qualification (e.g. *by and large* and *so to speak*), and many perform cross or multiple functions. For example, both *chicken out* and *drop the ball* are informative as well as evaluative, for the former informs the listener or reader with an evaluative message that a person referred to dishonorably did not do what he or she had promised to do, and the latter gives the information that someone failed in accomplishing something due to his or her own mistake. Without an understanding of the typical function an idiom plays and the connotation it carries, L2 learners may use it inappropriately, as Lattey (1994) demonstrates with examples of German ESL students' idiom production.

Useful Sources

In addition to the aforementioned corpora, there are many other useful sources available, in both traditional and electronic formats, for teachers to use in selecting idioms for instruction. An annotated selective list of such sources is provided as an appendix to this book. It includes primarily idiom dictionaries and student textbooks, although it also contains a few free online sources; the items are selected according to the following three criteria: contemporaneity (most published since 2000 and none before 1990), quality and quantity of the information provided (such as definition, explanation, examples, and learning activities), and soundness in idiom selection (many being corpus based). A few are included for their uniqueness (e.g. a sports idiom dictionary and a video teaching program).

ORGANIZING IDIOMS FOR INSTRUCTION AND RETENTION

After deciding on which idioms and what accompanying usage information to include for instruction, a teacher may want to consider how to classify and organize them in order either to present the idioms to students more effectively or to help the students retain them more easily. There are many different ways idioms may be organized. How to organize idioms for a curriculum or program will depend on several factors, such as the types of idioms selected and the students' age, learning goals, and learning styles. Organizing idioms appropriately can assist students' learning because it can help students see patterns, which, in turn, may lead to better understanding of idioms (Lattey, 1986). Of course, as Nation (2000) notes, learning lexical items that are related either syntactically or semantically may result in unnecessary interference, thus increasing learning difficulty. Teachers thus must be aware of such dangers and should watch out for and avoid them whenever possible. The following is a list of some methods for organizing idioms, each with a brief mention of its advantages and/or disadvantages. It is also important to note that some of the methods overlap.

1. *By grammatical structure.* Examples include:
   (a) phrasal verbs (*give in* and *come across*);
   (b) verb plus a noun structure (*jump the gun* and *bite the bullet*);
   (c) irreversible binominal and bi-adjective (*heart and soul* and *safe and sound*);
   (d) prepositional phrase (*down the drain* and *in hot water*);
   (e) ill-formed phrases (*by and large* and *all in all*);
   (f) complete sentences (*What's up?* and *When in Rome, do as the Romans do*).

   The strength of this grouping is that it may allow students to use different learning strategies for grasping the different types. For example, the ill-formed idioms will be best learned by memorization. A weakness is that such an organization is too broad. Too many idioms may go into any one of the categories.

2. *By grammatical function* (parts of speech). Examples include:
   (a) working as nouns (*back-seat driver* and *chip off the old block*);
   (b) functioning as verbs (*give in* and *dropped the ball*);
   (c) serving as adjectives (*fair and square* and *under the weather*);
   (d) performing as adverbs (*hand in glove* and *by and large*).

   This classification may help students remember better the part of speech of an idiom and may help them to use it more accurately in terms of grammar. Yet it is not easy to apply, because some idioms may perform multiple grammatical functions. For example, *fair and square* may function as either an adjectival or an adverbial phrase.

3. *By the motivating concept.* Examples include:
   (a) "anger is pent up steam" (*have steam coming out one's ears* and *blow off steam*);
   (b) "life is sport or competition" (*hit a home run* and *throw in the towel*);
   (c) "life is business" (*cash in* and *get more than one bargained for*);
   (d) "life is driving" (*spinning wheels* and *a two-way street*).

This grouping is especially helpful for teaching idioms based on concept-motivated metaphors. Research has shown that it may assist students in comprehending and memorizing such idioms. Yet there may be too many idioms motivated by the same concept for such a classification to be of high value for learning. Also, the large number of idioms with the same motivation concept may make students confused about them. It is thus important to emphasize the differences between them.

4. *By origin or source.*[2] Examples include:
   (a) from animals (*smell a rat* and *dog in a manger*);
   (b) from cooking or food (*a piece of cake* and *half-baked*);
   (c) from body parts (*all ears* and *head over heels*);
   (d) from farming (*cream of the crop* and *a needle in a haystack*);
   (e) from music (*low key* and *face the music*);
   (f) from fish and fishing (*a big fish in a small pond* and *let someone off the hook*);
   (g) religion (*preach/talk to the choir* and *a fallen angel*).

Research has shown that knowing the origin and source of an idiom helps students understand and remember it. Organizing idioms of the same origin together may assist students in remembering them. Yet it may also have the potential danger of creating confusion for students, because idioms with the same origin may interfere with one another. Both teachers and students should be cautious.

5. *By topic on which the idiom is used to comment.* Examples include:
   (a) difficulty/problem (*a pain in the neck* and *a hard nut to crack*);
   (b) abandoning effort (*throw in the towel* and *raise a white flag*);
   (c) agreement (*see eye to eye* and *be on the same page*);
   (d) advice (*bite the bullet* and *don't throw the baby out with the bathwater*);
   (e) cover-up/secret (*sweep something under the rug/carpet* and *a skeleton in the closet*);

(f) following trend (*jump on the bandwagon* and *go with the flow*);
(g) health (*under the weather* and *back on one's feet*);
(h) mood (*be on cloud nine* and *down in the dumps*);
(i) mistake (*get more than one bargained for* and *bite off more than one can chew*);
(j) preparation/getting started (*get one's feet wet* and *crank up*);
(k) study/work hard (*burn night oil* and *hit the books*);
(l) smooth and successful operation (*firing on all cylinders*);
(m) waste of time/effort (*fighting a losing battle, spinning wheels, beat a dead horse*).

This classification may not be helpful for instructional purposes because there are too many idioms for any given topics. It will be useful for retention purposes for students who possess a solid understanding of a lot of the idioms.

6. *By activity in or for which the idiom is often used.* Examples include:
   (a) dating (*go steady* and *hit it off*);
   (b) eating out (*go Dutch* and *pick up the tab*);
   (c) go to bed or to sleep (*turn in* and *sleep tight* or *like a log*).

This may be helpful when the instruction of a class is focused on such a topic but, again, work hard on the differences among the idioms on the same topic to help prevent interference or confusion.

7. *By key words.* Examples include:
   (a) "ball" (*drop the ball, have a ball,* and *the ball is in your court*);
   (b) "hand" (*give/lend someone a hand, have one's hands full,* and *wash one's hands of something*);
   (c) "water" (*be in hot water, do/does not hold water,* and *test the water*).

This may not be good for instructional purposes. It could be helpful for retention as it allows students to organize idioms in a way that may help them in remembering them.

8. *By semantics.* Examples include:
   (a) positive/praise (*hit a home run* and *cream of the crop*);
   (b) negative/criticism (*chicken out* and *beat about/around the bush*);
   (c) opposites (*on cloud nine* versus *down in the dumps* and *it's in the bag* versus *it's a long shot*);
   (d) same core meaning but degree of difference in connotation (*breathe one's last breath* versus *kick the bucket* and *strike out* versus *meet one's Waterloo*);
   (e) similar in form but different in meaning (*go through [successful]* versus *fall through [failed]*).

When using this classification, the teacher should focus not just on the similarity among the idioms in each category but also on the differences among the idioms in each category to help students understand and remember them and to avoid any confusion, or interference between similar idioms.

Given that these organizing strategies have their advantages and disadvantages, which one or ones to use will depend on a variety of factors, including the students' goals and learning styles and one's teaching purposes. For example, if your students want to learn to communicate effectively in functions like dating, eating out, etc., then organizing idioms around activities and functions may be a helpful practice.

PASSIVE VERSUS ACTIVE IDIOMS

Passive idioms are those that language learners understand when they encounter them but are not yet able to use in language production. As idiom acquisition also follows the "comprehension before production" sequence found in language acquisition in general, it can be assumed that when a learner first encounters and understands an idiom, it will initially be on the passive idiom list. After more exposure to the idiom, it may become an active one. Yet some idioms of low use frequency may remain in the receptive idiom repertoire for a long time (or perhaps forever) because there is hardly any opportunity or context for using them. To enhance idiom acquisition efficiency, it makes good sense to divide idioms that one wants to learn or is learning into active and passive categories. Such a division will allow a learner to focus more on the active ones, as these idioms require more effort to grasp. Generally speaking, for most learners the majority of phrasal verb idioms will be active idioms because they are common in speech. On the other hand, many proverb idioms will likely be passive idioms because they have a low frequency.

SUMMARY

Given the enormous number of idioms in a language and the difficulty involved in learning idioms, it is impossible for language learners to grasp all idioms, especially in a short period of time. Selecting appropriate idioms for instruction is thus very important. Researchers and teachers alike have identified some useful criteria for determining which idioms to include for instruction, such as students' learning needs, an idiom's usefulness and appropriateness, and its easiness for language learners to grasp. To help students learn how to use the idioms that they are studying, it is imperative that usage information regarding these idioms is provided, such as their formality, register, and functions. Idioms may be organized in many different ways to assist language learners in grasping them. Teachers need to understand how to organize their selected idioms interestingly and informatively so students will find the idioms not only interesting to learn but also easy to grasp.

Questions for Study and Discussion

1. From your experience, which of the criteria for selecting idioms for instruction mentioned in the chapter do you think are most important? Are there any other useful criteria that are not mentioned in the chapter? If so, what are they and why are they important?
2. Conduct a search of BNC regarding the frequency of the following idioms. If you do not have BNC, you may conduct the search online at http://view.byu.edu. Rank them in order of their frequency. Then decide whether the frequency information matches your intuitive view of the usefulness of the idioms.

    Cut corners; hang in the balance; hit or miss; in light of; it takes two to tango; keep track of; on the line; on the mend; (a) slap on the wrist; take its toll

3. Conduct a search of BNC or MICASE concerning the following idioms' register information—that is, the idioms' use frequency in the various subcorpora. Then divide them roughly into three groups: informal, in between, and formal. Do the results match or contradict your intuitive views about the idiom in terms of their register?

    as of; at the expense of; drop the ball; fool around; go hand in hand; in lieu of; off the record; pertain to; ring hollow; up to speed

4. Of the various idiom organization methods mentioned in this chapter, which one or ones do you think are the most helpful to your prospective students in learning idioms? Can you think of a few other ways of organizing idioms and explain how these might assist students in their learning?
5. Do you think you also have a passive idiom repertoire—that is, idioms you understand but rarely use in your speech and writing? If you do, give a few examples of them as well as a few of your active idioms and explain why you have classified them the way you did.

Chapter **8**

Idiom Pedagogy: Macro-strategies and General Approaches

INTRODUCTION

Because idioms are difficult to grasp, how to help students learn them effectively has long been a challenge and a topic of study for language educators and researchers alike (e.g. Abrahamsen and Smith, 2000; Boers, 2001; Boers et al., 2004a; Boers & Lindstromberg, 2005; Bromley, 1984; Cooper, 1998; Duquette, 1995; Grant & Nation, 2006; Irujo, 1986b; Latty, 1986, 1994; Lennon, 1998; Liu, 2000a; Otier, 1986). Their effort has borne some fruit. Based on their research, this chapter introduces and explores some useful macro-strategies and approaches for idiom learning and teaching. Some of these macro-strategies consist of micro-techniques. Thus, the discussion of the macro-strategies will also involve the introduction of the latter, but the majority of micro-strategies will be discussed in the next chapter. The chapter will end with a brief discussion of the pros and cons of using a proactive as against a retroactive approach to idiom instruction, a very important question in relation to macro-strategy.

RAISING STUDENTS' AWARENESS OF AND INTEREST IN IDIOMS

Idiom awareness is very important for L2 learners because, as second language acquisition (SLA) theory suggests, noticing is needed for language learning to take place (Ellis, 1997; Schmidt, 1990). More importantly, recent research (Jones & Haywood, 2004) has shown that raising students' awareness of formulaic expressions, including idioms, enhances their grasp of these expressions. By becoming aware of idioms, students learn to appreciate their importance in language and to understand how they are used. Furthermore, such awareness often leads learners to an increased interest in idioms and, in return, more incidental idiom learning, a welcome byproduct. In fact, some scholars believe that raising students' sensitivity to idioms is perhaps more effective than giving them lists of idioms to learn (Richards, 1996). This is because training students to notice the idioms that they encounter not only makes them more conscious of idiom use but also ensures that the idioms they learn are those of high frequency. This is because the idioms that learners encounter daily are usually those that are frequently used. As such, they are certainly more worthy of learning than those rarely used ones found in some teaching materials or in some of the lists prepared arbitrarily by teachers. While awareness of idioms is essential, an interest in idioms is equally important. This is because L2 idiom learning is a lifelong learning process due to their extremely large number. The following are some activities designed to raise students' awareness of and interest in idioms.

Developing a Habit of Watching for Idioms in Daily Language Use

First, demonstrate and explain to students that idioms are ubiquitous in language and then ask students to watch for them in their daily language use, including reading and listening. Of course, for students to engage in the activity successfully, we first need to train them so they will be able to recognize idioms when they encounter them. One training practice is to first select a passage with some idioms as a text and then have students identify the idioms in it. The passage can be used for either reading or listening, depending on its level of difficulty and the focus of instruction. When doing the activity the first time, have students work as a whole group. The rationale for making it initially a whole-class activity is that identifying idioms is not an easy task. Working as a class gives the teacher and students the opportunity to collaborate to ensure that all the students understand what they are looking for and know how to do it. Specific activities for helping students learn how to recognize idioms will be introduced in the next chapter in the section "Noticing and Identifying Idioms."

After students have learned how to find idioms, the teacher can ask them to do so individually and routinely when they read newspapers, listen to the radio, watch TV, etc. To make sure students practice regularly, the teacher can ask them to write down the idioms they encounter and their meaning or function in a notebook. Check the students' notebooks periodically to assess their work in terms of the number of idioms they identify and the meaning and usage information they put down. To motivate students, the teacher can conduct a contest among the students to see who identifies the largest number of idioms in a week, a month, or a semester. By doing the activity routinely, students should develop a habit of watching for idioms in their language learning.

Using Idiom Corner/Bulletin/File/Notebook

An idiom corner is a space on a wall of the classroom used to post idioms that students have encountered or that the teacher would like students to learn. It can appear in the form of an "Idiom of the Day" (Cooper, 1998). Usually the idiom(s) posted should be those that students either find interesting or have difficulty understanding. In the former case, the student who posts the idiom or idioms intends to share with the other students what he or she believes to be interesting and useful information. In the latter case, the person who posts the idiom or idioms wants to ask for help, to see if other students or the teacher can explain the idioms in question. In either case, students gain an extra idiom exposure opportunity. They also benefit from the interaction process itself. With the use of an idiom bulletin board or idiom corner, a friendly competition may also be conducted to see, for instance, who posts the highest number of idioms in a week or month, who posts the most challenging idiom(s) for the class (challenging in the sense of taking the longest time for the class to figure out its meaning), and who is the quickest in finding out or guessing correctly the meanings of the idioms posted.

Similarly, the teacher can work with the students to build an idiom file accessible to the entire class (Otier, 1986). The file may contain a list of idioms organized in several different ways, such as by theme, function, source origin, or structural pattern.

Exploring Idioms in Cartoons, Comic Strips, TV, and Other Media

Other activities that may help raise students' awareness and interest in idioms include reading and discussing idioms in cartoons and comic strips, watching TV, etc. These are fun but also very useful activities, especially for intermediate- and higher-level students (Irujo, 1986b). Reading and discussing idioms in cartoons should appeal especially to secondary and young college students.

Learning to Organize Idioms in a Variety of Ways to Promote Idiom Acquisition

Another way to increase students' sensitivity to and interest in idioms is to teach them the many different ways in which idioms can be organized, such as by theme, origin, function, and parts of speech (see Chapter 7 for a detailed description of the organization methods). Organizing idioms in different manners gives students the opportunity to review the idioms they have learned. It may also make some of the idioms easier to grasp and may enable students to better appreciate the value, functions, and usage patterns of idioms. As a result, students become more interested and motivated in learning idioms.

In fact, in addition to enhancing students' interest in and sensitivity to idioms, the above activities may also promote the incidental learning of idioms. This is because learners may pick up many of the idioms that they encounter when they read newspapers and other print media, listen to the radio, or watch TV.

INCORPORATING IDIOM LEARNING INTO THE ENTIRE CURRICULUM

In helping students learn idioms, we may devote some classes or some parts of a class exclusively to the teaching of idioms. Yet we should not rely mostly on such practice for idiom teaching, for two reasons. First, like other lexical items, idioms are best learned naturally in normal language use. It is thus not a good practice to teach idioms in a contrived language context, one that is often created in lessons designed solely for idiom learning. For this reason, some scholars (Cornell, 1999) have questioned the value and appropriateness of learning idioms separately and argued for learning them together with other language elements—that is, in regular language classes that focus on one or more of the four language skills. The second reason for not relying on idiom lessons to teach idioms is that the amount of time that can be allocated for such exclusive idiom instruction is very limited in most language teaching programs. Idiom teaching may thus be done much more effectively if it is incorporated naturally into the entire language teaching program. In other words, teachers should incorporate idiom teaching naturally into their regular lesson plans. As Irujo (1986b) points out,

> Learning idioms is, or should be, an integral part of vocabulary learning in a second language. Therefore it should not be put off until students reach advanced levels. Even at beginning levels, idioms can be added to the vocabulary being learned by including them in dialogues and stories which are created to supplement regular materials, and by providing idiomatic synonyms for vocabulary words which the students are learning. (p. 240)

For low-level students, some high-frequency, easy idioms can be taught by including them in the teaching material. This way, the teaching of idioms becomes natural.

In addition to incorporating idioms into the overall curriculum of a language teaching program, teachers may also want to include idioms in their instructional language or classroom speech as a whole whenever appropriate. In fact, as research indicates (Liu, 2000a), many teachers routinely use idioms in their instructional language, although they often do so unconsciously. Such a practice, as Perez (1981) reports, can enhance not only L2 students' oral proficiency but also their reading and hence overall language proficiency. Perez included many colloquial idioms in her teaching of Hispanic immigrant children and it helped the students to enhance their reading performance significantly. This is because the use of idioms in the instructional language increases L2 students' exposure to idioms in a natural fashion. Encountering and noticing new lexical items, including idioms, in normal communication situations is an ideal way of learning them. Yet the use of idioms in instructional language has to be done appropriately and carefully in order for it to help students acquire idioms. Otherwise, it may become a disservice to L2 students. For example, using idioms that the students do not know without offering some form of explanation or some comprehension compensation strategy may create learning barriers for L2 students in class. Using too many unknown idioms will frustrate students, resulting in instructional failures. Thus, the use of idioms in the instructional language has to be a principled practice. For example, teachers need to be careful about the idioms they use. They need to know, among other things, whether the idioms are familiar, semantically transparent, and decomposable, and how much contextual information there is for the idioms used.

When using idioms that are unfamiliar and/or semantically opaque, teachers will need to employ various assistance strategies to help the students not only to notice but also to understand them. Unfortunately Liu's (2000a) study showed that not many teachers provide assistance to their students when using difficult idioms in their instructional language. Therefore, it is vital that teachers become more informed about this issue and learn to develop and use strategies that will help their students better grasp the idioms embedded in the instructional language. While many instructors in Liu's study did not offer assistance to their students, some did, and fairly effectively. They used primarily three explanation strategies to help students understand unknown idioms: definition, elaboration, and paraphrasing, which will be introduced in detail with examples in the next chapter. Using these strategies allows a teacher to help students understand the unknown idioms without interrupting content instruction. Therefore, teachers should become familiar with these and other useful explanation strategies.

ADVANCING A HEURISTIC APPROACH WITH DISCOVERY LEARNING ACTIVITIES AND ADEQUATE CONTEXTUAL INFORMATION

Idiom comprehension plays a crucial role in idiom acquisition because a learner needs to understand an idiom before acquiring it. Thus, helping students understand idioms should be the main focus of idiom instruction. According to research reported in Chapter 4, L2 learners generally use a heuristic or problem-solving approach in idiom comprehension—that is, they employ a variety of strategies to work out the meaning of an idiom, including using pragmatic knowledge and guessing from context (Bulut and Çelik-Yazici, 2004; Cooper, 1999). Most idioms, especially figurative ones, lend themselves well to such a discovery approach. Given such information, teachers should try their best to use, whenever possible, learning activities that will advance the use of the said problem-solving strategies to help students understand and learn idioms. For such discovery learning to be effective, idioms need to be placed in context, with adequate discourse information. This is because in the absence of any contextual information, many idioms will be almost impossible to comprehend. Furthermore, providing adequate contextual information not only aids learners in understanding idioms but also, as research has demonstrated, enhances their memory and, in turn, promotes idiom acquisition. For example, in an experimental study Gibbs (1980) presented a list of idioms in three conditions to three randomly assigned groups of subjects (literal context condition, idiomatic context condition, and no context condition) and then asked the subjects to recall the idioms the next day. The results showed that the subjects in the context condition (both the literal and the idiomatic) performed significantly better in the recalling task than the other subjects. Abrahamsen and Smith's (2000) study yielded similar results.

There are two ways a teacher can have idioms contextualized. One is to create texts or vignettes with the idioms for instruction placed in them. The other is to select from corpora or other natural language sources passages that contain the idioms chosen for instruction. A teacher can use such authentic passages with or without modification or adaptation, depending on students' proficiency level or purpose of instruction. As a principle, authentic materials are far preferable to created texts because the latter can appear very contrived and may thus not be appropriate for language learning. Created texts may be used only when there is no authentic material available for teaching idioms that it is deemed necessary for students to learn. In such a case, the utmost effort should be exerted to make the text as natural as possible. Yet because of its nature, a created text will perhaps always betray some unnaturalness, as can be see in the following example, a passage developed for teaching some study-related idioms:

Tom is taking an honors English class this semester. The class are having their midterm next week. Their teacher has told them that there will be many critical reading questions on the midterm and asked them to not only *read the fine print* but also *read between the lines* of the assigned articles. Tom has not been doing well in the class. He wants to do better and he understands that the only way for him to do better is to *hit the books* and *make up* for his poor performance on the midterm. He may even need to *burn the midnight oil* like some of his classmates do.

Therefore, with corpora becoming increasingly more accessible, teachers are strongly encouraged to use them for finding idiom materials with adequate contextual information rather than using those created artificially.

Besides trying to encourage discovery learning with adequate contextual information, teachers should also endeavor to make sure that their teaching activities involve the use of the three processes that Nation (2000) argues are necessary for successful learning of lexical items: *noticing, retrieving,* and *generating.* These processes represent three different levels of processing in learning. *Noticing* means that learners pay attention to an idiom and realize that it is "a useful language item" (Nation, 2001, p. 63). There are many activities that help learners notice idioms, such as having idioms highlighted in a reading passage, pointing out and explaining an idiom, and having students look up an idiom in an idiom dictionary. *Retrieving* takes place when learners recall a previously learned idiom in either a comprehension (listening or reading) or a production (speaking or writing) activity. Each retrieval strengthens learners' grasp of the idiom. *Generating* occurs when a known idiom is encountered in a different context or used in a different way. Generative processing may vary in terms of degree of generation (Nation, 2001). Encountering an item used with a completely different meaning constitutes a high degree of generation, but meeting an item used simply in a different context without any change of meaning will be an instance of low degree of generation. Like retrieving, generating can also be either receptive (meeting a learned idiom in listening or reading) or productive (using an idiom in a new context). An example of receptive generative processing with a high degree of generation is when an L2 speaker who has learned the meaning of the phrasal verb idiom *turn on* in "*turn on* a light" encounters the idiom in the utterance "Their performance really *turned* the audience *on.*"

Depending on students' needs and the teaching objectives, the teacher may use activities that focus on just one or more of the three processes. It is necessary to note that while contextualization is very important in idiom learning, the process of noticing may entail some moments of decontextualization. "Decontextualisation occurs when learners give attention to a language item as a part of the language rather than as a part of a message," but it does not mean that the item "does not occur in a sentence context" (Nation, 2001, p. 64). It just means that the item is taken out of the message context for a moment to be examined as a linguistic item, such as when learners look up an idiom in a dictionary or try to negotiate the idiom's meaning with their teacher or peers. Research indicates that such moments of decontextualized learning are very helpful for acquisition of lexical items (Newton, 1995; Ellis et al., 1994).

One more issue teachers need to consider in designing and selecting idiom learning activities is that the activities should ideally draw students' attention to all the three key aspects of an idiom: form, meaning, and use. This three-element concept is borrowed from Larsen-Freeman's (2001) discussion of what grammar learning entails. Although idioms are not grammar per se, their use involves both vocabulary and grammar, especially those idioms containing a verb. "Form" in idiom learning refers to accuracy of the lexical items in an idiom, their sequence, and the tense (if a verb is involved). "Meaning" deals with whether the idiom conveys what the speaker or writer intends to express, including connotation. "Use" concerns whether the idiom is used in the right context involving time, place, and register. A solid grasp of an idiom involves a command of all three. Teachers should aim to help students develop this comprehensive command in idiom learning. Of course, we cannot expect learners to attain such a command after just one or two encounters with an idiom. The knowledge of an idiom, like that of any other lexical items, is developed incrementally. It takes time and a lot of effort.

PROMOTING "CONCEPTUAL MOTIVATION ANALYSIS" AND DEVELOPING L2 CULTURAL KNOWLEDGE

As has already been explained, extensive research (Boers, 2000a, b; Boers & Demecheleer, 2001; Boers et al., 2004b; Charteris-Black, 2002; Deignan et al., 1997; Kövecses and Szabó, 1996; Liu, 2000b, 2002) has shown that many idioms are conceptually motivated figurative expressions, not arbitrary linguistic structures with a special meaning. Furthermore, conceptual motivations or conceptual bases of idioms may sometimes vary from culture to culture. Certain conceptual metaphor-motivated idioms that exist in the L2 may be absent in learners' L1, thus causing difficulty for students (Boers & Demecheleer, 2001; Boers et al., 2004b; Charteris-Black, 2002). Research has shown that developing students' knowledge of L2 culture significantly enhances students' grasp of those idioms motivated by culture-specific concepts (Boers, 2000b; Boers et al., 2004b; Kövecses and Szabó, 1996).

In a small experimental study, Kövecses and Szabó (1996) taught ten phrasal verb idioms to two classes of Hungarian adult students (each consisting of fifteen language learners) using two different approaches. In the first class (Class A) they put the ten phrasal verb idioms on the board with their

Hungarian equivalents and explained their meanings. They then told the students to memorize the idioms. In Class B they used basically the same procedure but added the explanation of nine orientational metaphors underlying the idioms. For example, in English "completion is *up*" (e.g. *dry up* and *wind up*), "more is up" (e.g. *turn up* and *go up*) but "less is down" (e.g. *cut down* and *die down*). After the instruction, they gave both groups of students a test where the students had to fill in the particle of twenty phrasal verb idioms. Ten of them were the ones taught and ten had not been taught. Some of the latter ten bore the same metaphorical motivations and some not. Class B performed better than Group A on both the ten taught and the ten added idioms, suggesting that the teaching of the orientational metaphors was helpful. The fact that Class B's performance was much better on the ten untaught idioms (on some of which no orientational metaphors were given) suggests that these students "continued to use the *strategy* of thinking in terms of conceptual metaphors" (Kövecses & Szabó, 1996, p. 351). In other words, the use of the strategy of thinking in terms of conceptual metaphor may enhance students' understanding and acquisition of idioms motivated by the concept.

Similarly, Boers (2000b) conducted an experiment that used a similar design but involved a much larger sample. The results of his study indicated that the group of students to whom the phrasal verbs were presented under the headings of their underlying orientational metaphors performed better than the group who were introduced to the phrasal verbs without the headings of underlying orientational metaphors. Such a finding corroborates that of Kövecses and Szabó (1996).[1] Boers et al. (2004b) also report that giving students knowledge of the conceptual base of L2 idioms assisted students' grasp (recall) of them.

On the basis of the results of his empirical study showing that L2 learners experience serious difficulty in understanding idioms that are conceptually different from those in their L1, Charteris-Black (2002) argues that in teaching L2 culture-specific conceptual metaphor-based idioms, it is very important to raise students' consciousness of the difference in their metaphorical bases, but in teaching conceptual base-similar idioms, focus should shift to the linguistic differences (p. 128). He further emphasizes the importance of paying attention to the different connotations the L2 idioms may have.

Yet despite the importance of conceptual knowledge in L2 idiom learning, not many teachers seem to appreciate it fully. As Kövecses (2002) contends,

> one major stumbling block in understanding the nature of idioms and making use of this understanding in the teaching of foreign languages is that they are regarded as linguistic expressions that are independent of any conceptual system and that they are isolated from each other at the conceptual level. (p. 200)

It is important that teachers understand that most figurative idioms are conceptually motivated and that they should work hard to help their students develop and use conceptual and cultural knowledge in idiom learning. The following discusses a few strategies teachers can use to assist their students on this issue.

One strategy, based on the aforementioned research, is to highlight the concepts that motivate the idioms being taught by explaining the concepts or by presenting together idioms that are based on the same concepts to help students recognize the concepts behind them (specific activities will be presented in the next chapter). This strategy helps students understand and retain idioms more effectively. Another strategy, especially useful in the EFL context where students have a homogeneous L1, is to have students compare and contrast L2 idioms with L1 idioms based on conceptual motivations and linguistic forms. According to Deignan et al.'s (1997) contrastive study of English and Polish metaphors, L2 figurative idioms may be classified into four types: "same conceptual metaphor and equivalent linguistic expression," "same conceptual metaphor but different linguistic expression," "different conceptual metaphors," and "words and expressions with similar linguistic meanings but different metaphorical meanings" (p. 354). Contrastive analyses will surely heighten students' awareness of metaphorical idioms' conceptual bases, increasing their knowledge of those conceptual bases prominent in L2 but inconspicuous in their L1. Furthermore, according to the results of Charteris-Black's (2002) study of Malaysian students' understanding of English idioms, those that are "equivalent in form but different in conceptual basis" present the greatest difficulty. Such idioms are much more difficult than those that are different in linguistic form but have equivalent conceptual basis. They are more difficult even than those idioms that have no similarity with L1 idioms in either form or meaning. Therefore, identifying conceptually different idioms is of fundamental importance for students in the learning of figurative idioms.

One more strategy to help students develop the cultural knowledge necessary for understanding conceptually motivated idioms is to engage students in L2 cultural activities that are the source domains of its metaphorical idioms. For example, having students play or watch American football, baseball, and other sports will help them better understand many sports-based American English idioms, such as *drop the ball, hit a home run,* and *step up to the plate.* Watching movies and TV programs is also a useful activity (Duquette, 1995). In fact, according to Dörnyei et al.'s (2004) study, active participation in L2 social community is significantly correlated with the learners' level of success in acquiring formulaic sequences, including idioms. One more useful technique is to ask students to organize idioms according to cultural activities, which are often important source domains for idioms, such as cuisine, sports, and business practices. This activity will help students become familiar with the conceptual bases of many L2 idioms.

EMPLOYING A VARIETY OF ACTIVITIES TO DEAL WITH DIFFERENT TYPES OF IDIOMS AND TO ACCOMMODATE DIVERSE LEARNERS

As was mentioned in Chapters 5 and 6, factors such as idiom types and learner variables often affect the process of idiom comprehension and acquisition. It is of paramount importance that teachers consider these factors carefully when designing or selecting teaching strategies and activities. Different types of idioms may call for different teaching approaches. For example, compositional idioms, including all "idioms of encoding," will not require much instruction, due to their literal or transparent meaning and easy-to-analyze form. Knowing the exact wording and function is basically all that a learner needs in order to grasp such an idiom. Activities that focus on noticing and remembering such information will be very appropriate and should suffice for the learning of these idioms. In contrast, decomposable or figurative idioms will require substantially more work to understand and learn. Students will need to figure out the meaning of such idioms via close syntactical and semantic analyses, using linguistic, conceptual, and pragmatic knowledge as well as imagination in some cases. In teaching such an idiom, a teacher should resort to activities that make students use their all-around knowledge and skills to correctly understand the idiom's meaning and connotation. Some figurative idioms are based on unique conceptual metaphors or cultural practices. With these figurative idioms, the teacher may also need to provide students with the necessary background knowledge, including culture-specific concepts and the origin of the idiom being studied. Like figurative idioms, core or non-decomposable idioms, such as *by and large* and *pull someone's leg*, are not transparent in meaning. Yet unlike figurative idioms, these idioms are completely opaque in meaning—that is, their meaning cannot be figured out using linguistic and pragmatic knowledge. Therefore, according to Grant and Nation (2006), these idioms are best treated as single lexical items and then learned and memorized as such. Mnemonic activities will be most effective in learning these idioms.

Different learners also often call for different teaching approaches. For young students aged 7 through 11,[2] it may be better to teach most idioms as single lexical items and to use visual and other aids as well as games to compensate for their limited linguistic and conceptual ability. For example, the idioms *put the cart before the horse* and *take the bull by the horns* will be difficult for young students to understand if the teacher simply explains verbally what they each mean or if the teacher merely has the students decipher each idiom's meaning via linguistic analysis. However, the use of pictures illustrating the idioms will make them much easier to understand. Similarly, in teaching idioms to low- and lower intermediate-level adult learners, a teacher should avoid activities that require the use of complex language, because although these students are cognitively capable, their language is limited. For more advanced adult ESL students, a teacher can and perhaps should employ more challenging activities involving high levels of linguistic and cognitive analyses, such as figuring out an idiom's meaning inductively via corpus searches. Many specific useful teaching techniques for students of different age groups, proficiency levels, and learning modalities will be given in the next chapter. As for how to use teaching strategies to accommodate different intelligences, Cooper (1998, p. 260) offers excellent general suggestions (Table 8.1).

Also as a rule of thumb, the more varieties of learning and teaching activities teachers use, the more likely it is that they will be able to accommodate the many different learning styles and intelligences their students possess. It is also important for teachers to observe closely how students respond to teaching activities, assess students' learning results, and then make any necessary teaching adjustments accordingly.

USING DIRECT STUDY AS A SUPPLEMENT TO CONTEXTUALIZED LEARNING

While contextualization is extremely important for lexical learning, including idiom learning, research shows that direct study of lexical items out of context, such as using cards, notebooks, and dictionaries, can be a very useful practice (Nation, 2001). Students can learn many items in a short time and remember them for a lengthy period. Yet decontextualized study of idioms is effective for learning only certain aspects of idioms, such as an idiom's wording and definition. It is not useful for grasping usage information, such as when, where, and with whom a given idiom is usually used and contexts in which its use is inappropriate. Therefore, direct study of idioms should be used only as a supplement to contextualized learning, not a replacement. Of course, with more and more idiom dictionaries providing sentence examples from corpora, the use of dictionaries may become a learning practice often involving contextual information. How to use idiom dictionaries and idiom cards will be explored in detail in the next chapter.

TABLE 8.1
Summary Chart of Intelligences and Suggested Activities for Teaching and Learning Idioms

Intelligence	Core Components	Teaching Suggestions
Linguistic—being word smart	Sensitivity to the sounds, structure, meanings, and functions of words, and language	Discuss idioms and figurative speech; *Nacherzählung* (retelling) exercises; idioms from TV shows
Logical-mathematical—being logical smart	Sensitivity to, and capacity to discern, logical or numerical patterns; ability to handle long chains of reasoning	Choose idioms logically; sort idioms into thematic categories; add-on story; paragraph completion exercises with idioms
Spatial—being picture smart	Capacity to think in visual images and to recreate, transform, or modify images	Illustrate idioms to show the contrast between figurative and literal meanings; idioms from comic strips; idioms from cartoons; mobile of favorite idioms ("idiom of the day")
Bodily-kinesthetic—being body smart	Ability to control one's body movements and to handle objects skillfully	Act out the meaning of idioms; make idiom board game
Musical—being music smart	Ability to produce and appreciate rhythm, pitch, melody, and timbre	Idiom jazz chants
Interpersonal—being people smart	Capacity to understand and respond to moods, temperaments, motivations, and desires to other people	Define the social situations for the use of various idioms; interview classmates
Intrapersonal—being self smart	Ability to assess one's own emotional life and to have knowledge of one's own strengths and weaknesses	Students can create a dictionary of their favorite personal idioms and explain how the expressions give insights into understanding themselves

From Cooper (1998, p. 260). Two minor changes were made in the third column ("Teaching suggestions"): (1) omission of the references to the number of activities in his article and (2) the addition of "retelling" in parenthesis to explain the German word *Nacherzählung*. Reprinted by permission of the publisher, the American Council on the Teaching of Foreign Languages.

ENHANCING IDIOM RETENTION WITH EFFECTIVE MNEMONIC STRATEGIES

As was mentioned in Chapter 6, rote learning or memorization does have a role in idiom learning. It is especially useful for grasping non-compositional or non-figurative idioms such as *by and large, come by something, put up with*, and *so long*, because these idioms defy any logical analysis and understanding. It is also an excellent strategy for learning sememic or interpersonal idioms, such as *"Every cloud has a silver lining"* and *"Let's keep our fingers crossed."* Of course, instead of telling students the meaning of such an idiom and asking them to remember it, a teacher can have students figure out its meaning from context before asking them to memorize it. In this sense, the crucial role of memorization is not in the comprehension phase but in the intake phase of the idiom learning process—that is, in the phase of building an idiom into a learner's lexicon. In other words, memorization is useful for the retention of all types of idioms. Furthermore, memorization is a skill that can be enhanced by using various mnemonic techniques. Boers (2001), Boers and Lindstromberg (2005), and Lindstromberg and Boers (2005) have identified some effective mnemonic activities to assist students' retention of idioms, such as hypothesizing about idioms' origin and using alliteration and other sound features in idioms. These activities will be discussed in detail in the next chapter in the section on using mnemonic strategies to enhance idiom learning and retention.

TRAINING AND BOOSTING LEARNING STRATEGY USE

As was discussed in previous chapters, L2 students use a variety of strategies to understand and learn idioms, including guessing from context and using pragmatic and L1 knowledge. It should be an important part of a teacher's idiom instruction to include the training of learning strategies. While such training can be carried out in specially designed lessons, it is better and more practical to embed strategy training in regular lessons. This can be done effectively, for instance, by drawing students' attention to the strategy or strategies involved when engaging students in one or more of the micro-level learning activities and techniques introduced in the next chapter. One such learning activity is guessing the meaning of an idiom by using the cause–effect relationship indicated in the discourse in which the idiom is used: "John got promoted yesterday and today his wife delivered their first baby; he now really feels he's *on cloud nine.*" In this example, after students have figured out the idiom's meaning correctly the teacher can ask them how they arrived at the meaning, to make them conscious of the strategy they used. Furthermore, when students appear to have employed some learning strategy, complement them for doing so. Such positive feedback will help boost students' use of learning strategies.

CONDUCTING UNPLANNED TEACHING OF IDIOMS

Brown (2001) makes an excellent point regarding lexical instruction when he points out that vocabulary teaching is often unplanned—that is, it happens "when a student asks about a word or when a word has appeared that you feel deserves some attention" (p. 377). The same is often true of idiom instruction. Therefore, teachers should be prepared to conduct "unplanned" idiom teaching so they can carry it out effectively. When an impromptu moment for idiom teaching arises, the teacher should be able to choose from the aforementioned teaching strategies the most appropriate one for the students at the moment. For instance, if it is an idiom encountered in a listening or reading passage, the teacher may, depending on the type of idiom, ask students to guess its meaning by using contextual clues, conducting a syntactical and semantic analysis, resorting to their pragmatic knowledge, or tapping into any L1 idioms that are identical or similar in meaning and structure. Of course, in some cases the teacher may need to explain the idiom's meaning or provide some hints or information about its origin to facilitate students' understanding. Strategies for idiom explanation will be discussed in the next chapter in the section "Explaining Idioms to Help Students Notice and Understand Them."

OVERCOMING AVOIDANCE ERROR AND ENCOURAGING CREATIVE IDIOM USE

One of the problems in L2 idiom learning is that students often avoid using idioms, including even those that have identical equivalents in their L1 (Abdullah & Jackson, 1998; Irujo, 1986a, 1993; Laufer, 2000). Helping students overcome this avoidance error should be a high priority for teachers. Yet what can a teacher do? The first thing would be to create as many opportunities as possible for students to use idioms. Besides giving them idiom exercises in class, have students participate in "idiom corners" and other activities. With students of a homogeneous L1, it is helpful to compare and contrast L1 and L2 idioms so students understand which ones are identical in the two languages and which ones differ, and how. Consequently, they feel comfortable using the former type and know how and when to use the latter category. It is also important for teachers to give students positive reinforcement and encouragement. Praise them when they use idioms, especially when they use them appropriately and effectively. Modeling is another practice that a teacher can do to help. Via appropriate use of idioms, the teacher can show students when, where, and how idioms may be used. Of course, it is important that we do not go overboard in our effort to help students overcome the idiom avoidance problem by having them commit what Richards (1996) calls "idiomatosis"—the inappropriate overuse of idioms. We should warn students against using idioms for the sake of using them and help them understand that idioms are used only for effective communication. It is also imperative to let students know when and where not to use idioms (see the subsection "When and Where Not to Use Idioms" in Chapter 2 for information on this topic).

Given that idioms are generally fixed expressions, it is paramount that students use them as such—that is, use the exact words that make up an idiom. Yet as research has demonstrated, idioms sometimes do allow certain variation. While many idiom variations are rather systematic (see the discussion on idiom variation in Chapter 2), some do reflect the creativity of language use, such as "*pull another highway out of the hat*" and "*join the Proposition 36 bandwagon*" (corpus examples from Liu, 2003). Therefore, it behooves us not to discourage creative use of idioms that makes good sense in context.

PROS AND CONS OF PROACTIVE AND RETROACTIVE APPROACHES

Richards (1996) believes that there are two approaches to idiom instruction: a proactive and a retroactive approach. In the former approach, teachers actively seek out idioms to teach to students and make students use them as much as possible both in and outside class. In contrast, a retroactive approach does not actively teach any idioms. Instead, it only provides students with assistance concerning the idioms that they have already encountered and need help understanding and using. Richards argues that in idiom instruction, a retroactive approach is preferable to a proactive approach because proactive teaching of idioms often causes students to develop an overzealous drive to use as many idioms as possible. As has already been mntioned, this results, in turn, in what he calls idiomatosis, which is the serious problem of excessive and inappropriate use of idioms. Richards' point is certainly a very valid one and deserves close attention from language educators in approaching idiom instruction. At the same time, one can still argue for the use of a proactive approach in idiom teaching, for the following two reasons.

First, the overuse and inappropriate use of idioms may be a price students need to pay in learning idioms. Making errors and overusing certain linguistic structures and expressions has been known to be part of the language learning process. The overuse and inappropriate use of idioms are insufficient reasons for stopping active idiom teaching altogether. Second, if conducted cautiously and appropriately, proactive teaching of idioms should not lead to the problems Richard describes. It is reasonable to believe that if the teacher makes sure during instruction that students understand clearly the register and function(s) of the idioms taught, the chances of their overusing them and/or using them inappropriately are significantly reduced. Another practice a teacher can use to prevent students from overusing idioms is to remind them repeatedly not to use idioms just for the sake of using them. One more activity a teacher can use to help students avoid idiomatosis is to give them speech or writing samples that contain excessive and inappropriate use of idioms. The teacher can work with students on the samples trying to identify and correct the problems together. This activity will help students understand the negative effect of excessive idiom use, which, in turn, should enhance their sensitivity to inappropriate idiom use in general.

SUMMARY

This chapter has introduced some useful macro-strategies and approaches for enhancing students' learning of idioms identified by research. In practice, the use of these macro-strategies will need to be accompanied by the use of micro-strategies, which will be introduced in the next chapter. Teachers should also be keenly aware of the pros and cons of the proactive and retroactive approaches to idiom teaching in order to make appropriate instructional decisions based on their teaching context and students' needs.

Questions for Study and Discussion

1. Of the activities mentioned for increasing students' sensitivity to and awareness of idioms in the chapter, which one or ones have you used and, in your experience, how helpful are they? Evaluate the other activities against the ones you have used.
2. What challenges do you see in incorporating idiom teaching into an entire L2 curriculum? What can teachers do to confront the challenges?
3. Design one conceptual analysis activity to help your prospective students understand one prominent L2 cultural belief or conceptual motivation that lies behind some L2 idioms. The activity should involve some comparison and contrast between L1 and L2 cultural beliefs or conceptual models.
4. Why do different types of idioms require different instructional foci and practices? You need to mention at least two types of idioms as examples to support your point.

5. Discuss why and how idiom teaching activities should vary to better accommodate students who differ in age, language proficiency, and learning style. Give two specific examples in your answer.
6. Design one activity for training to use an idiom learning strategy. First, specify what learning strategy you plan to train your students to use, then describe the training activity, and finally explain how it may help students grasp and practice the learning strategy.
7. Describe your position on the debate between the proactive and retroactive approaches to idiom instruction, and then defend your position.

Chapter 9

Idiom Pedagogy: Micro-strategies and Techniques

INTRODUCTION

In the previous chapter we examined some macro-strategies for teaching and learning idioms. This chapter introduces a variety of effective micro-strategies and techniques[1] that research has identified. Before we proceed, it is necessary to note that these techniques are intended for use or adaptation for use primarily for regular L2 classes in which idioms may be encountered and dealt with. They are not meant mostly for "idiom classes" (that is, lessons designed for the sole purpose of teaching idioms), because, as was explained in the previous chapter, such classes are not the most effective instructional setting for idiom learning. Of course, the techniques can certainly be employed effectively in the latter type of class.

NOTICING AND IDENTIFYING IDIOMS

Given that noticing is an important process for learning lexical items, including idioms, teachers should help students learn and practice noticing and identifying idioms. There are a variety of activities for this purpose, including reading a passage with highlighted idioms, looking up an idiom in an idiom dictionary, guessing the meaning of an idiom from context, and teachers' explaining of idioms. As some of these activities will be discussed in the other sections of the chapter, the following covers only those uniquely concerned with noticing and identifying idioms.

Reading and Discussing Passages with Idioms Highlighted

One easy activity is to find a passage or excerpt from a corpus or some other natural language data that contains some interesting idioms. Highlight (that is, underline or put in bold face or italics) all the idioms in a reading passage, and ask students to read it and pay attention to the highlighted expressions. After the students finishing reading, the teacher will ask the students to discuss, either in pairs, small groups, or as a whole class, what the highlighted expressions mean, how they are unique, etc., so the students will not only notice but, hopefully, also understand the idioms. The following is an example. It is a short exchange at a White House news conference between President Clinton's spokesperson Dee Dee Myers and reporters about the President's dealings with the Congress on some difficult issues (from Barlow's CSPAE corpus, 2000). It contains some useful idioms (italicized) about political debates and dealings.

> Myers: As you know, the President met earlier this week with House and Senate leaders to discuss the crime bill. He's certainly been working very hard. I think 95 percent of that has been resolved between the houses, which is substantial progress. There are a few *stumbling blocks*, which I understand are being *worked out* among the members of the Congress right now.
> Voice: Well, they say it's _____
> Myers: Well, *It's not up to me, it's up to* the members of Congress to decide what the *stumbling blocks* are. I think certainly there are a couple of outstanding issues which they're addressing. I think the President hopes that they reach agreement soon and pass a crime bill and send it to his desk.
> Voice: Some of them suggested that *it's up to* him at this point to *come up with* a solution to the whole racial justice issue and remaining *stumbling blocks*, that it won't happen among them.
> Myers: He discussed it on Friday. I think they're aware of his position. We've certainly worked hard on this crime bill and we'll continue to do that. But I think the *ball is now with the members of Congress* who *are working out* some of the details.

As an alternative, the following activity suggested by Lennon (1998) may be used to help students notice and understand idioms. It is rather easy because the students are provided with an idiom in a sentence and an almost complete definition with just a key word missing, as shown in the examples below. Students only need to come up with the missing key word from a list of words provided. Such a spoon-feeding method aims to assist and encourage lower-level students in noticing and learning idioms.

IDIOM PEDAGOGY: MICRO-STRATEGIES 141

Please read each of the sentences, paying close attention to the italicized words. Then complete the paraphrase below by filling the blank with a word from the list provided. Each word can only be used once.

List of the words for completing the exercises: used, accomplish, important, good, risk.

He *put all his eggs into one basket* by investing in one company.
This means: He took a great _____ by investing in one company.

He *bit off more than he could chew* in taking up the project all by himself.
This means: He took on a task that he was not able to _____.

She *is calling the shots* here.
This means: She is making the _____ decisions here.

Every cloud has a silver lining.
This means: There is some _____ in every bad event.

The oil resources in this country will *run dry* in about 50 years.
This means: The oil resources in this country will be _____ completely in about 50 years.

Identifying Idioms in a Passage

In this activity the teacher will select a passage, as in the above activity, but it can be used for either reading or listening, depending on the students' language proficiency and the focus of language skill in the class. The teacher will not highlight the idioms in it but will, instead, ask the students to identify any unique or idiomatic expressions they find (by marking them in writing and pointing them out in listening) and discuss how these expressions are special in meaning and usage. When conducting this activity for the first time, the teacher should work with the whole class to demonstrate how to do it, because identifying idioms is not an easy task, especially for lower-level students. If students fail to mark some of the idiomatic expressions in the passage, the teacher can draw their attention to them by asking questions about these expressions. If the task appears too difficult for the students, the teacher should modify it by pointing out the idioms and simply asking the students to explain why and how these expressions are special. After the students learn what they are supposed to do and become familiar with it, have them practice the idiom identification activity in either pairs or small groups. The reason for asking them to work in pairs or small groups is that it not only allows them to help one another in accomplishing the difficult task but also provides them with the opportunity to communicate among themselves in the target language.

"Story quiz" is an interesting game developed by Lindstromberg and Boers (2005) that can be used to help students notice and identify idioms. In this game, adapt a traditional story (fairy tale or fable) by including in it some multiword expressions, some of which will be used literally and some figuratively. Have students either listen to or read the story. If the story is used for listening, give students a list of the expressions; for reading, simply mark them. The students are required to indicate whether each of the expressions is used literally or figuratively.

Identifying and Comparing Idioms in L1 and L2

In the case of a class composed of students of a homogeneous L1, the teacher may first have students read a passage in their native language and mark and discuss the idioms in it, because identifying idioms in one's native language is generally easier than doing it in an L2 and the activity may serve as a good warm-up or preparation for conducting it in an L2. Alternatively, give students two passages, one in the students' native language and one in the target language, and ask them to mark the idioms in them and discuss their meaning and usage. The two passages should be comparable in content and length and must contain some interesting and distinctive idioms. Of course, the idioms in the two passages can be either similar or different. After students have identified and discussed the idioms in each passage, the teacher can ask them to compare and contrast the idioms. By examining, comparing, and contrasting the idioms between the two languages, students become more conscious not only of the ubiquitous existence of idioms but also of the similarities and differences between idioms of different languages.

Conducting Corpus Searches for Idiom Examples

For intermediate and advanced students, when feasible have them conduct a corpus search to find authentic examples of the idioms they are learning. In doing so, students will repeatedly notice and read those idioms in authentic context. Students can and should be encouraged to read them for more in-depth understanding such as figuring out their connotation and context or register of use. In order to help your students better gather the latter information, you will need to make sure that the corpus search assignments are clearly specified—for example, asking students specifically to determine the context (formal or informal) and register (spoken, written, academic, fiction, etc.), or to decide whether an idiom is used negatively or positively in general (i.e. its meaning pattern), because most idioms do show a pattern. For example, while *chicken out* and *drop the ball* convey negative evaluations of an action, *hit a home run* and *take the bull by the horns* are positive expressions. Corpus searches of idioms can also be used for the purpose of generative processing of idioms. A teacher may have students search for idioms they have learned previously. In the process, students will very likely encounter the idioms used in new contexts with a new meaning—that is, in contexts and with meanings different from those they learned previously. It is important to remember that conducting corpus searches is a very challenging and complex task (see Chapter 7). According to Liu's (2007) study on using corpora in language learning and teaching, teachers should spend a lot of time demonstrating and modeling how to conduct corpus searches. Also, the search assignments have to be as specific as possible. Finally, continuous guidance is needed from the teacher.

UNDERSTANDING IDIOMS AND DEVELOPING INTERPRETATION STRATEGIES

The following activities are used to assist students in better understanding idioms and developing idiom interpretation strategies. The use of the strategies helps students not only notice idioms but also advance their heuristic approach to idiom learning, an approach that research advocates. All the following activities can be conducted with a class as a whole group, in small groups, in pairs, and individually. However, if a technique is used for the first time, it is better to make it an activity for the whole group so that the teacher can explain, demonstrate, and monitor as much as necessary to make sure students know how to use it.

Hypothesizing and Finding the Origin of Idioms

As has already been mentioned, research (e.g. Boers, 2001; Boers et al., 2004a; Nilsen & Nilsen, 2003) has shown that knowing an idiom's origin significantly enhances students' understanding of its meaning. Hence, it makes good sense to have students guess and/or search for an unknown idiom's origin. Such an activity, though challenging, can be interesting and fun. For example, it will surely lead to some lively discussion among students if they try to figure out the source of *bone up on something* and *burn night oil* (two of the aforementioned study-related idioms) because, for one thing, many of today's students perhaps have never seen a real oil-burning lamp. In turn, the discussion provides the students with an opportunity not only to explore the meaning of the idioms but also to practice their English. Generally speaking, to help guess the origin of an idiom, students should focus on the key words. Take, for example, the following idioms: *drop the ball, a backseat* _driver_, and _pull the plug_. The underlined words are each the key word in their respective idiom. They point to the source of the idioms: "ball" pointing to sports, as it is a common object used in playing games, "driver" to driving, and "plug" to power supply. Of course identifying the key words is sometimes not enough. Students will need to use pragmatic or world knowledge, and sometimes even imagination, in their endeavor. For low-level students or young learners, showing them or having them draw pictures that illustrate the literal meaning of an idiom will provide great assistance in understanding its origin.

It is necessary to point out, though, that this activity is useful only for figurative idioms and some core idioms. This is because most figurative idioms are metaphorical in nature, with a source and a target domain. Knowing the source domain of a figurative idiom often helps learners decipher its figurative meaning. As for core idioms, some of them have historical stories behind them. For example, _red herring_ is believed to have derived from the practice of drawing a trail of scent using a piece of strong-smelling smoked fish to mislead hunting dogs. Such source information certainly assists students in understanding the idiom. However, not all core idioms have such stories (e.g. _by and large_). Neither do most phrasal verb idioms.

Guessing Meaning from Context

An even more useful technique is to ask students to guess idioms' meaning by using the contextual information available. This is a very effective learning technique, as evidenced by research. More importantly, it is effective not only for figurative idioms but for all types of idioms, including what Grant and Bauer (2004) call "core idioms"—that is, non-compositional and non-figurative ones. Therefore, teachers should do their utmost to encourage and train students to use this strategy. Guessing the meaning of an unknown idiom is very much like guessing the meaning of an unknown word. Thus, Nation's (1990) step-by-step vocabulary guessing strategy should also work for guessing the meaning of idioms. First look at the idiom very closely to see what grammatical function it plays—that is, whether it is a complete predicate (_burn night oil_), a verb (_turn down_ . . .), or a noun (_a piece of cake_). Next, examine the immediate context (that is, the clause and sentence in which the idiom occurs), and then move on to the larger context (that is, the paragraph and beyond). The types of clues to look for to help figure out an idiom's meaning include, among others, the following:

Cause–effect

Examples:
1. Tom was laid off and his girlfriend had left him so he really felt *down in the dumps*.
2. Mary already had one ongoing project before she volunteered to take on this huge assignment. She has definitely *bitten off more than she can chew*.

In both examples a close reading will reveal a cause–effect relationship that helps pinpoint the meaning of the idiom.

Contrast/Antonym

Examples:
1. Although he said he was going to confront the boss at the meeting about the issue, he *chickened out* at the last minute.
2. While Mary is a very quiet person, her husband, Mike, is a *big mouth*.

In both examples a contrast is made between the main clause and the subordinating clause, helping divulge the meaning of the idiom in question. In a contrastive situation, one can also look for an antonym relation between the idiom and the contrastive word.

Explanation/definition

Examples:
1. Tom is full of *hot air*. He likes to think he knows everything and is eager to give unsolicited advice.
2. John is a well-known *backseat driver*. He constantly tells people around him what to do but seldom does any work himself.

In both examples the information immediately following the idiom serves as an explanation of the idiom.

Synonymous expressions

Examples:
1. Like his predecessor, who enjoyed using his power to order people around, this new CEO also likes to *throw his weight around*.
2. In high school she was always at the top in her class, but now, at Harvard, she is just an average student, so she constantly has the feeling she is *a small fish in a big pond*.

In both sentences the idiom has a synonymous expression in the previous clause.

Most of these reasoning activities can be conducted individually, in pairs, or in groups. Which type to use will depend on several factors, such as students' learning styles, class size, and time available. Conducting such activities individually allows students to use and develop problem-solving skills. Therefore, some scholars insist that teachers should always require students to decode idioms independently before resorting to help from teachers, peers, and/or reference books (Boers, 2000b; Lennon, 1998).

Guessing Meaning Using Pragmatic and Conceptual Knowledge as well as Imagination

Of course, contextual information is not the only thing students can use to guess an idiom's meaning. They can, and often should, resort to their pragmatic and conceptual knowledge, and sometimes even their imagination. This is especially true in dealing with figurative idioms. According to Grant (2007), in working out the meaning of a figurative idiom a person needs to first understand the literal meaning and recognize its "untruth" in the context, and then "pragmatically" reinterpret it to find the intended truth or meaning (p. 170). For example, in deciphering the meaning of *burn night oil* and *bite one's tongue*, a learner must first see the untruth of the expressions and then use pragmatic knowledge, or knowledge of the world, to reason that in the case of *burning night oil*, "burning night oil" means having a light on late at night; in doing that, a person must be staying up doing something—usually working or studying. As for *bite one's tongue*, our pragmatic knowledge will tell us that "biting one's tongue" is a fairly difficult undertaking and that when one bites his or her tongue, one will not be able to speak. From this pragmatic knowledge we can reason that *bite one's tongue* probably means to try very hard not to speak one's mind. Of course, to understand metaphorical idioms such as *throw a curve ball* and *the bottom line is . . .*, the learner will need to use conceptual knowledge that may be L2-culture specific. In such cases it is necessary to provide students with the necessary cultural knowledge. Training and helping students in developing such knowledge is an important task for idiom teaching. It will be discussed in detail below. In terms of using imagination, the informal idiomatic expression *hit the books* is a good case in point. Despite the help of contextual information, it requires some creative thinking on the part of the learner in order to arrive at the idiom's figurative meaning of "studying hard," for there is no connection, in the usual sense, between the word *hit* and the word *study*.

When helping students learn to decipher idioms' meanings by using pragmatic and conceptual knowledge, the teacher should provide whatever assistance is necessary, including making sure the students understand all the words in the idiom and the literal meaning of the idiom. The reason is that, in many cases, for students to work out the meaning of a figurative idiom they generally need to understand its literal meaning first. Furthermore, according to Boers (2000a), having students process the literal meaning of metaphorical idioms and then think about their possible figurative meanings facilitates in-depth comprehension and memorization of the idioms, since students will be encouraged to trace the idioms' literal meanings and explore all their possible meanings in the context in which they appear. For example, discussing the literal meaning of *scratching each other's back* and then trying to ascertain its figurative meaning will lead students to connect the literal image that the idiom projects and its figurative meaning, hence enhancing their understanding and retention. It is important to take note that all the guessing activities, including guessing from contextual information, not only help students work out idioms' meaning but also promote their cognitive, analytical skills.

Guessing Meaning Using Knowledge of L1 Idioms

The activity of guessing meaning using knowledge of L1 idioms can be conducted in a class of either homogeneous or heterogeneous L1 backgrounds. Of course, it may generate a greater variety of responses in the latter type of class. Yet in either case, the interlingual comparisons should result in an interesting discussion and a good exchange of information (Lennon, 1998). In selecting idioms for this type of activity, it is important to include a variety of idioms, such as those that have identical counterparts in students' L1 in both form and meaning, those identical in form but different in meaning, those similar in meaning but different in form, and those unique in L2 (that is, those having nothing in common with L1 idioms). *Big mouth* and *give the green light* are good examples in the first category because they are found in many languages. *Step up to the plate* (accept a challenge or responsibility) and *out in left field* (odd or misguided) fall into the last category (unique in L2) because they are purely American idioms derived from baseball, a popular home-grown sport in the United States. As an example of this guessing activity, the teacher may give students a list of L2 (i.e. English) idioms similar to the following:

Narrow-minded   *Rock the boat*
Be in hot water   *Dance in the end-zone*
Grease the wheels   *Score a touchdown*

Ask students whether they have idioms in their L1 that are similar in form—that is, idioms that contain similar words or ideas. If their answer is yes, have them explain what the L1 idioms mean. Finally, ask the students to guess the meanings of these English idioms on the basis of their L1 idioms. This process of relating new L2 idioms to those in their L1 "promotes the sort of cognitive analytic activity which will build a separate store of L2 idioms linked by meaning associations to the much richer L1 store" (Lennon, 1998, pp. 22–23).

Conducting Other Inductive Learning Activities to Assist Idiom Comprehension

Besides the above techniques, some other useful activities have been proposed, such as picture drawing and the dramatization of idioms. Most of these strategies are especially helpful for young learners and students with low English proficiency. Asking students to draw pictures or using other visuals such as graphs to represent the literal meaning of an idiom can also effectively enhance students' understanding of some idioms (Cooper, 1998; Gravois, 2002; Otier, 1986). For instance, drawing a picture of *put the cart before the horse* and one of *take the bull by the horns* can help illustrate their respective meaning clearly: "put things in the wrong order" and "forcefully and directly attacking a difficult situation or challenge." Similarly, showing a video clip of a baseball player *hitting a home run* plus an explanation of baseball rules makes it much easier for learners to figure out this idiom's metaphorical meaning: achieving a significant victory or success.

Dramatizing idioms can also be a very effective and interesting activity to help students understand the differences between an idiom's literal and figurative meanings (Cooper, 1998). In fact, research (Kenyon & Daly, 1991) has shown that writing and acting out skits portraying idioms produces better understanding and recall of the idioms than holding extended discussions of them. Many idioms, especially sports idioms, lend themselves readily to such dramatization. For example, *drop the ball* and *jump the gun* can be acted out by students so they have a clear understanding of their literal meanings, and the acting will, in turn, help students discover the idioms' figurative meaning. Teachers can also have some students act out literal interpretations of assigned idioms for other students to guess their likely figurative meaning. Many idioms are suitable for this type of activity. Examples include *bite one's tongue, bury the hatchet, put the cart before the horse, scratch each other's back*, and *spill the beans*. A special type of dramatizing is to create or have students create dialogues where a literal misinterpretation of an idiom or idioms occurs. The following is an interesting example from Irujo (1986b).

> Girl: Why don't you give me a ring some time?
> Foreign Boy: Oh, no. I don't know you well enough to marry you.
> Girl: You must be pulling my leg!
> Foreign Boy: How can I pull your leg? I'm not even near you!
>
> Discuss why the misinterpretation occurred. (p. 239)

Another effective activity for helping students better comprehend an idiom is to have them explain or illustrate the idiom using their personal experience. For example, asking students to illustrate the idioms *bite off more than one can chew* and *put one's foot in one's mouth* will help other students to relate to such experiences and comprehend them. Using this technique, students are better able to understand and recall the idioms they learn, because, according to Zigo (2001), having students go over an expression by making a highly personalized, storied exploration of their own experiences can significantly enhance their understanding of it. In short, as a rule of thumb, student-centered activities are very effective in developing students' understanding of idioms and other figurative language elements (Henry, 2006).

ANALYZING IDIOMS FOR REGISTER, CONNOTATION, AND OTHER IN-DEPTH UNDERSTANDING

In idiom learning, it is not enough, of course, merely to understand an idiom's denotational meaning. Learners should also know its connotation and register. Knowing such usage information is important for students if they want to use idioms correctly and appropriately. The following discusses a few useful strategies for helping students gain such information.

Understanding Register

One activity for understanding register information is what Cooper (1998) calls situational vignettes. In this activity, the teacher provides a brief scenario to elicit responses of different registers. After the students have given their responses, the teacher can work with the class in ranking their degree of formality. The following is an example from Cooper (1998, p. 262) that shows how responses of different registers can be made to a given scenario:

> Your friend seems to be unduly upset about something, and you try to calm him down. Some possible responses might be:
>
> 1) *Chill out, Jim.* (Slang)
> 2) *Take it easy, Jim.* (Colloquial)
> 3) *Don't worry about it. Everything will be all right.* (Standard)

Learning Connotation

Conducting corpus searches and checking reference books can be very effective strategies for finding register and connotation information. Such activities are appropriate for intermediate and advanced-level students only.

To help students conduct such searches effectively, the teacher will need to train them to appreciate the underlying messages of idioms from contextual information. In other words, students should learn to understand not just the denotational meaning of an idiom but also its underlying, often evaluative, message in a text (Littlemore, 2001, p. 335). The following is an example of an activity designed to help students appreciate such underlying messages or an idiom's connotation.

Read the following sentences, paying special attention to the idiomatic expressions in italics. Then decide whether the attitude and/or opinion expressed by the idiom in each of the sentences is positive or negative, and explain and support your evaluation.

[I]t seems to some of us that a large proportion of the World Cup referees *chickened out* of difficult and contentious decisions when they involved more powerful and vocal countries, but didn't hesitate to punish the lesser countries. (from BNC, *Rugby World and Post*, 1992)

He *took the bull by the horns* at the end of last season, slashing the club's wage bill by switching from expensive full-time players to part-timers, with dramatic results. (from BNC, *Today*, 1992)

Even the world's most boring beverage, Ovaltine, *jumped on the bandwagon* by using Steinski and Mass Media's parodic collage of kitsch fifties adspeak . . . (from BNC, *The Face*, 1990)

Identifying Idioms' Motivating Concepts or Sources

In this activity, based on the work of Boers (2000b) and Kövecses and Szabó (1996), first select and present to students one or more groups of idioms each based on the same motivating concept or source activity. Then have students discuss and identify the concept or activity behind the idioms to help them gain a more in-depth understanding and better retention of the idioms. The following are two examples.

1. Compare and contrast the phrasal verb idioms in A and B, paying special attention to the particles "up" and "down." (At the end of the discussion the class should understand that up usually means more, or functional, while down often indicates less, or not functional. In other words, the A idioms are based on the concept up is more and functional and the B idioms on the concept down is less and not functional.)

A: *bump up, go up, speed up, tune up, turn up*
B: *break down, die down, go down, shut down, turn down*

2. Identify the source of the following idioms. *(Identifying the source assists and strengthens understanding.)*

backseat driver, give the green light, (a) two-way street, spinning wheels, switching gears

Appreciating Differences Between L1 and L2 Idioms

In an L2 class of homogeneous L1 background, the teacher can engage the students in in-depth comparative and contrastive analyses between L1 and L2 idioms. For example, if there are L1 idioms that are similar but not identical to the L2 idioms being learned, ask the students to look for and discuss the similarities and differences, focusing, of course, on the differences between them. According to Lattey (1986), the similarities between the L1 and L2 idioms can be discussed but should not be emphasized, because students already know them well from their L1. The teacher can draw students' attention to the important differences by giving them a list of the types of things they need to focus on in the activity. The following is a list from Lattey (p. 232):

a. differences in form
b. differences in grammatical distribution (i.e. how many different parts of speech an idiom may function as)
c. differences in range of application
d. differences in interaction with other, similar and not-so-similar idioms
e. differences in conventional restrictions

As an example of this activity designed for a Chinese EFL class, ask students to compare and contrast the English idiom *bite off more than one can chew* with the Chinese idiom "ci bu liao, dou zhe zhou [could not finish eating what one asked for and had to carry it away with him/her]." The two idioms are rather similar in literal meaning but they differ significantly in their figurative meaning. The English idiom means "taking on a task or a responsibility that is more than the person can handle." The Chinese idiom, on the other hand, means "getting oneself into trouble or bringing trouble onto oneself." In terms of meaning, the Chinese idiom is actually closer to the English idiom *got more than one bargained for* than to *bite off more than one can chew*. The teacher can have the students examine the idioms very closely, and the discussion can help the students understand that idioms from two languages that are similar in form and literal meaning may have very different figurative meanings and vice versa. Such idiom comparison and contrast activities can also help students build a bridge from familiar L1 idioms to the L2 idioms they need to learn. In the above example, Chinese ESL students will gain a better understanding of the two English idioms because of their relation to their L1 idiom.

Learning about the Attitudes and Worldview behind L2 Idioms

Close analyses of idioms can also be used to help students learn about the attitudes and worldviews of native speakers of the target language, for, as Chaika argues, "one way to discover the attitudes of a people is to examine their idioms" (1982, p. 200). For example, the studies by Liu (2000b, 2002) and Liu and Farha (1996) on the prominent use of sports and business metaphorical idioms in American English illustrate how Americans tend to view life as a competitive game or business transaction. Here is an example of the activity.

Give the students the following list of English idioms. If some of them are unfamiliar, work with students to find out their origin and meaning. Then have them look closely at the idioms and their origin or source to see if the use of these idioms reveals anything about Americans' attitudes or views about life and the world:

> *bank on someone/something; (the) bottom line is . . .; cash in;*
> *get shortchanged; give one's two cents; got more than one bargained for;*
> *pay a price for something; put stock in someone/something*

With a close analysis and good discussion about the origin or source of the idioms, students should notice that all the idioms are business based. Then the question of why business-based idioms are used to depict non-business activities will probably lead the students to the conclusion that English speakers like to view life experience and activities in terms of business. Then the teacher can push further by asking again why English speakers do that. The question may lead to discussion of the United Kingdom and the United States, the two most prominent English-speaking countries, having been the business centers of the world as well as one of the world's oldest (United Kingdom) and the largest (United States) capitalist countries. This type of activity can significantly enhance L2 students' understanding of the idioms they are learning, which may encourage them to use these idioms.

RETRIEVING AND USING IDIOMS FOR COMPREHENSION

As retrieving is a necessary process for the learning of lexical items, teachers should use learning activities that promote the retrieving of idioms already studied. Many types of activities can be used for this purpose, including some simple and easy-to-prepare ones such as rereading and relistening to materials containing idioms and reviewing idiom cards. Other activities may require more preparation and perhaps more effort. Here are some examples.

IDIOM PEDAGOGY: MICRO-STRATEGIES

Telling What the Idiom Is by Using the Definition or Explanation Given

In this activity, give students definitions of idioms that they have learned or know and ask them to provide the idiom that fits the definition. For students to do this successfully, they will need to understand the idioms and be able to recall them correctly. The following are a few examples.

Definitions   **Matching idioms**

1. acquire, obtain   (*come by*)
2. be in trouble   (be *in hot water*)
3. lost an opportunity for achieving something   (*miss the boat*)
4. be attentive   (*be all ears*)
5. in general   (*by and large*)
6. tolerate   (*put up with*)

This activity can be conducted in pairs or groups. One party gives the definitions and the other party provides the idioms. The two parties should reverse roles to make sure they have equal opportunities.

Filling in Blanks with Appropriate Idioms

In this activity, select either sentences or passages with some idioms students know, or have just learned. Delete the idioms and leave them blank. Then have students fill the blank with the missing idioms (see example 1). An easier form of the activity will involve deleting just part (e.g. one word) of the idiom (see example 1 below). In such an activity, students only need to come up with the missing parts. The deleted part can be any word: a noun, preposition, or verb (see example 2). Sometimes the teacher may opt to delete only prepositions or verbs in order to draw students' attention to this special group of words and their role in idiom formation. By filling in the blanks with idioms, students recall the idioms they have learned and in the process reinforce their grasp of them:

Example 1: *Fill in the entire missing idioms*

Read the following sentences and fill in the blanks with appropriate idioms that you have learned in this lesson.

(Intended idioms include but are not limited to: *give me a break, work cut out, worn out, make up, catch up, screw up, hit the books.*)

Tom: Hey John. How's it going?
John: Not too good. I'm really worried about the math final. I _____ on my midterm so I've got to really do well on the final to _____ for my lousy job on the midterm. I really have my _____ for me. How about you?
Tom: I've been really _____ recently because of the research projects and the fraternity activities. So I'm also a little nervous about the math final, too.
John: You're nervous about math? _____. You've always been very good at math.
Tom: But I haven't worked on math in about a month. I really need to _____ on the last few chapters.
John: Then I guess we both need to _____ hard. Hopefully we'll both be fine.

Example 2: *Fill in part of an idiom:*

Use the words provided to complete the following idiomatic phrases. If the phrase is a verb, use the correct tense/form:

break, hit, cut, catch, out, screwed, up

Tom: Hey John. How's it going?
John: Not too good. I'm really worried about the math final. I _____ up on my midterm so I've got to really do well on the final to make _____ for my bad midterm. I really have my work _____ out for me. How about you?
Tom: I've been really worn _____ recently because of the research projects and the fraternity activities. So I'm a little nervous about the math final, too.
John: You're nervous about math? Give me a _____. You've always been very good at math.
Tom: But I haven't worked on math in about a month. I really need to _____ up on the last few chapters.
John: Then I guess we both need to _____ the books hard. Hopefully we'll both be fine.

Replacing Marked Expressions with Idioms

This activity is very similar to the one above, differing in that instead of a blank, a non-idiom is provided and the students are asked to replace the marked expression with an idiom they have learned. To help students, some hints about the idioms may be given, such as their source and conceptual base, as shown in the following example. As evidenced by research reported earlier, drawing students' attention to the source and conceptual base can enhance their understanding of the idioms in question.

Replace the underlined expression with an idiom that is based on the concept *"extreme happiness is being extremely high." (The intended answer is either "on cloud nine" or "in seventh heaven.")*

Tom was engaged last month and this morning he won a lottery. He is now underlined extremely happy.

Replace the marked expressions with idioms that came from baseball. *(struck out and hit a home run are the intended answers.)*

The candidate failed in his effort to change voters' view about him in the last debate. So, he has been working extremely hard preparing for the next debate, hoping to have a huge success.

For lower-level students, instead of having them provide the idiom, a list of choices may be given. The following is an example adapted from Otier (1986, pp. 31–32):

Replace the marked expression with the most appropriate idiomatic expressions provided.

One hundred years from now, people will see that when humanity faced its greatest crisis it came through *with a mark of honor*.

A) *with a grain of salt.* B) *with all stops out.* C) *with flying colors.* D) *with eyes wide open.*

Playing Idiom Games

Different games can be played to help students recall and practice the idioms they have learned. One is called "idiom charades," suggested by Irujo (1986b). In this game, first have students form groups and give them each a slip of paper with a figurative idiom. In each group, a member will act out first the literal and then, if possible, the figurative meaning of the idiom; then the other members of the group should try to guess what the idiom is. Some figurative idioms are easy to act out and thus suitable for this activity, such as *switch gear* and *throw in the towel*. To make the activity successful, "hand signals should be taught in order to designate whether it is the literal or idiomatic meaning, the number of words, which word is being acted out, the number of syllables, etc." (Irujo, 1986b, p. 240). The teacher measures the time it takes for each group to guess the idiom correctly. The group that finishes the game in the shortest time is the winner. Another game is the "idiom board game," proposed by Cooper (1998). This game usually involves "a road or path drawn on poster paper. The road would be divided into numbered segments. Each segment would correspond to a note card" that has an idiom on one side and a clue intended to help students figure out the idiom on the other side (p. 264). For example, for the idiom *be/feel down in the dumps*, the question for students to think about the idiom would be "How would you say you feel very bad or low in spirit?" and the clue would be "You are in a low place."

One more game that can be played is named "an operation." It is especially good for practicing action phrasal verbs (Larsen-Freeman, 2001; Nelson & Winters, 1993). In an operation, students perform a series of actions to complete a task by either following the teacher's commands or miming with the teacher the actions the latter describes verbally. The following is an example from Larsen-Freeman (2001, p. 260):

> I want to *call up* my friend. First, I *look up* the phone number. Then I write it down. I *pick up* the receiver and *punch in* the number. The number is busy. I *hang up* and decide to *call back* later.

Having students playing an "operation" game a few times will enable them to better understand and remember the meanings of the phrasal verbs involved. Of course, this game does not work for many of the figurative or opaque phrasal verb idioms.

RETRIEVING, GENERATING, AND USING IDIOMS FOR PRODUCTION

Output is an important part of language learning. Idiom acquisition is no exception. It is essential that students conduct production-required activities. Many production activities entail retrieving and/or generating processes of idioms because they require students to recall known idioms and use them in a new context. Such activities are suited especially for intermediate and advanced students. Of course, with more guidance, control in vocabulary and structure, and some modification, these activities may also be used for lower intermediate or even low-level students. The following are some examples of such activities.

Completing a Story or Paragraph with an Idiom

We begin production-required activities with this one because it is easy, requiring only minimal production from the students. To design such an activity, first find or create a short story or paragraph that ends with a sentence containing an idiom that the students have learned. Then delete the last sentence, or part of the sentence, including the idiom. Give the students the incomplete story or paragraph and have them complete it with an appropriate idiom they have learned or know. This activity is very similar to the fill-in-the-blank-with-an-idiom activity mentioned above in the comprehension practice activities, but it differs from the latter in that no list of idioms is provided. Students have to come up with the idiom themselves from their understanding of the story or passage. This activity is most suitable for figurative and some core idioms. Here are two examples:

1. Tom and his wife have been buying lottery tickets for three years without having won anything. So when his wife tells him that they've just won a million dollars, he doesn't believe it, thinking his wife is joking so he says to her . . . (Students can complete the sentence with "*You're pulling my leg*").

2. Mary successfully defended her dissertation yesterday, and today she has got a job offer from the university where she really wants to work. So she truly feels that . . . (Students can complete it with *she's on cloud nine* or *she's in seventh heaven*).

Making Sentences or Writing Passages or Stories Using Idioms

Ask students to make sentences or write a dialogue, short play, or story in which they have to use idioms they know or have just learned. For sentence writing, the teacher can ask students to use idioms motivated by the same concept or based on the same activity or knowledge. The activity will not only require retrieving and generating but also reinforce and deepen students' understanding of the idioms because it highlights the source and/or the conceptual base of the idioms. It can be done either individually or in pairs or groups. Here are two examples:

1. *Make two sentences describing a person who feels very unhappy and low in spirit by using two idioms that are based on the concept "being extremely unhappy is being in an extremely low place."* (The intended idioms are *be/feel low in the dumps* and *hit rock bottom*; if students have difficulty coming up with the idioms, the teacher may provide more hints or, as a last resort, the idioms themselves.)

2. *Make three sentences each using a phrasal verb idiom with the particle "on" that means continuing or continuing with great effort.* (The intended idioms are *carry on, go on, press on*.)

For writing plays (skits) or stories, group work may be preferable. More guided forms of the activity can be created for students with more limited English writing skills. For example, instead of having students write dialogues or plays themselves, a teacher can give students sentences, dialogues, or passages that contain some marked non-idiom expressions and ask them to reword or replace these expressions with appropriate idioms from the idioms they have learned, as in "Replacing marked expressions with idioms" in the previous section. The following is another example:

Read the following dialogue, paying special attention to the marked words or expressions. Then replace these expressions with appropriate idioms that you have recently learned.

(The following are the anticipated idioms: *be on the rocks, hit it off, go steady, have a lot in common, keep one's fingers crossed, opposites attract, what went wrong*; they are idioms students have recently learned or known for some time; the list will not be provided.)

Mike: I heard that Tom and Mary had some big fights recently and their relationship is <u>shaky</u>. I can't believe it, because they were talking about marriage just a couple of weeks ago.
Tony: Me, too.
Mike: Do you know <u>what caused the problem</u>?
Tony: I don't.
Mike: I thought they're your close friends.
Tony: Yes. In fact, we've been friends since high school.
Mike: Then is it true that they were high school sweethearts?
Tony: Yes. In fact, they <u>liked each other instantly</u> the first time they met. I think it was in our freshman year in an English class they both took.
Mike: Then they must <u>be very similar in their interests and personality</u>.
Tony: I'm not sure. As a matter of fact, they were quite different. Tom was rather quiet, a sort of nerd. Mary, on the other hand, was very outgoing. She was a cheerleader.
Mike: Then it must have been because <u>people are attracted to those with a totally different personality</u>.
Tony: I guess so because they began <u>to have a secure, long-term dating relationship</u> just after a few dates. I think they'll be fine, though, after things quiet down.
Mike: I hope so, too. Let's <u>pray for it</u>.

Acting Out/Role-playing Dialogues, Plays, and Stories that Students have Created

After students finish writing the dialogues, plays, or stories, the teacher may ask students to act them out or role-play them in class. This activity gives students an excellent opportunity to use the idioms again, further reinforcing their learning.

Retelling and Add-on Story

Two interesting activities that Cooper (1998) and Irujo (1986b) recommend are retelling, and using "add-on stories." In retelling, the teacher either selects or creates a story using some of the idioms just taught. The teacher tells the story to the students and then has the students retell or rewrite it. In their retelling or rewriting, students need to use as many of the idioms as possible.

In the "add-on story" activity, the teacher has a list of idioms written on the board, and the teacher speaks first by telling a story using one of the idioms. Then students, in turn, continue the story by each adding a sentence that makes use of one of the idioms.

Telling Stories Based on Pictures

Give students a picture story and ask them to say what is happening in each frame of the story by using idioms where appropriate. This activity is especially good for lower intermediate-level students to practice phrasal verb idioms. A good example would be to give students a picture series showing a person *getting up, putting on* glasses or clothes, *turning on* the light (radio/TV), etc., and then have students describe the actions taking place in the pictures.

USING EFFECTIVE MNEMONIC TECHNIQUES FOR RETENTION

The following are effective mnemonic techniques for helping students retain idioms more effectively.

Idiom Notebook and Flashcards

We begin with the idiom notebook and flashcards because these are common techniques that learners use to help retain all types of lexical items. Idiom notebooks and flashcards are easy to make and use. They can contain definitions, examples, and any other information regarding the use and register of given idioms. The information may even be in L1 if that is necessary or helpful for the students. Idiom cards and notebooks can be used for both receptive and productive learning purposes. Students can consult them if they want to use idioms in speaking and writing. Thus, teachers should encourage students to take advantage of this simple but probably helpful tool. It is necessary to recall, though, that idiom cards and notebooks are effective for learning only certain aspects of idioms, such as wording and definition. They are not useful for grasping usage information, and suchlike constraints on the use of a given idiom.

Semantic Association

Semantic association is a practice of relating a new idiom to idioms of similar meaning, or opposite meaning, that students already know. For instance, when teaching the idiom *kick the bucket*, have students recall any other idioms that express the meaning of "die." Students may come up with *pass away* or *bite the dust*. By relating the new idiom to what they already know, students reinforce their understanding and memory of not only the new idiom but also those already acquired. Similarly, *be in seventh heaven* can be associated with *be on cloud nine*, *tie the knot* with *walk down the aisle*. Of course, the teacher will need to help students understand the connotational or any other differences that exist between the related idioms in discussion. Otherwise, as research has shown (Nation, 2000), such association activities may cause students to be confused about the related idioms. Besides associating new L2 idioms with other L2 idioms, students can also connect them to those in their L1 that have a similar or the same meaning, or they can contrast L1 and L2 idioms that have similar form but different meaning, or vice versa.

Association of Idioms with Mental Images

Students should form a mental picture whenever possible for any idiom they learn (figurative idioms are especially conducive to the formation of mental images, such as *drop the ball, jump the gun*, and *throw in the towel*). Usually the mental image is based on the literal meaning of the idiom, but the image helps the learner derive the figurative meaning and in the process aids idiom understanding and retention. This strategy, recommended by Lindstromberg and Boers (2005), is based on the theory that "dual coding" enhances learning. The creation of a mental picture in processing an idiom enables students to have an imagistic coding component in addition to the usual linguistic component. Nippold and Duthie's (2003) study also shows that the mental images people have for idioms are a good indicator of their level of comprehension of the expressions.

Organizing Idioms in Ways that Best Assist Students' Memory

As was discussed in detail in Chapter 7, idioms may be organized in many different ways depending on their types and features. When idioms are organized appropriately, interestingly, and systematically, it becomes easier for learners to see their features and patterns, thus helping them remember them better.

Hypothesizing and Learning the Origin of Idioms

Hypothesizing and learning the origin of idioms is a practice that has been introduced for helping understand them. Yet as Boers (2001) and Boers et al. (2004a) have shown, the strategy can also help idiom retention. It is useful for most figurative idioms and some core idioms.

Paying Attention to Sound Features of Idioms

Paying attention to alliteration and other sound features of idioms is another practice that Boers and Lindstromberg (2005) have found to be effective in aiding idiom retention. According to their research, alliteration is a rather prominent feature of English idioms, as can be seen in examples such as *beat about the bush, neck and neck,* and *spick and span.* Furthermore, noticing alliteration and/or other sound features of an idiom entails a perceptual coding component in its comprehension process. It thus results in a dual coding process, which, in turn, produces better recall of the idiom.

Focusing on the "Idiom Key"

As was explained in Chapter 3, the "idiom key" is the word or words at which listeners recognize a phrase as an idiom. Although the position of the key may vary from one idiom to another, it is usually the first or second content word or words after the verb in idioms with a verb in them, such as *gun* in *jump the gun*. The idiom key is also the most important part of an idiom. While some parts of an idiom may be substituted with other lexical items, the "idiom key" usually is not replaceable. For example, one can say either *beat **about** the bush* or *beat **around** the bush*, yet the idiom key, *bush*, cannot be changed. Similarly, either ***get*** *cold feet* or ***develop/have*** *cold feet* will work, but the "idiom key" *feet* is not substitutable. Thus, it will be helpful for students to focus on the "idiom key" when memorizing an idiom. The "idiom key" can help learners recall known idioms more easily.

EXPLAINING IDIOMS TO HELP STUDENTS NOTICE AND UNDERSTAND THEM

Inductive learning is generally preferable to deductive learning. The same is true of idiom learning. Yet it sometimes takes a lot of time for students to figure out the meaning of an idiom. Hence, the practice may not be feasible or time cost-effective in a class whose focus is on other language skills and which is under severe time constraint. This is often the case in unplanned idiom teaching, a common instructional practice, as indicated in the previous chapter. In such a case, a teacher may have to simply explain the meaning of an idiom to help students understand it. For instance, a teacher may suddenly realize that he or she has just used an idiom in the instructional language that the students do not seem to understand and will need to explain it in order to continue the class successfully. Explaining idioms helps students notice them. Furthermore, research has shown that, when students listen to a story, briefly explaining vocabulary items increases lexical learning (Elley, 1989; Brett et al., 1996). Then, how to explain an idiom effectively in such a case becomes an important question. Liu's (2000a) study of fourteen college instructors' use of idioms in instructional language identified three common and helpful strategies: **definition**, **elaboration**, and **paraphrasing**. To help explain the techniques, real examples from some of the fourteen instructors' lessons are used.

Definition

In the definition strategy, the teacher simply gives the meaning of the idiom. The following excerpt from a professor's lecture on different business structures provides a good example: "There are several organizational designs. One is the simple structure. What a simple structure is is like a store, a *Mom and Pop store*. That's an American term. *What we mean is a family-owned business.*" Here the professor clearly defined the idiomatic expression *Mom and Pop store*. What is noticeable is that he used what I call a *definition marker*, "What we mean is . . ." Sometimes one may define an idiom without using a definition marker, as can be seen in the following excerpt from another professor's talk: "It needs someone to, as we say, *grease the wheels. . . . Grease the wheels. Make it operate much smoother* [definition]." This professor simply defined *grease the wheels* as "make it [referring to a project he was discussing] operate much smoother," without using any marker. Yet a definition marker can be very helpful, as it draws students' attention to the expression.

Elaboration

When using the elaboration technique, the teacher explains the meaning of the idiom by giving information or examples that will help students better understand it. The following lecture excerpt serves as an example:

> His biography says that he *jaywalked through life . . . jaywalked through life*, you know what the word "jaywalk" means? *It means you wandered around, crossed the street, not at the corner. You jaywalked through life, wandered around, didn't know what you were doing.*

Elaboration differs from definition in that rather than simply describing the meaning of the term, as in equating "make it operate much smoother" with "grease the wheels," you go further by offering whatever additional information or examples are deemed necessary.

Paraphrasing

In the paraphrasing strategy, the teacher uses a different expression that conveys the same meaning. The following is a good example found in a professor's talk about how to manage passive employees who have no initiative: "you gotta *kick them around*, you gotta *tell them what to do*." The professor paraphrased the slang idiom "kick people around" by the expression "tell them what to do" without calling attention to the idiom.

It is obvious that in explaining an idiom, we do not have to use just one technique or form. We can employ two or more simultaneously if necessary. In fact, researchers recommend that teachers and students examine various forms of definitions (Flowerdew, 1992). How many and which ones to use depends on the difficulty level of the idiom and the response from the students. Obviously, when one technique fails to work we should try another one and continue until students understand. Another point to bear in mind is that explanations need to be brief and clear because research suggests that brief explanations are most effective (Elley, 1989). In an EFL setting or a class with students of a homogeneous L1, explanations may be given in L1, a practice that some scholars promote (e.g. Laufer & Shmueli, 1997).

USING IDIOM DICTIONARIES

Dictionaries can be very helpful in learning lexical items if used appropriately. Studies suggest that the use of dictionaries can increase the number and the accuracy of the items learned (Knight, 1994; Hulstijin, 1993). Dictionaries can provide learners with useful information whenever needed, as long as the learners take the trouble to consult them. Such ready assistance is particularly valuable in idiom learning. As has already been mentioned, idiom learning is an incremental process. Learners need repeated exposure to an idiom in order to grasp it. Idiom dictionaries can be used as often as necessary both as a source of input (exposure) and an aid to the understanding of idioms encountered in and out of class. Students may use dictionaries for receptive, productive, and learning purposes. According to Nation (2001, pp. 281–281), the purposes of receptive use include:

- finding the meaning of unknown lexical items;
- confirming the meaning of partly known words;
- determining the accuracy of guesses of a word's meanings from context.

Productive use consists of, among other things

- finding the words one wants to use;
- obtaining information about the spelling, pronunciation, collocation; and usage information concerning partly known words;
- checking such information for known words.

For the purpose of learning, students can use dictionaries to

- select items to study;
- further their grasp of partly known items by obtaining more information about these items.

Learners may use idiom dictionaries for similar purposes. There are, however, a few things that learners typically look for when consulting dictionaries concerning idioms they want to use in speaking or writing. First, they check for the wording of an idiom, because idioms are fixed, or fairly fixed, expressions. It is not easy for learners to remember an idiom's exact wording. Second, they look for register, connotation, and language variety-related information about an idiom. For learners to use idiom dictionaries effectively, they should have a good understanding of the dictionaries they use and some basic dictionary use skills.

There are two major types of idiom dictionaries: monolingual and bilingual. In monolingual dictionaries, everything, including definitions and examples, is written in one language, the target language. Such idiom dictionaries are not appropriate for beginning or low-level students, due to the language proficiency required for interpreting definitions and examples. To help learners, some monolingual dictionaries use a controlled vocabulary in their definitions. For example, the *Cambridge international dictionary of idioms* (1998) employs a defining vocabulary of under 2,000 words. Yet even these dictionaries are still probably too difficult for low-level students. Bilingual dictionaries, on the other hand, use two languages, with the idiom and examples given in the target language and the definition(s) and other explanatory information in the user's first or native language. Sometimes there are L1 translations of the examples. Bilingual dictionaries can be used by L2 learners of all levels. It is of paramount importance to bear in mind, though, that the quality of bilingual dictionaries varies considerably. Some give inaccurate information, including erroneous definitions. Learners should thus use bilingual dictionaries with caution. When using a bilingual idiom dictionary, learners should check the information from it against that in a monolingual one if possible.

Some idiom dictionaries now contain usage information, such as information about the register and language variety in which a given idiom is used. These dictionaries are more helpful than those that do not provide such information. It is always wise to pay attention to usage information. To obtain and understand usage information, learners will need to know the coding system used in the dictionary. Frequently used codes include *informal, humorous, old-fashioned,* and *British, American, etc.* The following entry from the *Cambridge international dictionary of idioms* (p. 154) illustrates how such codes are used:

Get away with you! *British & Australia,*
Old-fashioned
something that you say when someone says something that is silly, surprising or not true
- *"Be honest with me, do I look fat in these trousers?" "Get away with you!"*

Idiom dictionaries usually provide information about their coding system at the beginning. Learners should refer to the coding system whenever necessary in order to use idiom dictionaries more effectively.

Another important issue related to idiom dictionaries is that the number of entries varies tremendously from one dictionary to another. There are two reasons for the significant variation. First, as was mentioned in Chapter 1, there is no consensus on what an idiom is. Different dictionaries often use different criteria in selecting their entries. Second, idioms are often language variety specific. Idioms in British English may not be used in American English, and vice versa. Learners should be aware that no idiom dictionary contains all the idioms that exist. In looking up an idiom, they may sometimes need to consult several dictionaries before finding it. Sometimes they may need to go to a specialist idiom dictionary, such as Palmatier and Ray's (1993) *Dictionary of sports idioms*.

SUMMARY

This chapter has introduced some useful micro idiom learning and teaching strategies and techniques. It is paramount that a teacher selects the most effective ones according to the students' age, level, and learning styles as well as the type of idioms being learned. Teachers should also try to use a variety of activities to promote both discovery learning and the three levels of processing to help students learn idioms successfully.

Questions for Study and Discussion

1. Explain, with specific examples, how the information about the origin or source of an idiom can help students understand an idiom.
2. Idioms may be taught as single lexical items or approached by having students analyze them structurally, semantically, and functionally to guess the meaning accordingly. Which is a better approach in general, and why? It has also been mentioned in this book, however, that some idioms may be better approached by one of the two methods. Recall and discuss the rationale with specific examples.
3. In trying to figure out the meaning of an unknown idiom, a learner can look for textual clues such as causal and contrast relationship. Besides the types of clues mentioned in the chapter, are there any other clues you have found useful? Give examples in your answer.
4. Comparing and contrasting L2 idioms with L1 idioms has been found to be very helpful not only in assisting students in understanding idioms but also in enabling them to build a separate store of L2 idioms (distinct from the L1 store). The activity also promotes cognitive analytical skills. Can you think of an L1 and an L2 idiom that may be good for such comparison and contrast? Illustrate how.

5. In addition to those mentioned in the chapter, think of and describe any other mnemonic activities for enhancing students' retention of idioms.
6. The chapter has listed a variety of techniques that teachers can use to teach idioms. Do you know any other useful techniques or activities that are not mentioned in the chapter? If you do, explain what they are and how they can be used.

Chapter 10

Error Treatment and Assessment in Idiom Instruction

INTRODUCTION

This chapter addresses the issues of error treatment and assessment in idiom learning. As is the case with the learning of any other aspect of language, error treatment and assessment are two very important tasks. Effective error treatment assists students in improving their idiom learning. Appropriate assessment is crucial in helping teachers gain information about students' progress, including both their successes and their difficulties. Such information, in turn, enables teachers to adjust their teaching to make it more effective.

ERRORS AND THEIR TREATMENT

Students make errors in idiom learning for a variety of reasons, including negative L1 transfer and failure to understand the connotation of an idiom. There are both comprehension and production errors. With regard to comprehension errors, often it is difficult for teachers to recognize such errors unless students respond inappropriately or incorrectly to an idiom used in speaking or they give an incorrect response regarding an idiom in reading comprehension. When noticing such comprehension errors, teachers may need to take appropriate steps to let students know of them. Production errors, on the other hand, are much easier to identify, and they usually draw more attention from teachers in error treatment. Thus, they will be the focus of discussion in this chapter.

Because making errors is part of the learning process, teachers should neither be too concerned nor overreact. This does not mean that they should not try to help students to learn from their errors and eventually eliminate them. In order to deal with students' errors effectively, teachers need to understand the types of errors L2 learners make and the causes of those errors. Before we explore the types of errors, we should recall that many L2 learners suffer from avoidance error. Therefore, teachers should keep this in mind and be extremely sensitive in approaching students' errors. Otherwise, a teacher's error treatment may end up making students more hesitant in idiom use, a scenario that no teacher would like to see. To make sure that this does not happen, teachers should follow established principles in error treatment. The following are some of the principles: "Do not try to correct every single error; focus, instead, on those that impede communication or occur frequently." "Don't correct your students' errors during their performance (language production) or in front of other students." "Use recasting instead of directly pointing out the mistake," unless pointing out the mistake is warranted by the context (for example, if requested by the students)."

Now let us turn to some of the major types of errors in L2 idiom use. While there are many different kinds of errors, they can be roughly grouped into the following key categories: inaccurate wording or structure, wrong connotation, use in inappropriate context, semantic overextension, and incorrect register. Of course, a particular error may sometimes be classified as belonging to more than one category. For example, an idiom used with wrong connotation may simultaneously be produced in an inappropriate context. The categories are, therefore, not mutually exclusive.

1. Inaccurate wording and incorrect structure: This is a frequent type of error in L2 idiom use because, despite some variations, idioms are generally fixed multiword expressions. It is not easy for L2 learners to remember accurately all the lexical items in an idiom. They sometimes miss a word, often an article, as shown in the phrase *in red* (meaning in deficit) for *in the red* and *once in while* instead of *once in a while*. Other times, they use a wrong word, as in *pain in the back* rather than *pain in the neck* and *hit about the bush* for *beat about the bush*. Occasionally, they may add a word or words that are unnecessary, as in "*He's a pain in the neck to me*," an utterance cited by Lattey (1994, p. 306),[1] where the added prepositional phrase "to me" makes the idiom sound extremely awkward. One special type of structural error is the use of the wrong tense, as in the following examples from Lattey: "I just got the brush-off from M. I even suppose that *she only pulled my leg* when she told me she loved me" (ibid., p. 303). Here, *pull someone's leg* is erroneously put in the simple past tense, for this idiom is usually used in the progressive, although occasionally it may be used in the perfect aspect (e.g. "I think you have had your leg pulled." The consequences of inaccurate wording vary. In many cases it does not affect communication; it merely sounds awkward or

ERROR TREATMENT AND ASSESSMENT 171

strange. In other cases, it causes confusion, making it difficult for the listener to understand.

2. Wrong connotation: problems of this type occur when idioms expressing negative evaluations are used in a situation requiring a positive or neutral expression or vice versa. Take, for example, the idiomatic phrase *take advantage of*. When it is followed by something such as an opportunity, it is rather positive, but when the object of the preposition is human, it often conveys a rather negative meaning, as in "The teacher *took advantage of* his students by having them wash his car." Yet ESL speakers sometimes do not understand the difference and use the idiom incorrectly, as shown in the note reportedly posted in the guest rooms of a hotel in Thailand: "Our distinguished guests, please *take advantage of* our maids between 12:00 and 2:00 during your stay." As another example, the idiom *drag one's feet* also expresses a negative evaluation. Thus, it does not sound appropriate in the following statement: "I don't think the project makes sense. We need to *drag our feet* on it."

3. Inappropriate context: this refers to an instance where a person uses an idiom with the wrong interlocutor, in the wrong place, or for the wrong situation. An example of "wrong interlocutor in the wrong place" would be for a student to say to his or her professor, "I *have a bone to pick with you*. I don't understand why you gave me a C on the paper." The following example from Lattey (1994, p. 303) is an instance of an idiom used in the wrong situation:

> A: Excuse me, can you please show me the way to the White House on my map?
> B: Sure, I know Washington inside out. I'm just on my way to see the president. If it *suits you to a T*, you can accompany me right now.

The idiom *suit someone to a T* in B's utterance is not appropriate for the situation because the idiom is never used in an *if* conditional clause; it is used in a declarative sentence only.

4. Semantic overextension: like vocabulary in general, some idioms are used in certain domains but not others. For example, *be the spitting image of someone* is used only to express physical likeness. Lattey's German ESL students, however, employed the idiom to depict similarities in behavior, as demonstrated in the following example: "Fred seems *to be the spitting image of* George. Once he has discovered a new hobby, he puts all his time and money into it" (1994, p. 305). A more subtle semantic extension can be seen in the following example from Lattey (ibid., p. 307).

> A: I think there's no use staying together any longer . . . our relationship *has come to a standstill.*
> B: Do you really think so? In my opinion we should try again.

The idiom *come to a standstill* applies to the cease of movement in literal or physical sense. When used metaphorically, it is often used to depict negotiations and competitions, not relationships. Such nuance differences in semantics are very difficult for ESL students to grasp, thus calling for some instructional activities.

5. Incorrect register: this is also a common type of error in L2 idiom use because learners often are not cognizant of an idiom's register. An example would be writing the following sentence in an academic paper reporting findings from a study "Students all *gave their best shot* on the test." The idiom is register-inappropriate because *give one's best shot* is usually used in informal speech. Another example would be the use of the phrasal verb idiom *put out* in a legal document: "the residents *put out* the fire at 6 o'clock..." Here, the formal verb "extinguish" is much more register-appropriate.

What can teachers do to help students address these various types of errors? In dealing with an error in idiom use, the first thing teachers should do is to try to understand its cause or source. Knowing the source of an error will allow a teacher to treat it more effectively. As we know, some of the errors are the result of L1 transfer, especially in cases where L1 and L2 both have an idiom identical in form but different in meaning. For example, according to Lattey (1994), the addition of "to me" in the utterance *a pain in the neck to me* was likely the result of transfer from German, because such use of a prepositional phrase is typical in idiomatic expressions in German. Besides L1 transfer, overgeneralization is often another common cause of errors. An example is the German ESL students' use of *spitting image* to refer to similarities in behavior.

After learning the source of an error, a teacher needs to let students notice or make them aware of the problem. For example, if students use an idiom with the wrong connotation or in the wrong context, they need to be made aware of it in a subtle, non-embarrassing fashion. Then the teacher can explain or explore with the students the cause of the problem, with appropriate examples. Finally, the teacher should have students do some exercises designed to reinforce their understanding of the problem. Take, for instance, the aforementioned misuse of *drag one's feet* and *sit on the fence*. The teacher should first make the students understand the negative connotation—that is, the negative evaluation each of the idioms conveys—by using various authentic examples of the idiom in context. Then, the teacher should give the students exercises to strengthen their understanding of this particular semantic feature of the idiom, such as constructing sentences that contain the idiom used appropriately. Of course, errors from different causes may require different approaches. For instance, while a contrastive analysis between L1 and L2 will be helpful for transfer errors, an exploration of semantic constraints of an idiom will make better sense in dealing with overgeneralization errors. Furthermore, there are many different techniques a teacher can use to treat student errors, including recasting and teacher-guided group or peer correction. Choose the practice that is best for your students, but whichever technique is selected, make sure the correction is done with sensitivity so it will not discourage idiom use.

ASSESSMENT

Assessment is an indispensable part of any language instruction, and idiom teaching is no exception. Teachers need always to be informed about how successful their students are in grasping the idioms they are learning. Therefore, the best practice of assessment is ongoing because it provides the teacher with continuous, up-to-date information about students' progress, allowing the teacher to make timely instructional adjustment to ensure effective teaching. Ongoing assessment can be carried out in different forms, such as quizzes, tests, and observation of students' performance in class. Yet quizzes and tests, when given frequently, may take away too much time from instruction. A more sensible ongoing assessment practice is to embed it in the lessons—that is, to integrate it into classroom learning activities. In other words, teachers can use some learning activities simultaneously as assessment tools to measure students' grasp of the idioms being taught. Many of the idiom learning activities and exercises discussed in the previous chapter can be used for this purpose, including "matching idioms with definitions or pictures that illustrate them," "filling in blanks with appropriate idioms," "story quiz," and "story writing using idioms learned." When using these learning activities as assessment tools, it is, of course, necessary for the teacher to rate (or score) students' performance and keep a record of it.

Another point to note is that classroom idiom learning activities may be comprehension based, production oriented, or both. Given the comprehension-before-production sequence in idiom acquisition, assessment of idiom learning should, if possible, follow the same order—that is, assessing idiom comprehension before production. Furthermore, in selecting assessment tools, teachers need to take into consideration students' variables such as age, learning style, and language proficiency level, because these variables may affect an assessment tool's appropriateness and effectiveness. For example, for testing young or low-level students, matching idioms with pictures may be more appropriate than matching them with definitions. Similarly, when using fill-in-the-blanks as an assessment tool, providing a list of idioms for students to select from will be more appropriate for lower-level students than for higher-level ones. Perhaps the most important issue in assessing idiom learning deals with whether the assessment conducted covers all the three important aspects that the learning of an idiom involves: form (structure), meaning (semantics), and use (pragmatics). As was explained in the previous chapter, having a solid and complete grasp of an idiom entails all three of the aspects. A valid assessment of idiom learning should, therefore, also include all three if possible.

Of course, the acquisition of idioms, like the acquisition of other lexical items, is incremental. We cannot expect students to grasp every aspect of an idiom and gain a full breadth and depth of knowledge about it all at once. This is especially true of idioms that have multiple meanings; many phrasal verb idioms fall into this category. Students are very unlikely to grasp all the meanings of such an idiom the first time they learn it. Therefore, it is vital to take this into consideration when assessing idiom learning. The aspects of an idiom and the breadth and depth of knowledge about it that a teacher should test may thus vary according to, among other things, teaching objectives and the students' age and language proficiency.

Finally, it is necessary to point out that, in addition to directly measuring students' learning performance, assessment of idiom learning may also be carried out indirectly via surveys and interviews as well as comparing teaching objectives with what is actually taught. These tools may provide additional information about students' learning, hence triangulating the data and enhancing the validity and reliability of one's assessment.

SUMMARY

Error treatment and assessment are two very important issues in idiom instruction. Teachers need to understand the sources and types of errors students make in order to render effective treatment. Regarding assessment of idiom learning, it needs to be ongoing in order for it to be effective. Many idiom learning activities and exercises can be used as assessment tools. Using these learning and assessment activities makes ongoing assessment feasible.

Questions for Study and Discussion

1. Besides those discussed in the chapter, describe any other type of errors students make in idiom learning. Try to explain the cause of the errors and discuss any strategies that can be used to help students address such errors.
2. Examine the following idioms ESL students have produced and identify any errors in them. Then determine the type and the source or cause of each of the errors.

    tighten loose ends, make advantage of, be on a sideline
    We should *beat about the bush* on this issue.

The young man *came by* a large inheritance from his uncle [in a legal document].

3. Explain why teachers should be extremely sensitive in treating idiom errors, perhaps more so than in treating errors in other areas of language learning. Then think of one or two strategies or activities that may help students understand their errors but may simultaneously encourage and promote their idiom learning.
4. Select two assessment activities or tools that are appropriate for evaluating lower-level students' idiom learning and two for upper intermediate or advanced students. Describe the activities and explain why they are appropriate for the level of student you use them for.
5. Explain how error treatment and assessment may help teachers improve their teaching of idioms. Give specific examples in your answer.

Glossary

Active idioms idioms that a learner is able to use both receptively and productively.

Anomalous collocations uniquely or unusually formed collocations, including four subcategories "ill-formed collocations," "cranberry collocations," "defective collocations," and "phraseological collocations" (see the respective terms).

Cohesive function of idioms the function of idioms to provide textual cohesiveness; it is the primary function of some idioms, such as *in turn*. It is a type of "relational" or "textual" function in contrast with "ideational" and "interpersonal" functions.

(The) compositional analysis hypothesis the theory that idiom comprehension uses normal language processing together with a pragmatic interpretation of the idiom in its discourse context.

Compositional idiomatic expression one whose meaning is the sum of the meanings of its parts, e.g. *breathe one's last breath*.

Core idioms a term Grant and Bauer (2004) use to refer to a small number of idioms that are non-compositional (non-literal) and non-figurative in meaning, e.g. *kick the bucket*.

Cranberry collocations those that contain items in them that are peculiar to the collocation—that is, the items do not exist in other collocations, e.g. *kith and kin*.

Defective collocations those that one cannot comprehend entirely on the basis of compositional analysis, due to the fact that either one component has a unique meaning not found elsewhere or one or more components contain no meaning of their own.

(The) dual idiom representation hypothesis the theory that idiom comprehension involves both normal linguistic processing and direct memory retrieval.

(The) figurative first (also known as "direct access") hypothesis the theory that in idiom processing, speakers rarely process an idiom literally; instead, they often directly access its figurative meaning.

Fixed expressions a generic term used to refer to any expression that allows very little, or no, variation in form and which often has a specialized meaning; also called "formulaic expressions/sequences" or "formulae."

Formulae or formulaic expressions/sequences see **fixed expressions**.

Heuristic approach in idiom processing a theory about L2 idiom comprehension; it postulates that L2 idiom processing uses a variety of strategies rather than following any of the established L1 idiom processing models.

Ideational function of idioms the function of providing information; most idioms are used for this function, e.g. Tom *chickened out*.

Idiom key the word in an idiomatic phrase at which the listener recognizes the phrase as an idiom.

(The) idiom principle the theory that word choices or combinations are not random and that language users often resort to preconstructed or semi-preconstructed phrases. This principle works jointly with the "open choice principle" in human language production.

Idiomatosis excessive and inappropriate use of idioms.

Idioms of decoding those that have a non-literal meaning, e.g. *red herring*.

Idioms of encoding stable collocations peculiar to a language, e.g. *take a taxi* (not *ride a taxi*); also called "phraseological idioms."

Idioms of restricted variance idioms that allow some limited variance in wording.

Ill-formed idioms/collocations those that are either syntactically abnormal (*see* **syntactically abnormal idiom**) or syntactically normal but violate the usual word collocation and semantic restriction rules, e.g. *crack a joke*.

Incorporating verbs compound verbs, e.g. *eavesdrop*.

Interpersonal function of idioms the function primarily of interacting with other people; idioms used for this function are mostly formulaic sayings, e.g. *What's up?*

Invariant idioms those that do not allow any variance in wording.

Irreversible binominals structures composed of two nouns in a fixed order, e.g. *safe and sound*.

Lexemic idioms those that are noun or verb phrases used as lexical items as opposed to "sememic" or sentential idioms; also referred to as phrasal idioms.

Lexical idioms those composed of a polymorphemic word whose meaning cannot be derived from its composing morphemes, e.g. *greenhouse*. Only a few scholars consider such words to be idioms.

(The) literal first (also known as "idiom list) hypothesis the theory that in idiom processing, speakers first process an idiom literally, but when the context does not allow a literal interpretation, they access the meaning of the idiom in a special idiom list.

(The) open choice principle the theory that in constructing phrases and sentences, language users possess relative freedom in word choice, a freedom restricted only by grammaticality. This principle works jointly with the "idiom principle" in human language production.

Passive idioms idioms a speaker uses only in reception, not production.

Phrasal compounds compound nouns and adjectives, e.g. *stalemate*.

Phrasal idioms see **lexemic idioms**.

Phrasal verb a verb used together with one or two particles to function as a whole unit and, often, express an idiomatic meaning, e.g. *fall through*.

Phraseological collocations those with some limited variance in wording, e.g. *in/with regard to*. Consult also **idioms of encoding**.

Prefabricated or preconstructed expressions see **fixed expressions**.

Pseudo-idioms compound words or phrases in which one of the constituents is a cranberry morph, e.g. *chit-chat*.

Relational function of idioms *see* **cohesive function**.

Semantically decomposable idiom one whose constituting parts have either literal or figurative meanings that contribute independently to the string's overall idiomatic or figurative meaning, e.g. *be in the dark about* something.

Semantically non-decomposable idioms idioms whose individual components do not contribute to the phrase's figurative meaning, e.g. *shoot the breeze*. Consult also **core idioms**.

Sememic idioms idiomatic expressions longer than phrasal or lexemic idioms, often complete utterances, e.g. *What's up?*

(The) simultaneous processing or lexical representation hypothesis the theory that in idiom processing, speakers process an idiom both literally and figuratively at the same time until they decide on the appropriate interpretation based on context.

Stable collocation words that are often used together, such as *assets and liability*.

Syntactic and semantic processing disassociation hypothesis the theory that there is a disassociation between the syntactic and the semantic processors in idiom comprehension.

Syntactically abnormal idiom one that violates syntactical rules in formation, e.g. *by and large*.

Syntactically frozen idiom   one that does not allow passive transformation—that is, it loses its idiomatic meaning when used passively, e.g. *kick the bucket.*

Textual function of idioms   see **cohesive function**.

Tournures   idioms each made up of a verb plus at least two words, e.g. *bite the bullet.*

Truncated idiom   an idiom with a part (a word or phrase) being omitted, e.g. *a bird in hand.*

Annotated List of Selective Idiom Reference Books and Textbooks
(grouped by publishers)

Addison-Wesley/Longman/Pearson Education (New York, etc.)

Essential idioms in English: Phrasal verbs and collocations (5th ed.) (2003) by R. J. Dixson.
  Presents over 500 idioms with definitions/illustrations and a variety of learning exercises.

Everyday idioms for reference and practice (two-book series) (1997) by R. E. Feare (Addison-Wesley).
  Contains high-frequency and popular idioms but not enough register and contextual use information.

The Idiom advantage: Fluency in speaking and listening (1995) by D. Watkins (Addison-Wesley).
  Offers some interesting learning activities; but also some out-of-date or low use-frequency idioms.

Longman American English idioms dictionary (1999) ed. by R. Urbom.
  Contains over 4,000 entries of frequently used idioms with definitions written with the Longman 2,000-word defining vocabulary and example based on sentences from the Longman Corpus Network; also has a few illustrative pictures.

Longman phrasal verb dictionary (2000) by R. Courtney.
  Contains over 5,000 entries with the same notable features as those found in its sister idiom dictionary.

Longman grammar of spoken and written English (1999), ed. by D. Biber, S. Johansson, G. Leech, S. Conrad and E. Finegan.
  Although not an idiom dictionary, it contains extensive corpus-based information on idiom use.

Barron's (Hauppauge, NY)

A dictionary of American idioms (3rd ed.) (2004) by A. Makkai, M. T. Boatner, and J. E. Gates.
  Contains over 8,000 entries with definitions and sample sentences.

American idioms and some phrases just for fun (1999) by E. Swick.
  Offers many interesting activities designed to make idiom learning easy and fun.

Handbook of commonly used American idioms (3rd ed.) (2004) by A. Makkai, M. T. Boatner, and J. E. Gates.
  Contains over 2,500 entries with register information; concise, small, and easy to carry around.

Cambridge University Press (Cambridge)

Cambridge dictionary of American idioms (2003) ed. by P. Heacock.
  Contains over 5,000 entries; definitions written using a carefully controlled defining vocabulary of under 2,000 words; examples given all based on sentences from the Cambridge International Corpus; register information also provided.
Cambridge international dictionary of idioms (1998).
  Contains over 7,000 entries with the same notable features.
Cambridge international dictionary of phrasal verbs (1997).
  Contains over 4,500 entries with the same notable features.
English idioms in use (2002) by M. McCarthy and F. O'Dell.
  Over 1,000 commonly used idioms explained clearly in context with practice activities and an answer key.
English phrasal verbs in use (2004) by M. McCarthy and F. O'Dell.
  Presents over 1,000 useful phrasal verbs in context with practice activities and an answer key.
In the know: Understanding and using idioms (2005) by C. Leaney.
  Over 1,000 useful idioms presented and practiced in contexts with an answer key.

Collins COBUILD (London)

Collins COBUILD Idioms Dictionary (2nd ed.) (2002) by E. Schuhbeck.
  Corpus-based with over 6,000 entries and a thematic index.
Collins COBUILD phrasal verb dictionary (2nd ed.) (2002) by J. Sinclair.
  Corpus-based with 4,500 entries and 12,000 examples; register information provided.

Heinle & Heinle (Boston)

Against all odds: Speaking naturally with idioms (1991) by M. H. Eichler.
  With two audiotapes; idioms presented in context with interactive activities.
All clear! Idioms and pronunciation in context (three-book series) (1993 and 1997) by H. K. Fragiadakis.
  Focuses on 200 high-frequency idioms with activities for listening and speaking, especially pronunciation.

McGraw-Hill (Columbus, Ohio), including titles from the former National Textbook Company

Dictionary of sports idioms (1993) by R. A. Palmatier and H. L. Ray. (NCT).
  Excellent reference about sports idioms' meanings and origins.
Essential American idioms (3rd ed.) (1999) by R. A. Spears.
  Each entry illustrated with at least two examples in full sentences.

ANNOTATED LIST OF REFERENCE BOOKS   **183**

Idioms for everyday use (2001) by M. Broukal.
  Interesting activities with appealing illustrations.
McGraw-Hill's American idioms dictionary (4th edition) (2006) by R. A. Spears.
  Contains 14,000 entries each exemplified with contextual sentences.
McGraw-Hill's dictionary of American idioms and phrasal verbs (2006) by R. A. Spears.
  Contains over 24,000 entries with sentence examples.
NTC's super-mini American idioms dictionary: the most practical and up-to-date guide to contemporary American idioms (1996) by R. A. Spears.
  Over 1,500 entries provided; concise and easy to carry around.
Phrases and idioms (1998) by R. A. Spears.
  Over 2,300 difficult American idioms listed and illustrated.
Practical idioms: Using phrasal verbs in everyday contexts (1993) by L. A. Berman and L. Kirstein.
  Over 1,000 phrasal verb idioms with useful learning activities.

Oxford University Press (Oxford)

Can you believe it? Stories and idioms from real life (three-level series) (2000) by J. Huizenga and L. Huizenga.
  Useful idioms presented in story context with practice activities, comic-style illustrations, and cassettes.
Oxford idioms dictionary for learners of English (2001) ed. by J. Toby.
  Over 10,000 entries with information regarding idioms' origin, register, connotation, and English variety.
Oxford phrasal verbs dictionary for learners of English (2001) ed. by D. Parkinson.
  Contains over 6,000 entries with the same notable features.
The Oxford Dictionary of Idioms (2nd ed.) (2005) ed. by J. Speake.
  Contains over 5,000 entries with the same notable features.

Scholastic, Inc. (New York)

Scholastic dictionary of idioms (revised ed.) (2006) by M. Terban.
  Easy-to-understand definitions with information about the origins of over 600 idioms; illustrations.
20 Hands-on activities for learning idioms (2002) by M. Gravois.
  Innovative idiom teaching activities designed especially for young and lower-level students.

Other Publishers

The American heritage dictionary of idioms (2003) by C. Ammer, Boston: Houghton Mifflin.
  Over 10,000 entries with clear definitions, examples, and origins.
Body idioms and more for learners of English (2005) by M. Pare, Tujunga, CA: Mayuree Pare.
  Interesting discussion of idioms based on body parts; written by an ESL speaker.
Dictionary of idioms and their origins (2000) by L. Flavell and R. Flavell, London: Kyle Cathie.
  Excellent source about the origins of idioms.

A dynamic approach to everyday idioms (2005) by C. Malarcher, Tokyo: Hokuseido.
Covering 300 common idioms in 30 lessons targeted for high beginners; colorful and humorous; accompanied by a useful CD.

Easy American idioms: Hundreds of idiomatic expressions to give you an edge in English (2006), New York, NY: Random House Living Language.
Useful idioms in daily functions with interesting activities, including four audio CDs.

Idiom organizer (1999), J. Wright, Hove, England: Language Teaching Publications.
Over 1,800 idioms organized in four different ways; plus exercise to practice the idioms.

Illustrated everyday idioms with stories 1 and 2 (2003) by C. Malarcher, San Antonio: Compass Publishing.
Easy-to-read examples of 600 common idioms each accompanied by a short definition; two examples of correct usage shown in context within a story.

The Penguin Dictionary of English Idioms (2001) by D. M. Gulland and D. G. Hinds-Howell, London: Penguin.
Organized by theme, making it easy to compare synonymous idioms or those on the same subject.

Spotlight on two-word verb idioms (revised ed.) (1998) by C. P. Gilman, Berlingame, CA: Alta Book Center.
Phrasal verb idioms presented in fun stories.

Vidioms: Activating idioms for ESL (1991) by J. F. Chabot, Niagara Falls, NY: Full Blast.
A unique three-tape video program with a student workbook consisting of fifteen lessons on idioms.

Webster's New World American idioms handbook (2003) by G. Brenner, Indianapolis, IN: Wiley.
Over 1,000 entries with register and other useful information and examples.

A year in the life of an ESL student: Idioms and vocabulary you can't live without (2004) by E. J. Francis, Victoria, BC, Canada: Trafford.
A unique book with over 8,000 entries embedded in a story about an international student's one-year experience in an English-speaking country, with definitions and exercises.

Online sources (all free, easy to access, and user-friendly)

Dictionary of English idioms and idiomatic expressions at http://www.usingenglish.com/reference/idioms/

English idioms: Sayings and slang by W, Magnuson at http://www.idioms.myjewelz.com/. Print version available.

ESL idiom page on Dave Sperling's ESL Café at http://eslcafe.com/idioms/id-mngs.html

Idioms and Phrases at http://idioms.thefreedictionary.com/

The idiom connection at http://idiomconnection.com/

Notes

Chapter 1 Idiom Definition and Classification

1. For a thorough examination of the issue of idiom definition, consult Fernando (1996), Grant and Bauer (2004), Makkai (1973), Moon (1998), and M. M. Wood (1981).
2. *Brewer's dictionary of phrase and fable* (p. 158) sets out another theory about the origin of this idiomatic phrase: the idiom came from the suicide practice of hanging oneself by kicking away the bucket one was standing on.
3. Scholars have used many other terms to refer to "formulae" such as "chunks," "fixed expressions," and "formulaic sequences." For further information about formulaic language, consult Wray's (2002) and Schmitt's (2004) comprehensive books on the topic.
4. Based on Kövecses' (2002) analysis, the difference between metaphor- and metonymy-based idioms is that in the former, the vehicle and the target are from two different domains (for example, in the statement "The test was a *piece of cake*," "test" is academic work but "cake" is food); in the latter, the vehicle and the target belong to the same domain (in "He *met his Waterloo*," Waterloo is the place Napoleon suffered his defeat and it stands for defeat in both the vehicle and the target domain). For more information on the issue, consult Kövecses (2002, pp. 143–162).

Chapter 2 Idiom Use: Function, Variation, Frequency, and Register

1. Of course, by the term "idiom" in his "idiom principle," Sinclair refers to a much broader concept than that discussed in this book; it includes collocations and many other prefabricated expressions. Yet at the same time it does cover those idiomatic expressions that are the concern of this book. Hence, Sinclair's idiom principle applies to the idiomatic expressions we are discussing.

2. To see how Halliday treats logical and organizational functions both as ideational (below clause level) and textual (above clause level) components, read Halliday's (1994) chapter 6, "Below the clause: Groups and phrases" (pp. 179–214), and chapter 9, "Around the clause: Cohesion and discourse" (pp. 308–339). In arguing for the treating of logical relationships as ideational functions, Halliday writes, "in interpreting group structures we have to split the ideational component into two: EXPERIENTIAL and LOGICAL," with the latter component expressing "meaning as organization of experience" and "certain very general logical relationships" (p. 179).
3. Barlow's (2000) CSPAE corpus is made up of speeches at American professional conferences and the White House news conferences. Liu's (2002) CSAME consists of transcripts of American TV programs downloaded from the major TV networks such as ABC, NBC, and CNN.
4. For a complete discussion of the types of variations, the reader is referred to Fernando (1996, pp. 43–52), Liu (2003, pp. 682–684), and Moon (1998, pp. 121–177). Most of the examples about idiom variations mentioned here are from Moon and Liu. Some of the variation types identified by Moon are not discussed here, primarily because of (1) lack of space, and (2) because they overlap with those that are addressed in this section—for example, what Moon calls "idiom schema"-related variations (e.g. *shake in one's shoes* versus *quake in one's shoes*, and *shake in one's shoes* versus *quake in one's boots*) may also be considered verb and noun variations.
5. I use "metaphorically based idioms" as a generic term to mean not only idioms based on metaphor but also those based on "metonymy" and "conventional or pragmatic knowledge." While the distinction is often not made, there is a technical difference among the three categories in linguistic terms, one that Kövecses (2002) explained very clearly. According to Kövecses, for example, the figurative idiom *sit on one's hands* is, strictly speaking, based on metonymy (that is, "hand" standing for activity) and conventional knowledge (for example, the knowledge that when sitting on one's hands, one cannot do anything). Such technical differences are not very important for the purpose of this book, however, and hence will not be emphasized in the discussion on metaphor-based idioms in the remainder of the book.

Chapter 3 L1 Idiom Processing and Comprehension

1. When Titone and Connine (1999) first proposed the model, they also drew on Cacciari's (1993) and Glucksberg's (1993) work and they called the model a "hybrid model of idiom comprehension" (p. 1666). Building on Titone and Connine's work, Abel (2003) strengthened the model by using findings from his study and renamed it the *dual idiom representation* model. The two terms *hybrid* and *dual* are really synonymous, because by *hybrid*, Titone and Connine meant dual idiom processing, too. I am using Abel's term instead of Titone and Connine's simply because it is clearer, as it explicitly indicates the two idiom representation modes in the model. Another point that needs to be made here is that this model is somewhat similar to the *simultaneous processing* or *lexical representation* hypothesis but it differs from the latter in that this model takes into consideration the compositionality of an idiom in determining how an idiom is processed. It suggests that a non-decomposable idiom may have only an idiom representation but a decomposable one may have both a conceptual and an idiom represen-

tation. This latter hypothesis, allowing a compositional idiom to be processed both as conceptual representation and as idiom representation, further distinguishes the *dual idiom representation* model from the *simultaneous processing/lexical representation* hypothesis as the latter allows for only one representation—that is, as either a literal or a figurative term. The most important difference lies, of course, in the fact that the *simultaneous processing/literal representation*, as Glucksberg (1993) points out, is simply a "direct look-up" processing model like the *literal first* and the *figurative first* hypotheses, while the *dual representation* model encompasses both compositional analysis and direct retrieval.
2. According to Abel, the term "representation" used here is synonymous with processing, "because the manner of representation directly influences processing," although he also argues that, if examined more closely, "assumptions about the mental representation of language should be located at an even more abstract and 'higher' level than those about processes" (2003, p. 342). By "conceptual representation" Abel means non-linguistic world knowledge at a general cognitive level, and it "must not be confused with semantic knowledge" (2003, p. 342).
3. Abel's *dual idiom representation model* finds support in or is similar to Wray's (2002) "dual-system model" for language processing in general. Wray's language processing model consists of "analytical processing" and "holistic processing," with the former being in charge of encoding and decoding "novel, or potentially novel linguistic material" and the latter in charge of producing and retrieving prefabricated strings [formulaic expressions] stored in memory" (ibid., p. 14). In both Abel's and Wray's processing models, if an expression is already stored in a speaker's memory, direct retrieval will most likely ensue.

Chapter 4 L2 Idiom Processing and Comprehension

1. Some researchers (Abdullah and Jackson, 1998; Irujo, 1986a) examined their subjects' understanding of idioms in isolation—that is, out of context.
2. It is important to emphasize that according to some studies, conceptual knowledge is not always activated in idiom comprehension. For example, Glucksberg et al.'s (1993) study indicates that usually conceptual knowledge is not accessed when people do not have the time to apply analogies using their conceptual knowledge. The findings of Gibbs et al. (1997) also suggest that conceptual knowledge is not activated on certain metaphorical idioms. In fact, Keysar and Bly (1999) even argue that there are no conceptual structures existing independently of language, and the interpretation of the meaning of an idiom is not motivated largely by conceptual structures; rather, it is the result of the working of "the mind's interpretive strategies" (p. 1559).

Chapter 5 Factors that Affect Idiom Comprehension

1. The study also examined the effects of idioms' syntactic frozenness; we will cover that issue below.
2. Consult Fraser (see Chapter 1) on this issue.
3. Syntactically abnormal idioms are part of what Gibbs et al. (1989) and Moon (1998) call "ill-formed idioms," although the latter term is more inclusive, for "ill

formed idioms" may also include idioms that are not syntactically abnormal but abnormal because of their violations of usual word collocations and semantic restrictions. In other words, while syntactically abnormal idioms are all ill-formed, not all ill-formed idioms are syntactically abnormal. For example, *by and large*, *happy go lucky*, and *in the know* are syntactically abnormal and hence ill-formed; yet *crack a joke*, *pop a question*, and *drive a hard bargain* are ill-formed but not syntactically abnormal because they do not violate any syntactical rule. They are ill-formed because they break the traditional collocations or the semantic restrictions of word usages. We usually "make" a joke, "ask" a question, etc.

Chapter 6 Idiom Acquisition and Its Importance in Language Development

1. Of course, rote learning may be the strategy for grasping what Grant and Bauer (2004) call "core idioms"—that is, those that defy any syntactical and/or semantic analysis, such as *by and large*.

Chapter 7 Selection and Organization of Idioms for Learning and Instruction

1. It is important to note, according to experts on corpus linguistics (e.g. Biber et al., 1998), that the number of words is not the only issue to look at in considering the issue of the size of a corpus. The number of texts included should also be taken into account. Without a sufficient number of different texts, a corpus may still not be representative even if it has a very large number of words.
2. Flavell and Flavell's *Dictionary of idioms and their origins* (1992) is an excellent source for this type of classification of idioms. Boers (2001) and Boers et al. (2004a) also offer a wealth of useful information about the origin of idioms.

Chapter 8 Idiom Pedagogy: Macro-strategies and General Approaches

1. Yet concerning the effect of the strategy of thinking in terms of conceptual metaphor on the students performance on phrasal verbs that were *not* taught, Boers' (2000) study did not support Kövecses and Szabó's findings, for the group who were presented the phrasal verbs under the orientational metaphor headings did not perform better than the other group on the *untaught* phrasal verbs. The finding raises some questions about the transferring effect of the training on the strategy of thinking in terms of conceptual metaphor in dealing with phrasal verb idioms.
2. The reason for not including children under the age of 6 is that, according to research, these young children have not developed the figurative competence needed for comprehending idioms—that is, they do not possess the cognitive and linguistic competence needed to understand idioms, most of which are figurative in nature. In the remainder of the book, any reference to teaching idioms to young learners means teaching them to children aged 7 and above.

Chapter 9 Idiom Pedagogy: Micro-strategies and Techniques

1. In order to avoid confusion arising from the use of different terms, I am following Brown in using the word "technique" as "a superordinate term to refer to various activities either teachers or learners perform in the classroom" (2001, p. 129). Techniques, thus, may mean activities, procedures, tasks, strategies, etc. However, other terms such as "activities," "procedures," and "strategies" may still be occasionally used when warranted by, among other things, discourse context or the need to avoid word repetition. Furthermore, while, in the strictest sense, teaching and learning strategies are technically not the same, the distinction is not always clear or necessary. For example, having students figure out an idiom's meaning is in and of itself both a teaching and a learning activity, depending on whether one looks at it from the teacher's or the students' perspective. From the former, having students do it is a teaching activity, but from the students' perspective doing it is a learning activity. Therefore, in this chapter some of the techniques are referred to as both teaching and learning strategies.

Chapter 10 Error Treatment and Assessment in Idiom Instruction

1. Besides this example, several others in my discussion below are from Lattey (1994), in which he examined the issue of universals versus language-specifics in L2 acquisition by analyzing the problems his German EFL students experienced in learning English idioms. Because his focus was the extent to which the use of idioms was language-specific (i.e. not universal), his classification and the terms he used for depicting the errors were often not exactly the same as mine.

References

Abdullah, K. & Jackson, H. (1998). Idioms and the language learner: Contrasting English and Syrian Arabic. *Language in Contrast, 1*, 83–107.
Abel, B. (2003). English idioms in the first language and second language lexicon: A dual representation approach. *Second Language Research, 19*, 329–358.
Abrahamsen, E. P. & Smith, R. (2000). Facilitating idiom acquisition in children with communication disorders: Computer vs. classroom. *Child Language Teaching and Therapy, 16*, 227–239.
Aijmer, K. (1996). *Conversational routines in English: Conversation and creativity.* London: Longman.
Austin, J. L. (1962). *How to do things with words.* Cambridge, MA: Harvard University Press.
Bahns, J., Burmeister, H., & Vogel, T. (1986). The pragmatics of formulas in L2 learners' speech: Use and development. *Journal of Pragmatics, 10*, 693–723.
Bardovi-Harlig, K. (2002). A new starting point? Investigating formulaic use and input in future expression. *Studies in Second Language Acquisition, 24*, 189–198.
Barlow, M. (2000). Corpus of spoken professional American English [CD-ROM]. Houston, TX: Athelstan.
Biber, D., Conrad, S., & Reppen (1998). *Corpus linguistics: Investigating language structure and use.* Cambridge: Cambridge University Press.
Biber, D., Johansson, S., Leech, G., Conrad, S., & Finegan, E. (1999). *Longman grammar of spoken and written English.* Harlow, England: Pearson Education.
Bobrow, S. & Bell, S. (1973). On catching on to idiomatic expressions. *Memory and Cognition, 1*, 343–346.
Boers, F. (2000a). Enhancing metaphorical awareness in specialized reading. *English for Specific Purposes, 19*, 137–147.
Boers, F. (2000b). Metaphor awareness and vocabulary retention. *Applied Linguistics, 21*, 553–571.
Boers, F. (2001). Remembering figurative idioms by hypothesizing about their origin. *Prospect, 16*(3), 35–43.
Boers, F. (2003). Applied linguistics perspectives on cross-cultural variation in conceptual metaphor. *Metaphor and Symbol, 18*, 231–238.

Boers, F. & Demecheleer, M. (1997). A few metaphorical models in (Western) economic discourse. In W. A. Liebert, G. Redeker, & L. Waugh (Eds.), *Discourse and perspective in cognitive linguistics* (pp. 115–129). Amsterdam: John Benjamins.

Boers, F. & Demecheleer, M. (2001). Measuring the impact of cross-cultural differences on learners' comprehension of imaginable idioms. *ELT Journal, 55*, 255–262.

Boers, F., Demecheleer, M., & Eyckmans, J. (2004a). Etymological elaboration as a strategy for learning figurative idioms. In P. Bogaards and B. Laufer (Eds.), *Vocabulary in a second language: Selection, acquisition, and testing* (pp. 53–78). Amsterdam: John Benjamins.

Boers, F., Demecheleer, M., & Eyckmans, J. (2004b). Cross-cultural variation as a variable in comprehending and remembering figurative idioms. *European Journal of English Studies, 8*, 375–366.

Boers, F. & Lindstromberg, S. (2005). Finding ways to make phrase-learning feasible: The mnemonic effect of alliteration. *System, 33*, 225–238.

Bolinger, D. (1975). *Aspects of language* (2nd ed.). New York: Harcourt Brace Jovanovich.

Brett, A., Rothlein, L., & Hurley, M. (1996). Vocabulary acquisition from listening to stories and explanations of target words. *The Elementary School Journal, 96*, 415–422.

Brewer's dictionary of phrase and fable (centenary ed.; revised by I. H. Evans). (1975). London: Cassell.

Bromley, K. D. (1984). Teaching idioms. *The Reading Teacher, 38*, 272–276.

Brown, H. D. (2001). *Teaching by principles: An interactive approach to language pedagogy*. White Plains, NY: Longman.

Bulut, T. & Çelik-Yazici, Y. (2004). Idiom processing in L2: Through rose-colored glasses. *The Reading Matrix, 4*, 105–116.

Cacciari, C. (1993). The place of idioms in a literal and metaphorical world. In C. Cacciari & P. Tabossi (Eds.), *Idioms: Processing, structure, and interpretation* (pp. 27–55). Hillsdale, NJ: Lawrence Erlbaum.

Cacciari, C. & Levorato, M. C. (1989). How children understand idioms in discourse. *Journal of Child Language, 16*, 387–405.

Cacciari, C. & Tabossi, P. (1988). The comprehension of idioms. *Journal of memory and language, 27*, 668–683.

Celce-Murcia, M. & Larsen-Freeman, D. (1999). *The grammar book: An ESL/EFL teacher's course* (2nd Ed.). Boston: Heinle & Heinle.

Chaika, E. (1982). *Language: The social mirror*. Rowley, MA: Newbury House.

Charteris-Black, J. (2002). Second language figurative proficiency: A comparative study of Malay and English. *Applied Linguistics, 23*, 104–133.

Cooper, T. C. (1998). Teaching idioms. *Foreign Language Annals, 31*, 255–266.

Cooper, T. C. (1999). Process of idioms by L2 learners of English. *TESOL Quarterly, 33*, 233–262.

Cornell, A. (1999). Idioms: An approach to identify major pitfalls for learners. *IRAL, 37*, 1–21.

Cowie, A. P. & Mackin, R. (Eds.) (1975). *Oxford dictionary of current idiomatic English.* 2 vols. Oxford: Oxford University Press.

Cronk, B. C. & Schweigert, W. A. (1992). The comprehension of idioms: The effects of familiarity, literalness, and usage. *Applied Psycholinguistics, 13*, 131–146.

Cummins, J. (1979). Linguistic interdependence and the educational development of bilingual children. *Review of Educational Research, 49*, 222–251.

Cummins, J. (1991). Interdependence of first- and second-language proficiency in bilingual children. In E. Bialystok (Ed.), *Language processing in bilingual children* (pp. 70–89). New York: Cambridge University Press.

REFERENCES

Deignan, A. (2003). Metaphorical expressions and culture: An indirect link. *Metaphor and Symbol, 18*, 255–272.
Deignan, A., Gabrys, D., & Solska A. (1997). Teaching English metaphors using cross-linguistic awareness-raising activities. *ELT Journal, 51*, 352–360.
Dew, P. & Holt, E. (1988). Complainable matters: The use of idiomatic expressions in making complaints. *Social Problems, 35*, 398–417.
Dew, P. & Holt, E. (1995). Idiomatic expressions and their role in the organization of topic transition in conversation. In M. Everaert, E.-J. van der Linden, A. Schenk, & R. Schreuder (Eds.), *Idioms: Structural and psychological perspectives* (pp. 117–132). Hillsdale, NJ: Erlbaum.
Dörnyei, Z., Durow, V., & Zahran, K. (2004). Individual differences and their effects on formulaic sequence acquisition. In N. Schmitt (Ed.), *Formulaic sequences* (pp. 87–106). Amsterdam: John Benjamins.
Douglas, J. D. & Peel, B. (1979). The development of metaphor and proverb translation in children Grade 1 through 7. *Journal of Educational Research, 73*, 116–119.
Duquette, G. (1995). Developing comprehension and interaction skills with idiomatic expressions. In G. Duquette (Ed.), *Second language practice: Classroom strategies for developing communicative competence* (pp. 35–42). Clevedon, England: Multilingual Matters.
Elley, W. B. (1989). Vocabulary acquisition from listening to stories. *Reading Research Quarterly, 24*, 174–187.
Ellis, R. (1997). *Second language acquisition.* Oxford: Oxford University Press.
Ellis, R., Tanaka, Y., & Yamazaki, A. (1994). Classroom interaction, comprehension and the acquisition of word meaning. *Language Learning, 44*, 449–491.
Emanation, M. (2002). Congruence by degree: On the relation between metaphor and cultural models. In R. W. Gibbs & G. J. Steen (Eds.), *Metaphor in cognitive linguistics* (pp. 205–218). Amsterdam: John Benjamins.
Erman, B. (2007). Cognitive processes as evidence of the idiom principle. *International Journal of Corpus Linguistics, 12*, 25–53.
Erman, B. and Warren, B. (2000). The idiom principle and the open choice principle. *Text, 20*, 29–62.
Fernando, C. (1978). Towards a definition of idiom, its nature and function. *Studies in Language, 2*, 313–343.
Fernando, C. (1996). *Idioms and idiomaticity.* Oxford: Oxford University Press.
Flavell, L. & Flavell, R. (2000). *Dictionary of idioms and their origins.* London: Kyle Cathie.
Flores d'Arcais, G. B. (1993). The comprehension and semantic interpretation of idioms. In C. Cacciari & P. Tabossi (Eds.) *Idioms: Processing, structure, and interpretation* (pp. 79–98). Hillsdale, NJ: Lawrence Erlbaum.
Flowerdew, J. (1992). Definitions in science lectures. *Applied Linguistics, 13*, 202–212.
Forrester, M. A. (1995). Topic implicature and context in the comprehension of idiomatic phrases. *Journal of Psycholinguistic Research, 24*, 1–22.
Fraser, B. (1970). Idioms within a transformational grammar. *Foundations of Language, 6*, 22–42.
Fraser, B. (1996). Pragmatic markers. *Pragmatics, 6*, 167–90.
Galka, M. & Flahive, D. (2005, March/April). Cross-cultural interpretations of textually embedded grammatical metaphors. Paper presented at the Thirty-ninth TESOL Annual Convention, San Antonio, TX.
Gass, S. & Selinker, L. (Eds.) (1983). *Language transfer in language learning.* Rowley, MA: Newbury House.
Genzel, R. B. (1991). *Getting the hang of idioms and expressions.* New York: Maxwell Macmillan.

Gibbs, R. W. (1980). Spilling the beans on understanding and memory for idioms in conversation. *Memory and Cognition, 8,* 148–164.
Gibbs, R. W. (1983). Do people always process the literal meanings of direct requests? *Journal of Experimental Psychology: Learning, Memory and Cognition, 9,* 524–533.
Gibbs, R. W. (1983). Literal meaning and psychological theory. *Cognitive Science, 8,* 275–304.
Gibbs, R. W. (1987). Linguistic factors in children's understanding of idioms. *Journal of Child Language, 14,* 569–586.
Gibbs, R. W. (1990). Psycholinguistic studies on the conceptual basis of idiomaticity. *Cognitive Linguistics, 1,* 417–451.
Gibbs, R. W. (1991). Semantic analyzability in children's understanding of idioms. *Journal of Speech and Hearing Research, 34,* 613–620.
Gibbs, R. W. (1992). What do idioms really mean? *Journal of Memory and Language, 31,* 485–506.
Gibbs, R. W. (1993). Why idioms are not dead metaphors. In C. Cacciari & P. Tabbossi (Eds.), *Idioms: Processing, structure, and interpretation* (pp. 57–78). Hillsdale, NJ: Lawrence Erlbaum.
Gibbs, R. W. (1994). *The poetics of mind: Figurative thought, language, and understanding.* Cambridge, UK: Cambridge University Press.
Gibbs, R. W. (1995). Idiomaticity and human cognition. In E. Everaert, E.-J. van der Linden, A. Schenk, & R. Schreuder (Eds.), *Idioms: Structural and psychological perspectives* (pp. 97–116). Hillsdale, NJ: Lawrence Erlbaum.
Gibbs, R. W. (1999). Taking metaphor out of our heads and putting it into the cultural world. In R. W. Gibbs & G. J. Steen (Eds.), *Metaphor in cognitive linguistics* (pp. 145–166). Amsterdam: John Benjamins.
Gibbs, R. W., Bogdanvich, J. M., Sykes, J. R., & Barr, D. J. (1997). Metaphor in idiom comprehension. *Journal of Memory and Language, 37,* 141–154.
Gibbs, R. W., Nayak, N., & Cutting, C. (1989). How to kick the bucket and not decompose: Analyzability and idiom processing. *Journal of Memory and Language, 28,* 576–593.
Gibbs, R. W. & O'Brien, J. (1990). Idioms and mental imagery: The metaphorical motivation for idiomatic meaning. *Cognition, 21,* 100–138.
Glucksberg, S. (1993). Idiom meanings and allusional content. In C. Cacciari & P. Tabbossi (Eds.), *Idioms: Processing, structure, and interpretation* (pp. 3–26). Hillsdale, NJ: Lawrence Erlbaum.
Glucksberg, S., Brown, M., & McGlone, M. S. (1993). Conceptual metaphors are not automatically accessed during idiom comprehension. *Memory and Cognition, 21,* 711–719.
Grant, L. E. (2005). Frequency of "core idioms" in the British National Corpus (BNC). *International Journal of Corpus Linguistics, 10,* 429–541.
Grant, L. E. (2007). In a manner of speaking: Assessing frequent spoken figurative idioms to assist ESL/EFL teachers. *System, 35,* 169–181.
Grant, L. E. & Bauer, L. (2004). Criteria for re-defining idioms: Are we barking up the wrong tree? *Applied Linguistics, 25,* 38–61.
Grant, L. E. & Nation, I. S. P. (2006). How many idioms are there in English? *International Journal of Applied Linguistics, 151,* 1–14.
Gravois, M. (2002). *20 Hands-on activities for learning idioms.* New York, NY: Scholastic.
Halliday, M. A. K. (1973). *Explorations in the functions of language.* London: Edward Arnold.
Halliday, M. A. K. (1978). *Language as social semiotic: The social interpretation of language and meaning.* London: Edward Arnold.
Halliday, M. A. K. (1994). *An introduction to functional grammar* (2nd ed.). London: Edward Arnold.

REFERENCES

Henry, L. (2006). Figurative language: Teaching idioms. Retrieved online from http://www.readwritethink.org/lessons/lesson_view, June 20.
Hockett, C. F. (1958). *A course in modern linguistics.* New York: Macmillan.
Holme, R. (2004). *Mind, metaphor, and language teaching.* New York: Palgrave Macmillan.
Honeck, R. P. & Temple, J. G. (1994). Proverbs: the extended conceptual base and great chain metaphor theories. *Metaphor and Symbolic Activity, 9*(2), 85–112.
Howarth, P. (1998). Phraseology and second language proficiency. *Applied Linguistics, 19*, 24–44.
Hulstijin, J. H. (1993). When do foreign language readers look up the meaning of unfamiliar words? The influence of task and learner variables. *Modern Language Journal, 77*, 139–147.
Hulstijin, J. H. & Marchena, E. (1989). Avoidance: Grammatical or semantic causes? *Studies in Second Language Acquisition, 11*, 241–255.
Irujo, S. (1986a). Don't put your leg in your mouth: Transfer in the acquisition of idioms in a second language. *TESOL Quarterly, 20*, 287–304.
Irujo, S. (1986b) A piece of cake: Learning and teaching idioms. *English Language Teaching Journal, 40*, 236–242.
Irujo, S. (1993). Steering clear: Avoidance in the production of idioms. *IRAL, 31*, 205–219.
Johnson, J. (1989). Factors related to cross-language transfer and metaphor interpretation in bilingual children. *Applied Psycholinguistics, 10*, 157–177.
Johnson, J. (1991). Developmental versus language-based factors in metaphor interpretations. *Journal of Educational Psychology, 83*, 470–483.
Johnson, J. & Rosano, T. (1993). Relation of cognitive style to metaphor interpretation and language proficiency. *Applied Psycholinguistics, 14*, 159–174.
Jones, M. & Haywood, S. (2004). Facilitating the acquisition of formulaic sequences: An exploratory study in an EAP context. In N. Schmitt (Ed.), *Fomulaic sequences* (pp. 268–292). Amsterdam: John Benjamins.
Jordens, P. (1977). Rules, grammatical intuitions and strategies in foreign language learning. *Interlanguage Studies Bulletin, 2*(2), 5–77.
Katz, J. J. (1973). Compositionality, idiomaticity, and lexical substation. In S. Anderson & P. Kiparsky (Eds.), *A festschrift for Morris Halle* (pp. 357–376). New York: Holt, Rinehart, & Winston.
Katz, J. J. & Postal, P. (1963). The semantic interpretation of idioms and sentences containing them. *MIT Research Laboratory of Electronic Quarterly Progress Report, 70*, 275–82.
Kellerman, E. (1977). Towards a characterization of the strategy of transfer in second language learning. *Interlanguage Studies Bulletin, 2*(1), 58–145.
Kellerman, E. (1979). Transfer and non-transfer: Where we are now. *Studies in Second Language Acquisition, 2*, 37–57.
Kennedy, G. (1998). *An introduction to corpus linguistics.* New York: Longman.
Kenyon, P. & Daly, K. (1991). Teaching idioms. *Perspectives in Education and Deafness, 9*, 12–14.
Keysar, B. & Bly, B. M. (1999). Swimming against the current: Do idioms reflect conceptual structure? *Journal of Pragmatics, 31*, 1559–1578.
Knight, S. M. (1994). Dictionary use while reading: The effects on comprehension and vocabulary acquisition for students of different verbal abilities. *Modern Language Journal, 78*, 285–299.
Kövecses, Z. (1999). Does it constitute or reflect cultural models? In R. W. Gibbs & G. J. Steen (Eds.), *Metaphor in cognitive linguistics* (pp. 167–188). Amsterdam: John Benjamins.

Kővecses, Z. (2002). *Metaphor: A practical introduction.* Oxford: Oxford University Press.
Kővecses, Z. & Szabó, P. (1996). Idioms: A view from cognitive linguistics. *Applied Linguistics, 17,* 326–355.
Lamb, S. (1962). *Outline of stratificational grammar.* Berkeley: ASUC.
Larsen-Freeman, D. (2001). Teaching grammar. In M. Celce-Murcia (Ed.), *Teaching English as a second language* (2nd ed.) (pp. 251–266). Boston: Heinle & Heinle.
Larsen-Freeman, D. (2007, March). The dynamics of change. Plenary speech given at the Forty-first TESOL Annual Convention, Seattle, WA.
Larzar, R. T., Warr-Leeper, G. A., Nicholson, C. B., & Johnson, S. (1989). Elementary school teachers' use of multiple-meaning expressions. *Language, Speech, and Hearing Services in Schools, 20,* 420–430.
Lattey, E. (1986). Pragmatic classification of idioms as an aid for the language learner. *IRAL, 24,* 217–33.
Lattey, E. (1994). Inference and learnability in second language acquisition: Universals vs. language-specific phenomena in the domain of idiomatic expression. In R. Trancy & E. Lattey (Eds.), *How tolerant is universal grammar?* (pp. 295–312). Tübingen, Germany: Niemeyer.
Laufer, B. (1991). Words you know: How they affect the words you learn. In J. Fisaik (Ed.), *Further insights into contrastive analysis* (pp. 573–593). Amsterdam and New York: John Benjamins.
Laufer, B. (2000). Avoidance of idioms in a second language: The effect of L1–L2 similarity. *Studia Linguistica, 54,* 186–196.
Laufer, B. & Shmueli, K. (1997). Memorizing new words: Does teaching have anything to do with it? *RELC Journal, 28,* 89–108.
Lennon, P. (1998). Approaches to the teaching of idiomatic language. *IRAL, 36,* 12–30.
Levorato, M. C. (1993) The acquisition of idioms and the development of figurative competence. In C. Cacciari & P. Tabossi (Eds.), *Idioms: Processing, structure, and interpretation* (pp. 101–128). Hillsdale, NJ: Lawrence Erlbaum.
Levorato, M. C. & Cacciari, C. (1992). Children's comprehension and production of idioms: The role of context and familiarity. *Journal of Child Language, 19,* 415–433.
Levorato, M. C. & Cacciari, C. (1995). The effects of different tasks on the comprehension and production of idioms in children. *Journal of Experimental Child Psychology, 60,* 261–283.
Levorato, M. C. & Cacciari, C. (1999). Idiom comprehension in children: Are the effects of semantic analysability and context separable? *European Journal of Cognitive Psychology, 11,* 51–66.
Lindstromberg, S. & Boers, F. (2005). Means of mass memorization of multi-word expressions, Part 1: The power of sounds. *Humanizing Language Teaching, 7*(1). Available from www.hltmag.co.uk.
Littlemore, J. (2001). The use of metaphor in university lectures and the problems that it causes for overseas students. *Teaching in Higher Education, 6,* 333–349.
Liu, D. (2000a, March). Idioms in the instructional language. Paper presented at the Thirty-fourth TESOL Annual Convention, Vancouver, Canada.
Liu, D. (2000b). "Hitting singles" and "scoring runs": Sports metaphor in American English and American life as sports. *Alpha Vision: An Interdisciplinary Journal of Higher Education, 1,* 10–16.
Liu, D. (2001). Corpus of Spoken American Median English compiled from transcripts of a variety of U.S. TV programs.
Liu, D. (2002). *Metaphor, culture, and worldview: The case of American English and the Chinese language.* Lanham, MD: University Press of America.
Liu, D. (2003). The most frequently used spoken American English idioms: A corpus analysis and its implications. *TESOL Quarterly, 37,* 671–700.

REFERENCES

Liu, D. (2007, March). Corpora and lexicogrammar in grammar learning and teaching. Paper presented at the Forty-first TESOL Annual Convention, Seattle, WA.

Liu, D. & Farha, B. (1996). Three strikes and you're out: A study of the use of football and baseball jargon in present-day American English. *English Today: The International Review of the English Language, 12.*1, 36–40.

Lodge, L. & Leach, E. (1975). Children's acquisition of idioms in the English language. *Journal of Speech and Hearing Research, 18,* 521–529.

Makkai, A. (1972). *Idiom structure in English.* The Hague, the Netherlands: Mouton

Makkai, A. (1976). Idioms, psychology, and lexemic principles. In *The 3rd LACUS forum* (pp. 467–478). Columbia, SC: Hornbeam.

Makkai, A. (1993). Idiomaticity as a reaction to *L'Arbitraire du Signe* in the universal process of semeio-genesis. In C. Cacciari & P. Tabossi (Eds.), *Idioms: Processing, structure, and interpretation* (pp. 297–324). Hillsdale, NJ: Lawrence Erlbaum.

McElree, B. & Nordie, J. (1999). Literal and figurative interpretations are computed in equal time. *Psychonomic Bulletin and Review, 6,* 486–494.

McMordie, W. (revised by Goffin, R.) (1972). *English idioms.* Oxford: Oxford University Press.

Moon, R. (1998). *Fixed expressions and idioms in English.* Oxford: Clarendon Press.

Nagy, W. (1978). Some non-idiom larger-than-word units in the lexicon. In D. Farkas, W. M. Jacobsen, & K. W. Todrys (Eds.), *Papers from the parasession on the lexicon, Fourteenth Regional Meeting of the Chicago Linguistics Society* (pp. 289–300).

Nation, I. S. P. (1990). *Teaching and learning vocabulary.* Boston: Heinle & Heinle.

Nation, I. S. P. (2000). Lexical vocabulary in lexical sets: Dangers and guidelines. *TESOL Journal, 9,* 6–10.

Nation, I. S. P. (2001). *Learning vocabulary in another language.* Cambridge: Cambridge University Press.

Nattinger, J. R. and DeCarrico, J. S. (1992). *Lexical phrases and language teaching.* Oxford: Oxford University Press.

Nayak, N. & Gibbs, R. W. (1990). Conceptual knowledge in the interpretation of idioms. *Journal of Experimental Psychology: General, 119,* 315–330.

Nelson, G. & Winters, T. (1993). *Operations in ESL.* Brattleboro, VT: Pro Lingua.

Newton, J. (1995). Task-based interaction and incidental vocabulary learning: A case study. *Second Language Research, 11,* 159–177.

Nilsen, A. P. & Nilsen, D.L.F. (2003). A new spin on teaching vocabulary: A source-based approach. *The Reading Teacher, 56,* 436–439.

Nippold, M. J. & Duthie, J. K. (2003). Mental imagery and idiom comprehension: A comparison of school-age children and adults. *Journal of Speech, Language, and Hearing Research, 46,* 788–799.

Nippold, M. A. & Martin, S. T. (1989). Idiom interpretation in isolation versus context: A developmental study with adolescents. *Journal of Speech and Hearing Research, 32,* 59–66.

Nippold, M. A. & Rudzinski, M. (1993). Familiarity and transparency in idiom exploration: A developmental study of children and adolescents. *Journal of Speech and Hearing Research, 36,* 728–737.

Nippold, M. A. & Taylor, C. L. (1995). Idiom understanding in youth: Further examination of familiarity and transparency. *Journal of Speech and Hearing Research, 38,* 426–433.

Odlin, T. (1989). *Language transfer.* Cambridge: Cambridge University Press.

Odlin, T. (2005). Crosslinguistic influence and conceptual transfer: What are the concepts? *ARAL, 25,* 3–25.

Ortony, A. Schallert, D. L., Reynolds, R. E., & Antos, S. (1978). Interpreting metaphors and idioms: Some effects of context on comprehension. *Journal of Verbal Learning and Verbal Behavior, 7,* 465–77.
Otier, M. H. (1986). Teaching idiomatic expressions: Letting the cat out of the bag. *Zielsprache English, 16,* 31–33.
Palmatier, R. A. & Ray, H. L. (1993) *Dictionary of sports idioms.* Lincolnwood, IL: National Textbook Company.
Papagno, C., Curti, R., Rizzo, S., Crippa, F., & Colombo, M. R. (2006). Is the right hemisphere involved in idiom comprehension? A neuropsychological study. *Neuropsychology, 20,* 598–606.
Perez, E. (1981). Oral language competence improves reading skills of Mexican American third graders. *The Reading Teacher, 35,* 24–27.
Peterson, R. R. & Burgess, C. (1993). Syntactic and semantic processing during idiom comprehension: Neurolinguistic and psycholinguistic dissociation. In C. Cacciari & P. Tabossi (Eds.), *Idioms: Processing, structure, and interpretation* (pp. 201–225). Hillsdale, NJ: Lawrence Erlbaum.
Peterson, R. R., Burgess, C., Dell, G. S., & Eberhard, K. M. (2001). Dissociation between syntactic and semantic processing during idiom comprehension. *Journal of Experimental Psychology: Learning, Memory, and Cognition, 27,* 1223–1237.
Pollio, H. R., Barlow, J. M., Fine, H. J., & Pollio, M. R. (1977). *Psychology and the poetics of growth.* Hillsdale, NJ: Lawrence Erlbaum.
Pollio, M. R. & Pollio, H. R. (1974). The development of figurative language in children. *Journal of Psycholinguistic Research, 3,* 185–201.
Prinz, P. M. (1983). The developmental of idiomatic meaning in children. *Language and Speech, 26,* 263–272.
Quirk, R., Greenbaum, S., Leech, G., & Svartvik, J. (1985). *A comprehensive grammar of the English language.* London: Longman.
Richards, J. C. (1996). Idiomatically speaking. *Zielsprache Englisch, 26,* 32–33.
Ruhl, C. E. (1989). *On metonymy.* Buffalo: SUNY Press.
Schachter, J. (1974). An error in error analysis. *Language Learning, 24,* 205–214.
Schmidt, R. (1990). The role of consciousness in second language learning. *Applied Linguistics, 11,* 129–158.
Schmitt, N. (Ed.) (2004). *Formulaic sequences.* Amsterdam: John Benjamins.
Schuster-Webb, K. (1980). A study of cognitive processing strategies for the encoding of English idioms into long-term memory. Ann Arbor, MI: University of Michigan Microfilms International.
Schweigert, W. A. (1986). The comprehension of familiar and less familiar idioms. *Journal of Psycholinguistic Research, 15,* 33–45.
Schweigert, W. A. & Moates, D. R. (1988). Familiar idiom comprehension. *Journal of Psycholinguistic Research, 17,* 281–296.
Searle, J. R. (1969). *Speech acts.* Cambridge: Cambridge University Press.
Searle, J. R. (1979). *Expression and meaning: Studies in the theory of speech acts.* Cambridge: Cambridge University Press.
Sinclair, J. M. (1987). Collocation: A progress report. In R. Steele & T. Thomas (Eds.), *Language topics: Essays in honor of Michael Halliday, II* (pp. 319–331). Amsterdam: John Benjamins.
Steinberg, D. D. (1993). *An introduction to psycholinguistics.* London: Longman.
Strässler, J. (1982). *Idioms in English: A pragmatic analysis.* Tübingen, Germany: Gunter Narr.
Stubbs, M. (2001). *Words and phrases: Corpus studies of lexical semantics.* Oxford: Blackwell.
Swinney, D. A. & Cutler, A. (1979). The access and processing of idiomatic expressions. *Journal of Verbal Learning and Verbal Behavior, 18,* 523–534.

REFERENCES

Tabossi, P. & Zardon, F. (1993). The activation of idiomatic meaning in spoken language comprehension. In C. Cacciari & P. Tabossi (Eds.), *Idioms: Processing, structure, and interpretation* (pp. 145–162). Hillsdale, NJ: Lawrence Erlbaum.

Tabossi, P. & Zardon, F. (1995). The activation of idiomatic meaning. In E. Everaert, E. J. Van der Linden, A Schenk, & R. Schreuder (Eds.), *Idioms: Structural and Psychological perspective* (pp. 273–282). Hillsdale, NJ: Lawrence Erlbaum.

Titone, D. A. & Connine, C. M. (1994). Descriptive norms for 171 idiomatic expressions: Familiarity, compositionality, predictability, and literality. *Metaphor and Symbolic Activity, 9,* 247–270.

Titone, D. A. & Connine, C. M. (1999). On the compositional and noncompositional nature of idiomatic expressions. *Journal of Pragmatics, 31,* 1655–1674.

Trosborg, A. (1985). Metaphoric productions and preferences in second language learners. In W. Paprotte & R. Derven (Eds.), *The ubiquity of metaphor* (pp. 525–557). Amsterdam: John Benjamins.

Underwood, G., Schmitt, N., & Gaplin, A. (2004). The eyes have it: An eye-movement study into the processing of formulaic sequences. In N. Schmitt (Ed.), *Formulaic sequences* (pp. 153–172). Amsterdam: John Benjamins.

Vosniadou, S. & Ortony, A (1983). The emergence of literal–metaphor–anomalous distinction in young children. *Child Development, 54,* 154–161.

Weinert, R. (1995). The role of formulaic language in second language acquisition: A review. *Applied Linguistics, 16,* 180–205.

Weinreich, U. (1969). Problems in the analysis of idioms. In J. Puhvel (Ed.), *Substance and structure of language* (pp. 23–81). Berkeley, CA: University of California Press.

Winner, E. (1988). *The point of words: Children's understanding of metaphor and irony.* Cambridge, MA: Harvard University Press.

Wood, D. (2002). Formulaic language in acquisition and production: Implications for teaching. *TESL Canada Journal, 20,* 1–15.

Wood, M. M. (1981). *A definition of idiom.* Bloomington: Indiana University Linguistics Club.

Wray, A. (1999). Formulaic language in learners and native speakers. *Language Teaching, 32*(4), 213–231

Wray, A. (2000). Formulaic sequences in second language teaching: Principle and practice. *Applied Linguistics, 21,* 463–489.

Wray, A. (2002). *Formulaic language and the lexicon.* New York: Cambridge University Press.

Wray, A. (2004). "Here is one I prepared earlier": Formulaic language learning on television. In N. Schmitt (Ed.), *Formulaic sequences* (pp. 249–268). Amsterdam: John Benjamins.

Wright, J. (1999). *Idioms organizer.* Hove, England: Language Teaching Publications.

Yorio, C. A. (1980). Conventionalized language forms and the development of communicative competence. *TESOL Quarterly, 14,* 433–442.

Yorio, C. A. (1989). Idiomaticity as an indicator of second language proficiency. In K. Hyltenstam and L. K. Obler (Eds.), *Bilingualism across the lifespan: Aspects of acquisition, maturity and loss.* Cambridge: Cambridge University Press.

Yu, N. (1995). Metaphorical expressions of anger and happiness in English and Chinese. *Metaphor and Symbolic Activity, 10*(2), 59–92.

Yu, N. (2000). Figurative uses of *finger* and *palm* in Chinese and English. *Metaphor and Symbol, 15*(3), 159–175.

Zigo, D. (2001). From familiar worlds to possible worlds: Using narrative theory to support struggling readers' engagements with texts. *Journal of Adolescent and Adult Literacy, 45,* 62–70.

Index

Abdullah, K., 65–70, 87, 102, 112, 135, 187
Abel, B., 54–55, 60, 65, 73–74, 78, 100, 186–187
Abrahamsen, E. P., 121, 126
acculturation, 103
acquisition, *see* idiom acquisition and language acquisition
active idioms, 118–119, 177
activities for: assessing idiom learning, 173–175; cultural learning, 130; error treatment, 172–173, 175; guessing idiom meanings, 146–147; learning and teaching idioms, 89, 114, 118, 122–166; mnemonic learning, 131, 134, 167; raising awareness of and interest in idioms, 122–124, 127, 131, 139; retrieving and generating. 152, 156–159
add-on (stories), 133, 159
Aijmer, K., 27
alliteration, 131, 164
anomalous collocation, 19, 177
Arabic, 67, 69
as good as gold, 19
As of, 7, 9, 119
assessment (of idiom learning), 132, 169, 173–175, 189; *see also* tests
Austin, J.L., 28
avoidance (error), 69, 88, 102, 135–136, 170

awareness of idioms, 104, 121–123, 130

back-seat driver, 20, 34–35, 115, 144–145, 151
Bahns, J., 27
Bardovi-Harlig, K., 103
Barlow, M., 29, 140, 186
Bauer, L., xiii, 3, 11–14, 16, 20–22, 101, 144, 177, 185, 188
beat a dead horse, 24, 36, 38, 117
beat about (around) the bush, 81, 161–162, 170, 174
beg the question, 19, 32, 89
Bell, S., 48
Biber, D., 15, 25, 39–40, 109, 181, 188
binominals, 17, 115, 178
bird in hand (a) (is worth two in the bush), 36, 180
birds of a feather (flock together), 18, 36
bite the bullet, 17, 115–116, 180
bite more than one can chew, 21
blind date, 7
blue film, 11
Bly, B. M., 187
BNC (British National Corpus), 110, 113–114, 119, 150
Bobrow, S., 48
Boers, F., xiii, 21, 41–42, 65, 70–71, 100, 121, 128–129, 134, 142–143, 146–147, 150, 161, 188
Bolinger, D., 9, 27

break the ice, 50, 85
Brett, A., 162
brevity is the soul of wit, 17–18
Bromley, K. D., 121
Brown, H. D., 135, 189
Bulut, T., 54, 65–66, 68–70, 73–74, 79, 87, 126
Burgess, C., 56–59, 64
Burmeister, H., 27
burn one's candle at both ends, 11, 70
by and large, 7, 9, 12, 19, 28, 31–32, 70, 81, 100–101, 114–115, 131, 134, 144, 153, 179, 188
by any stretch of the imagination, 28
by the same token, 32, 114
by word of mouth, 16

call it a day, 15, 34, 114
Cacciari, C., 51, 56, 59–61, 80, 82–86, 93–94, 98, 100–101, 186
cash in, 116, 152
Celce-Murcia, M., 22
Çelik-Yazici, Y., 54, 65–66, 68–70, 73–74, 79, 87, 126
Chaika, E., 152
Charteris-Black, J. 41, 65–66, 68–69, 71–72, 94, 102, 128–130
chicken out, 33, 114, 117, 142
Chinese: history, 41; idioms, 41, 71, 151; language, 41; opera, 41; psyche, 41; speakers and students, 41, 71, 151
classification of idioms, *see* idiom classification
cohesive function, 28–29, 38, 177, 179; *see also* relational function or use of idioms; textual function or use of idioms
cold feet, get/develop/have, 10, 62, 162
come up (with), 6, 24, 40, 140
compare apples and oranges, 21
comparison and contrast, 63, 130–131, 137, 142, 149, 151, 166; *see also* contrastive analysis
compositional analysis hypothesis (The), 47, 51–52, 54–55, 57, 63, 177
compositional idiomatic expressions, 3, 9, 13–14, 16, 19, 24, 26–27, 32, 40, 49, 51, 55, 61–62, 88, 97, 105, 108, 111, 141, 146, 150, 155, 162, 172, 177, 179

comprehension of idioms, *see* idiom comprehension
conceptual knowledge, 71, 73, 89, 129, 146, 187
conceptual motivation, 128, 130, 137
conceptually: different idioms, 129–130; motivated idioms, 41, 89, 128, 130
Connine, C. M., 54–55, 100, 186
connotation, 107, 114, 117, 128–129, 131, 142, 149–150, 160, 165, 169–172
Conrad, S., 181
contextual information, 49, 54–57, 61, 66, 73, 79, 82, 84, 98, 125–127, 132, 144, 146–147, 150
contrastive analysis (L1 and L2 contrast), 42, 130, 135, 137, 142, 151, 160, 166, 172; *see also* comparison and contrast
Cooper, T. C., xiii, 3, 39, 54, 65–66, 68–70, 73–74, 79, 87, 112, 121, 123, 126, 132–133, 148–149, 156, 159
core idioms, 11–12, 14, 16, 20, 100–101, 144, 157, 161, 177, 179, 188
Cornell, A., xiii, 3, 109, 124
corpus: searches, 109, 113, 132, 143–143, 149; wild card search, 111
Cowie, A. P., 15
cranberry collocations, 19, 177
Cronk, B. C., 50, 78, 80–81
CSAME (Corpus of Spoken American Media English), 29–32, 109, 186
CSPAE (Corpus of Spoken Professional American English), 29–31, 109–110, 140, 186
culture and idiom use, 41–42
culture-specific idioms, 41–42, 68, 71–72, 75, 99, 101, 128–129, 131, 146
Cummins, J., 88
cut and dried, 20
cut the cackle, 21
Cutler, A., 49, 50

Daly, K., 148
DeCarrico, J. S., 27
decomposable, 52, 54–55, 79–80, 112, 125, 131, 179, 186; *see also* semantically decomposable idioms
defective collocations, 19, 177
definition: of idioms, *see* idiom

INDEX

definition; of idioms as a teaching practice, 125, 162–163, 165, 173
Deignan, A., 41, 128, 130
Demecheleer, M., 41–42, 70–71, 128
Dew, P., 32
dictionary, 15, 21–22, 113–114, 127–128, 133, 139, 165–166, 181–185, 188
direct access hypothesis (The), 47, 50–51, 54, 56–57, 63, 178
discourse, 21, 87, 109, 126, 134; analysis, 28; cohesiveness, 37, 42; context, 51, 59, 177, 189; functions, 25; information, 126; processing, 56
dog days (the), 20
dog in a manger (a), 12, 14, 116
Dörnyei, Z., 103, 130
Don't put all the eggs in one basket, 17, 141
Don't throw the baby out with the bathwater, 26, 116
Douglas, J. D., 93–94, 101, 112
dropped the ball, 8, 28, 32, 115
dual coding 161
dual idiom representation hypothesis/model (The), 47, 54–56, 73–74, 178, 186–187
dual processing, 50, 53, 63, 74; *see also* lexical representation hypothesis
Duquette, G., 104, 121, 130
Duthie, J. K. 84, 93–94, 161

eat one's words, 5, 24
elaboration of idioms as a teaching practice, 125, 162–163
Elley, W. B., 162, 164
Ellis, R., 121, 128
Emperor's new clothes, 20
Erman, B., 26–27
error: causes and sources, 170–172, 174; correction, 173; treatment, 169–170, 174–175
ESL: idiom publications, 15, 181–184; educators and professionals, xiii–xv; learners and students, xiv, 12, 22, 54, 66–67, 71, 73, 75, 101, 106, 112, 114, 132, 151, 171–172, 174; speakers, 86, 171, 183
evaluative, 28, 30, 32–34, 42, 72, 103, 114, 150; message, 114, 150; use, 32
every cloud has a silver lining, 19, 26, 134, 141
explaining idioms, 135, 162

eye for an eye (an), 19

factors affecting idiom comprehension: idiom as, 87–89, 112–113, 115, 131; learner and user as, 87–89, 98, 107, 115, 118, 131, 146
fall through the cracks, 38
Farha, B., 152
fat chance, 10–11
Fernando, C., 3, 9–11, 13–14, 16, 18–21, 24–25, 27–29, 32, 34–36, 40, 103, 185–186
figurative: competence, 94–98, 101, 105, 188; first hypothesis (The), *see* direct access hypothesis; idioms, 6–9, 11–12, 14, 20, 22, 49, 51–52, 54, 56–59, 61, 69, 78–81, 86, 88, 94–103, 105, 126, 128, 130–131, 133–134, 142, 144, 146–149, 151, 155–157, 160–161, 177–179, 186–188; proficiency, 94
Fine, H. J., 198
Finegan, E., 181
first language, 67, 72; *see also* L1
fixed expressions, 9, 11, 14, 19, 42–43, 136, 164, 178–179, 185
flashcard, 160
Flahive, D., 65
Flavell, L., 183, 188
Flavell, R., 183, 188
Flores d'Arcais, G. B., 51–53, 56, 59–62
Flowerdew, J., 163
foot the bill, 18–19
forefronting, 22
formulae, 9, 11, 14, 19, 26–27, 97, 99, 103–104, 121, 130, 178, 185, 187
formulaic: expressions, *see* formulae; sequences, *see* formulae
Forrester, M. A., 78
Fraser, B., 7–8, 13–14, 27, 187
friend or foe, 17

Galka, M., 65
Gass, S., 66
generating, 127, 156–157; *see also* activities for retrieving and generating
Genzel, R. B., 21
get a raw deal/have a raw deal, 36
get more than one bargains for, 21, 24, 116–117
get/give the cold shoulder, 37, 70

Gibbs, R. W., 41, 48–51, 70–71, 79–80, 82, 87, 94, 101, 126, 187
give in, 16–17, 22, 24, 32, 115
give me a break/rest, 29, 153–154
Glucksberg, S., 56, 186–187
Grant, L. E., xiii, 3, 11–14, 16, 20–22, 100–101, 109, 121, 131, 144, 146, 177, 185, 188
Gravois, M., 148, 183

habitual collocations, 9–11, 16
Halliday, M. A. K., 20, 28, 186
hang in the balance, 20, 119
have a bone to pick with someone, 12, 171
have designs on something, 20
Haywood, S., 121
Henry, L., 149
heuristic approach, 73–74, 79, 87, 126–128, 143, 178
high frequency idioms, 33–34, 39–40, 42, 103, 109, 113, 122, 125, 181–182
hit a home run, 17–18, 21, 24, 41, 70, 108, 112, 116–117, 130, 143, 155
Hockett, C. F., 3–4, 13–14
Holme, R., 41
Holt, E., 32
Honeck, R. P., 54
hot potato, 16
Howarth, P., xiii, 27
Hulstijn, J. H., 88, 102, 164
hypothesis: about idiom acquisition, 98; about idiom comprehension and processing, 56–60, 63–64, 68, 177–179, 186–187; *see also* direct access hypothesis; dual idiom; representation hypothesis; lexical representation hypothesis; literal first hypothesis,

ideational: function of idioms, 20, 28–30, 32–35, 42, 178; use, 28–29
idiom: acquisition, xiii–xv, 12, 27, 66, 69, 91, 93–94, 97–106, 118, 121, 124, 126, 128–129, 131, 156, 173–174, 188–189; *see* also idiom learning; classification, 16–21, 24, 28, 97, 107, 115–118, 188; comprehension, i, xv, 21, 47–48, 50–51, 53–60, 63, 65–75, 77–78, 80, 82–90, 93, 95–96, 98–102, 105, 118, 125–127, 131, 147–148, 152, 157, 161, 169, 173, 177–178, 186–187; corner, 123, 135;

definition, 3–16, 23–24, 185; file, 123; function, 42–43, 68, 88, 103–104, 108, 110, 113–114, 116, 118–119, 124, 177–179; importance of acquisition of, 93, 103–106, 188; key, 47, 53, 56, 59–60, 62–63, 161–162,178; learning, 25, 40, 100, 107, 110, 118–119, 121–122, 124, 127–130, 132–135, 137–140, 143, 149, 162, 164, 166, 169, 173–175; *see also* idiom acquisition; list hypothesis, *see* literal first hypothesis; organization, *see* organization of idioms; origin, 12, 116, 124, 131, 134–135, 143–144, 152, 161, 188; principle, 25–26, 42, 103, 178–179, 185; processing, 21, 47–49, 53–56, 58–61, 63–65, 73–74, 82, 99, 186; teaching, i, xiv–xv, 3–4, 12, 16, 21, 25, 39, 105, 107, 109, 113–114, 116, 118, 121–122, 124–127, 129, 131–133, 135–139, 143, 146, 160, 162, 166, 169. 173–175, 188–189
idiom-list hypothesis (The), 48, 50, 56, 63, 73, 179; *see also* (the) literal first hypothesis
idiomatosis 105–106, 135–136, 178
idioms: of decoding, 6, 9, 14, 16, 178; of encoding, 6, 9, 16, 131, 178; of restricted variance, 10, 178
ill-formed idioms and collocations, 11, 19, 89, 115, 178, 187–188
in hot water, 7, 20, 61, 115, 117, 147, 153
in the long run, 16, 37
incorporating verbs, 17, 178
informative, 42, 65, 84, 103, 114
intelligences and multiple intelligences, xi, 132–133
interference of L1, 66, 70, 72, 89
interpersonal function or use of idioms, 20–21, 28–30, 32–33, 40, 42, 100, 133–134, 178
invariant idioms, 10–11, 13, 15–16, 19, 23, 26, 178
irreversible binominals, *see* binominals
Irujo, S., xiii, 65–69, 88, 102, 111–112, 121, 123–124, 135, 148, 155, 159, 187
ive got to run, 32

Jackson, H., 65–70, 87, 102, 112, 135, 187

INDEX

Johansson, S., 181
Johnson, J., 71, 84, 86–88
Jones, M., 121
Jordens, P., 88, 102
jump on (join) the bandwagon, 30, 32–33, 117, 136, 150

Katz, J. J., 3, 5–8, 14, 16
Kellerman, E., 66, 88, 102
keep a low profile, 20
Kennedy, G., 110
Kenyon, P., 148
Keysar, B., 187
kick the bucket, 3, 5, 9, 16–18, 36, 39, 52, 55, 80, 106, 117, 160
kill two birds with one stone, 12, 14, 104
Knight, S. M., 164
knock it off, 29–30
know the ropes/learn the ropes/show someone the ropes, 36–37
knowledge: conceptual, *see* conceptual knowledge; L1 cultural, *see* L1 cultural knowledge; pragmatic, *see* pragmatic knowledge; world, *see* world knowledge
Kövecses, Z., xiii, 21, 41, 65, 70, 128–129, 150, 185, 186, 188

Lamb, S., 6
language: acquisition, xv, 27, 66, 99–101, 118, 121; variety, 38, 109, 113, 165–166
Larsen-Freeman, D., xiv, 22, 128, 156
Larzar, R. T., 39, 94
Lattey, E., 20, 27, 114–115, 151, 170–172, 189
Laufer, B., 69, 88, 102, 135, 164
learning strategies, 134–138
learning styles, 115, 118, 132, 138, 146, 166, 173
Leech, G., 181
Lennon, P., 121, 140, 146–148
let the cat out of the bag, 33
Levorato, M. C., 51, 80, 82–86, 93–101
lexemic idioms, 16–18, 32, 178
lexical idioms 5, 16, 179
lexical representation hypothesis, 47, 49–50, 53, 56, 63, 179, 186–187
Lindstromberg, S., xiii, 21, 100, 121, 134, 142, 161

literal first hypothesis (The), 47–50, 56, 63, 73, 179, 187; *see also* (the) idiom-list hypothesis
literal idioms, xiii–xiv, 5–16, 18–20, 22–24, 34, 47–52, 54, 56–62, 66–67, 69–70, 78–86, 95–99, 101, 126, 131, 133, 142, 144, 146–148, 151, 155, 160, 177–179, 187
Littlemore, J., 65–66, 71–72, 150
Liu, D., i–iv, 3, 25, 29, 36–37, 39–41, 71, 108–109, 121, 125, 128, 136, 143, 152, 162, 186
Lodge, L., 93–94
L1: acquisition, 101; conceptual knowledge and transfer, 70, 72, 128–130; *see also* conceptual knowledge; cultural knowledge, 70, 73, 137; equivalents, 66–67, 102, 135; idiom comprehension and processing, 47, 65, 73–74, 77, 88, 178; influence, 66–67, 69, 72, 75, 87–89; knowledge, 67, 134, 137, 143; *see also* L1 conceptual knowledge; proficiency, 88, 94; research, 102; speakers, 24, 73–74, 82; transfer, 89, 169, 172, 188; translation, 68, 165; use of, 66, 68, 70, 112, 130, 134–235, 147–148, 151, 160, 164
L2: acquisition, xv, 66, 121; idiom comprehension and processing, 54, 65–69, 73–75, 77, 88, 90, 178; learners xiii–xiv, 13, 15–16, 19, 21, 35, 65–70, 72–75, 86–88, 102–106, 114, 121, 126, 129, 165, 170

Mackin, R., 15
macro-strategies, 121–137
Makkai, A., xiii, xiv, 5, 6, 9, 13–14, 16–18, 21, 24, 32, 39–40, 181–182, 185
Marchena, E., 102
Martin, S. T. 82–84, 94
McElree, B., 48–49
McMordie, W., 15
memorization, 100, 105, 115, 134, 147; *see also* activities for mnemonic learning
mental images, 160–161
met his/her/one's Waterloo, 21, 24, 117, 185
metaphorical competence, 94
metaphorical idioms, 32, 41–42, 68,

70–73, 88–90, 93, 95–96, 101, 105, 112, 130, 146–147, 152, 187
metonymic idioms, 95–96
MICASE (Michigan Corpus of Academic Spoken English), 40, 110, 113, 119
micro-strategies, 139–167
mnemonic: learning, *see* activities for mnemonic learning strategies, 100, 134
Moates, D. R., 78, 82
Moon, R., 3, 10–11, 14, 19, 21, 25–29, 32–34, 36–40, 78–79, 103, 185–187
MWU (Multi word unit), 12, 20

Nagy, W., 27
Nation, I. S. P., xv, 12, 100–101, 115, 121, 127, 131–132, 144, 160, 164
native language, 69, 73, 87, 102, 106, 142, 165
Nattinger, J. R., 27
Nayak, N., 70–71
neck and neck, 161
negative: attitude, 35; connotation, 172; consequence, 69; effect, 137; meaning, 34, 171; transfer, 68
Nelson, G., 156
Newton, J., 128
Nilsen, A. P., 143
Nilsen, D.L.F., 143
non-decomposable, 52, 54–56, 70, 79–81, 99, 112, 131, 179, 186; *see also* semantically non-decomposable idioms
non-literal, 6, 9, 12–14, 16, 18–20, 23–24, 34, 47, 51, 177–178
Nippold, M. J., 82–84, 86, 93, 94, 161
no pain, no gain, 17
Nordie, J., 48–49
noticing, 121–122, 125, 127, 131, 139–140, 161; *see also* activities for raising awareness of idioms

O'Brien, J., 71
Odlin, T., 66
off the top of my head, 20
on the contrary, 21, 31
on the fence, 20, 172
on the other hand, 21
opaque idioms, 3, 9–11, 13–14, 19, 22, 72, 80–82, 101, 112, 125, 131, 156

open choice principle (The), 25–26, 42, 103, 179
Operation (an idiom game), 156
organization of idioms: by activity, 117; by grammatical functions, 115; by grammatical structure, 115; by key words, 117; by motivating concept, 116; by origin or source, 116; by semantic, 117
Ortony, A., 48–49, 82, 86, 93, 94
Otier, M. H., 121, 123, 148, 155
out in left field, 38, 147

pain in the neck (a), 20, 116, 170, 172
Palmatier, R. A., 166, 182
Papagno, C., 54
paraphrasing of idioms as a teaching practice, 125, 162–163
particle xiv, 7–8, 17, 22–23, 36, 110, 129, 150, 157, 179
pass(ed) out, 28
passive idioms, 118, 179
Peel, B., 93–94, 101, 112
Perez, E., 125
Peterson, R. R., 56–59, 64
phrasal compounds, 17, 179
phrasal idioms, 5, 20, 23, 179
phrasal verbs, 7–8, 14, 16–17, 21–23, 35, 102, 104, 110, 113, 115, 118, 127–129, 144, 150, 156–157, 159, 172, 174, 179, 188
phraseological collocations, 19, 177
piece of cake (a), 21, 43, 75, 112, 116, 144, 185
Pollio, H. R., 39, 102
Pollio, M. R., 39, 102
Postal, P., 3, 5–8, 14, 16
pragmatic knowledge, 54–56, 69–70, 73, 79, 126, 131, 135, 146, 186; *see also* world knowledge
prefabricated or preconstructed expressions, 179, 185
Prinz, P. M., 93–94
proactive idiom teaching, 121, 136–138
processing of idioms: in L1, 47–64, 73, 178; in L2, 65–75, 178
production of idioms, 67–68, 88, 93, 98–103, 105–106, 114, 118, 127, 156, 169–170, 173
pseudo-idioms, 17, 179
pull a rabbit (a highway) out of the hat, 37–38, 136

INDEX

pull someone's leg, 7, 16, 19, 39, 49, 100, 131, 170
pure idioms, 10–11, 16, 18, 23–24, 39–40
put one's foot in the mouth, 5
put out, 35, 172
put the cart before the horse, 20, 131, 148
put up with, 16–17, 22–24, 134, 153

Quirk, R., 22

Ray, H. L., 166, 182
red herring, 6, 16, 20, 144, 178
recall(ing), 67, 126–127, 129, 148–149, 153, 155–156, 160–162, 166, 170
register, 25–26, 40, 42–43, 107–109, 111, 113–114, 119, 128, 137, 142, 149, 160, 165, 170, 172
relational function or use of idioms, 20–21, 28–29, 177, 179; *see also* cohesive function; textual function or use of idioms
retention of idioms, 100, 117, 134, 147, 150, 159–162
retrieving, 127, 152, 156–157, 187; *see also* activities for retrieving
retroactive idiom teaching, 121, 136–138
Richards, J. C., 105–106, 122, 136
right on the money, 21, 30, 33
rock the boat, 20, 51, 147
Rosano, T., 71, 86–88
rote learning, 94, 98–100, 105–106, 134, 188
Rudzinski, M., 82, 84, 86
Ruhl, C. E., 13, 24

safe and sound, 17, 19, 115, 178
Schmidt, R., 121
Schmitt, N., 27, 104, 185
Schuster-Webb, K., 104
Schweigert, W. A., 50, 78, 80–82
Searle, J. R., 26–28
second language, xiii–xiv, 4, 67, 104, 121, 124; *see also* L2
seize/grasp the nettle, 10
Selinker, L., 66
semantic association, 160
semantically decomposable idioms, 52, 54–56, 70, 79–81, 112, 125, 131, 179, 186
semantically non-decomposable idioms, 52, 54–56, 70, 79–81, 99, 112, 131, 179, 186
sememic idioms, 16–18, 32, 40, 179
semi literal, 10–11, 13–14, 16, 18–19, 23–24, 47
sequence of idiom acquisition, 97, 100–101, 103–105, 108, 118, 130, 173
shake a leg, 35
Shmueli, K., 164
simultaneous processing *see* lexical representation hypothesis
Sinclair, J. M., 25–26, 42, 103, 182, 185
skeletons in the cupboard/closet, 33, 36, 116
smell a rat, 10, 116
Smith, R., 121, 126
so long, 12, 18, 30, 100–101, 108, 134
so to speak, 20, 31, 34, 49, 114
sources of: errors, *see* error causes and sources; idioms, *see* idiom origins; idiom teaching materials, 107, 114, 126, 141, 184
spill the beans, 3, 11, 20, 148
stable collocations, 6–7, 11, 179
Steinberg, D. D., 27
step up to the plate, 17, 75, 104, 130, 147
stepping stone, 19
stick one's neck out/with one's neck stuck out, 36
Strässler, J., 27, 35
strategies: for learning idioms, *see* learning strategies; training the use of, 122–123, 134–138, 188
Stubbs, M., 27, 28
Swinney, D. A., 49–50
switch gears, 31–32, 34, 75
syntactic and semantic processing disassociation hypothesis, 56, 63–64, 179
syntactically abnormal idioms, 81, 178–179, 187–188
syntactically frozen idioms, 81, 180

Tabossi, P., 3, 56, 59–62, 64
take the bull by the horns, 17, 131, 143, 148
target language, 68, 73, 94, 102, 104, 112, 141–142, 152, 165
Taylor, C. L., 82, 84, 86, 93–94
teachers, 12, 17, 40, 73, 89–90, 105–107, 109–111, 114–116, 118–119, 122, 124–132, 135–139,

143–144, 146, 148, 152, 160, 163, 166–167, 169–174, 189; in training, xiv
teaching idioms. *See* Idiom teaching tests; *see also* assessment: completion, 101; comprehension, 101, 129, 174; multiple-choice, 83, 85, 98, 101
textual function or use of idioms, 28–29, 32–34, 42, 177, 180, 186; *see also* cohesive function; relational function or use of idioms
the bottom drops out, 20
the bottom line is . . ., 21, 32, 87, 146, 152
the shoe drops, 20
the straw that breaks the camel's back, 20
the truth of the matter is, 20
three strikes and you're out, 38, 87
throw in the towel, 19, 116, 155, 160
Titone, D. A., 54–55, 100, 186
to make a long story short, 29
tournures, 16–18, 39, 180
training in learning strategy use, *see* strategy training and use
Trosborg, A., 88, 94
truncated idioms, 36, 180
turn back the clock, 20
turn down, 22, 110, 113, 144, 150
twist somebody's arm, 20
two wrongs don't make a right, 7

Underwood, G., 27
unplanned idiom teaching, 135, 162
use of idiom dictionaries, 127, 139, 165–166

variance (variation): of idioms, 7–11, 13–16, 23–24, 36, 178; limited, 178–179
variety of: activities ix, 131, 139, 166; learning, exercises,181; factors, 118; functions, 27, 35, 42; strategies, 73–74, 79, 126, 134, 178
Vogel, T., 27
Vosniadou, S., 86

Warren, B., 26
Weinert, R., xiii, 99, 104
Weinreich, U., 6–11, 13–14, 48
What's up, 4, 21, 24, 26, 28, 32, 100, 108, 115, 178–179
whole nine yards (the), 21, 104
Winner, E., 70, 86, 93–96, 155
Winters, T., 156
Wood, D., 103
Wood, M. M., 3, 8–10, 14
world knowledge, 69–70, 44, 187; *see also* pragmatic knowledge
wouldn't hit a lick at a snake, 38
Wray, A., 26–28, 100, 103–104, 185, 187
Wright, J., 21, 184

You bet, 26, 29, 111
You made my day, 29
Yorio, C. A., xiii, 27, 104, 108
Yu, N., 41

Zardon, F., 3, 56, 59–62, 64
Zigo, D., 149